THOSE BLUE REMEMBERED HILLS

7'

Those Blue Remembered Hills

by

PATRICK GORDON-DUFF-PENNINGTON

The Memoir Club

This edition first published in 2004
by The Memoir Club

First published in 2004 by
The Memoir Club
Stanhope Old Hall
Stanhope
Weardale
County Durham

British Library Cataloguing in
Publication Data.
A catalogue record for this book
is available from the
British Library.

ISBN: 1 84104 126 2

Typeset by George Wishart & Associates, Whitley Bay.

Printed and bound by Antony Rowe Ltd, Eastbourne

Dedicated to Catriona Bechtel

Acknowledgements

I would like to acknowledge the assistance of the following people: my editor, Meg Ross; Patience Wheatcroft, for writing the Foreword; Catriona Sutherland my portrait painter; Karen Bennett; Tina Chandler; Jo Hall for translating my awful handwriting; and including friends I have loved and insulted without malice and those I have loved and excluded with unwonted tact.

Contents

List of Illustrations ix

Foreword xi

Chapter 1 1

Chapter 2 27

Chapter 3 42

Chapter 4 52

Chapter 5 67

Chapter 6 82

Chapter 7 93

Chapter 8 101

Chapter 9 108

Chapter 10 126

Chapter 11 136

Chapter 12 144

Chapter 13 165

Chapter 14 191

Chapter 15 196

Chapter 16 214

Chapter 17 218

Chapter 18 236

List of Illustrations

Duffy with her grandchildren 4

My grandfather, Thomas Craven 5

Father, Geordie Gordon-Duff 8

Bridget Toynbee 13

Sister Elspeth, aged 15 16

Mother Rosemary, aged 44 28

Eaton Hall OCTU, March 1952 44

Mother-in-law Veronica, Lady Pennington Ramsden 53

Donald MacDonald at Ruskich 55

Robin McCall with Kirstie at Ruskich 60

PTGD 1955 63

Sir William Pennington-Ramsden 69

Some of my friends, Aberarder Farm 70

Aberarder Farm, 1955 70

Wife Phyllida Pennington, 1955 73

PTGDP with Prunella and Dearg 76

Kirkland of Tynron 83

Daughters, 1964 97

In the garden at Muncaster 169

PTGDP with Sir Christopher Harding 172

In the kitchen at Muncaster 180

Peter Frost-Pennington and family 190

Muncaster 217

Catriona Bechtel, aged 11 221

Buckingham Palace with Iona and Anthea 226

Phyllida and Patrick Gordon-Duff-Pennington 238

Foreword

MY LIFE WOULD HAVE BEEN the poorer had not Patrick Gordon-Duff-Pennington entered it via the correspondence column of *The Times*. He read a letter my husband had penned, taking issue with something I had written, and he got in touch.

Getting, and staying, in touch is a Patrick speciality. Whether politicians, extended family, neighbours, assorted eccentrics or those who would merely like to think of themselves as friends, Patrick encourages their better qualities and enjoys their idiosyncrasies. His reminiscences provide a wonderful parade of humanity, some merely glimpsed and some portrayed in more telling detail.

He introduced himself to me as 'Patrick of the Hills' and it is in the guise of poet that his deepest thoughts surface. Some of these poems are included in this volume but the entire autobiography has a poetic feel to it as he romps through his memories of a life which would be unimaginable to children who spend most of their time in front of a screen.

He evokes the thrill of being a child with the moors and their wildlife beckoning and the fears of losing that freedom for incarceration at boarding school. He reports back from his ventures abroad, conveying his first impressions with all the observant freshness of events just passed rather than experiences of decades ago.

This remarkable man refuses to be bound by the normal strictures. He is not the conventional result of an Eton and Trinity education but he is a fine advertisement for it. His enduring love of literature and ever-inquiring mind illuminate this book. From his childhood to his time in the services and then his relationships with the bureaucrats who meddle (as he tends to see it) in agriculture, Patrick has always been prepared to find himself at odds with officialdom.

He is a natural rebel as his early nannies decided and misguided politicians have come to learn, as he has delivered brusque judgement on their efforts. He is also a wonderful friend and confidant, who has made me eternally grateful for my husband's letter to *The Times*.

Patience Wheatcroft
City and Business Editor, *The Times*

Chapter 1

'What a wonderful boy he is!' said my mother.
'I'm feared he turn out a conceited gowk,' said old Barnet, the Minister's man.

James Hogg 1770-1835
The Private Memories and Confessions of a Justified Sinner

As I start to write on Aunt Katharine's 99th birthday, my memory is long and my boredom threshold short and I don't want to be 99. Life has been interesting and filled with a long list of kind and courteous friends – and a few shits! Good memory and fierce determination were gifts from my mother, together with an expensive and liberal education which taught that 'diplomacy is the art of telling plain truths without giving offence'. My father, a good gardener, was a true Duff. A cousin once said the trouble with them all was they liked mucking about with mud – a blessed gene which led to farming to the horror of my stepfather who had mapped out for me a bright future in a company he had resurrected in the Depression, making bathroom fittings in Croydon, Surrey. On hearing my foolish hopes my mother stated firmly that my grandfather had lost a lot of money playing cards and 'she wasn't having another gambler in the family!' My birth was awaited at home in Moray, but my mother, on a visit to her father at 12A Kensington Palace Gardens, now the Nepalese Embassy, got stuck in the lift with her friend, Kat Pelham Burn, a lovely lunatic Irishwoman, also having a baby. As a result I was born at 6 a.m. on 12 January 1930 within the sound of Bow Bells – the first and most supreme insult!

The christening was conducted by Randal Davidson, Archbishop of Canterbury, assisted by the Primus of Scotland, Arthur Maclean, Bishop of Moray and Nairn, together with a generous endowment of four godparents. Two were never heard of again; one died who had a sister, an eminent historian with whiskers on her chin; and the fourth gave a devastating demonstration of a Sportsman's Advice to his Son by not taking the cartridges from his gun when he shot off his toe crossing a fence near Peebles in 1931 – not humorous, but a generous gesture to my future involvement with firearms!

Eventually we returned to Moy House, near Forres, an elegant place greatly enhanced by my father's gardening skills. Willie, the under gardener, taught us – my sister Elspeth arrived in 1933 – how to crawl under the old fishing nets to help ourselves to the strawberries which never tasted so good again. We had our own tiny garden, surrounded by a box hedge, where we planted columbines, ox-eye daisies, and dusty millers whose velvet fragrance is still more perfect than that of any other flower.

1

There were dogs in handfuls, a piebald pony, and white ducks, one of which had to be dosed with castor oil in the kitchen. It died. After tea we were allowed downstairs to the drawing room to eat one sweet and be inspected by parents and visitors. Sometimes we hid behind the curtains watching the moon. On the tick of ten to six we were kissed by the grown-ups and sent to bed, mounting the stairs one step at a time to see how long we could take. Often there was thunder which terrified us, and in winter the Northern Lights.

Nanny Munro, our keeper, spoilt us. She thought I was angelic having been nursemaid to Michael Baillie, later Lord Burton, a boy of uncertain temper who minded about his possessions even then. Sixty five years later I went into the Dunain Park Hotel outside Inverness. In the hall Nanny's daughter Ann, a substantial lady, was holding court among her visitors in her chef's hat and white overalls. On seeing me she shouted to her husband, 'Edward, Edward, come quick! You must come and see Mummy's little angel boy!' The visitors had hysterics.

We had our quota of ailments, each one regarded as life threatening. We were attended by Dr Adams who took out my tonsils on the nursery table, sewed up my head after my sister had thrown an iron at me, and later treated me for impetigo.

My father trained dogs with endless patience. Three or four times a week he went shooting and otherwise was found up to his waist fishing the waters of the Findhorn or the Spey. He was an elegant shot, a brilliant fisherman, a scratch golfer, and at the balls reputed to leap higher than anyone else dancing the Highland Fling, but he was a sad man, probably a relic of his time in the trenches and in Ireland during the Black and Tans.

Our Moray childhood was sheltered. People working on the land were badly off but always laughing and smiling in a way that those in the street never do seventy years later despite comparative affluence. Farming dominated life and our treat as children was to go to Wellhill with Nanny to visit her cousins. We rode in the cart at turnip time behind Prince, the Clydesdale gelding, and gathered eggs from the brown hens in well-strawed nesting boxes. In the kitchen there were oatcakes and raspberry jam. It wasn't so good when Nanny left to marry Alastair Shaw of Slackbuie by Inverness, a farmer with hands like soup plates. Her place was taken by Peggie, the nursery maid, who ultimately married somebody called Hutchinson and lived in a cottage with roses around the door and everlasting peas at the garden gate. The only remembered good she did was to produce a boyfriend who took me on the back of his motorbike and once found me a yellowhammer's nest. Two days after Nanny Munro's marriage she sent a piece of wedding cake which Peggie confiscated because I had escaped from her on my tricycle on the way home from Wellhill. She sent me to bed, and worse, allowed my sister to play with my golf clubs. Predictably, I screamed. Later she suspended our cousin, Romayne, over the banisters by her hair – after which she was invited to find another place! Undoubtedly we were spoilt.

We went to tea parties with our parents' friends whose children we invariably disliked. Once I pushed a boy with buck-teeth off a bench, to Nanny's delight. One summer my Craven grandmother took Blervie and taught us to hunt for fairies underneath the pines among red toadstools with white spots. In winter we went to meets of the Fort George Beagles, and in summer on picnics to the Culbin Sands, where we listened for the bells of the church buried in the great storm of 1692. Once we were taken to see James Brander Dunbar who bred curly-coated retrievers and had made his name in the Boer War by shooting more Boers than anyone alive or dead. They tried to kill him, but as he was left handed they aimed at his feet, his head being the wrong side of the rock. He was the original of John Buchan's poaching hero, John MacNab. He lived with a woman of a different colour, no mean feat in 1930 Moray, and under his bed he kept his coffin, on which was written:

> In Memory of James Brander Dunbar of Pitgaveny
> The most loveable rogue on earth and the most unspeakable villain.
> There was no room in hell for Satan and him.

Another shooting eccentric was Rose of Kilravock who kept ferrets in his pockets and hens in the drawing room, and always said, 'I say, you know, I say.' As Sir Thomas Woodcock was lowered into his grave at Nairn, a voice from the back of the mourners was heard to exclaim: 'I say, you know, I say – very bad year this year for woodcock!' The humour was not lost on the assembled mourners. In summer we went by day with our cousins, the Astells and the Torins, to Findhorn where we got splinters in our fingers from the beach huts and had to bathe, which I hated. There were jellyfish. Sometimes we stayed at Hopeman with our Duff grandmother who had an outdoor aviary of budgerigars and a parrot which vandalised the backs of the books in the library. We ate loganberries in the garden and white raspberries in the woods, and fed ourselves on the chickens' bran in the bin in the shed. Duffy had moved to Hopeman Lodge when she left Drummuir after Grandfather died. He had built it in the 1880s and it eventually became one of the houses of Gordonstoun School. At Hopeman we usually saw Aunts. Aunt Consie was disagreeable with a deep voice, married to Wyn Astell who she divorced. June and David, the children, were nice but have had unlucky lives. Aunt Margaret, a spinster, known as Git or Aunt Ratstails, was reputed to be the thinnest woman in the north of Scotland, her backbone meeting her stomach which caused endless bother. She taught me – with difficulty – to ride a bicycle and eventually emigrated to Dorset where she lived in a wooden house with a wooden roof constantly attacked by woodpeckers. When gardening she hung her wig on her fork, and much later had her toes run over by a bus in London.

Aunt Katharine was the youngest and favourite. She married Leo Fraser-Mackenzie who died, and had one son, Thomas, who died in the 1940s. In 1926 she had married again, Chum Torin who was in the Shropshire Light Infantry.

Duffy with her grandchildren, Joanna Torin, Thomas Fraser Mackenzie, June Astell, Patrick Gordon-Duff, Elspeth Gordon-Duff, Duffy with Priscilla Torin, Elspeth Torin, David Astell.

There were three daughters, Joanna, Elspeth and Priscilla. Uncle Randal, a submariner, was married unsuccessfully to Mollie and killed in HMS *Culver* in 1942. Uncle David was a tea planter in Ceylon, married to an Australian – Aunt Nell.

There was a maid, Madge, and Violet the cook, and a pervasive smell of mince and boiled potatoes. On the dining room table were silver owls for pepper and salt. Upstairs at night we watched the fishing fleet sail up the Firth on the evening tide and occasionally ships from the Royal Navy moved out from Invergordon through the Souters. At the far end of the moonpath was Morven in Caithness as we sat in the window.

We still lived in the shadow of the 1914 War in whose mud my eldest uncle, Lachlan, had died, but there seemed no reason why our idyllic life should not last for ever – until disaster struck! In 1934 my mother's father died. Early in 1935 my grandmother moved from Kensington Palace Gardens to 8 Kensington Court where we stayed from 18 January–27 March. I was photographed in my kilt with the champion Shetland at the Islington Pony Show – our first and only acquaintance! My parents separated and eventually divorced. Life was never quite the same again.

Perhaps we should have been sensitive enough to know it was happening. On 19 September 1934 I was a page at my cousin Posie's wedding to Rodney Palmer

My grandfather, Thomas Craven.

in Keith. Their only son eventually became British Ambassador to Cuba and to the Vatican. On the way home my stepfather was showing off to my mother by driving too fast – probably 35 m.p.h. – in his Ford V 8. Where the road ran between pine trees west of Elgin I was sick down my lace jabot and my kilt and all over the back of the car. We were never told what happened about the divorce, but spent much time with our grandmothers at Hopeman and in London. By then both grandfathers were dead. The following August, my Craven grandmother, Gang-Gang, rented the shooting at Trinafour in Perthshire. One day I fell in the burn underneath the bridge below the post office on the Kinloch Rannoch road. That evening when my mother came upstairs to kiss me goodnight I said: 'Good night, Mrs Duff.' She answered, 'I'm not Mrs Duff any more. I'm Mrs Mayer.' I suppose it was the start of never quite knowing where I really belonged which still persists. Later she told us how she had fallen in love with Uncle Edward, but didn't know what to do about it when, by luck, our father fell in love with our stepmother, Sheila Davison. My mother had money, my father not much, and it was a problem for young minds to decide whether we only preferred staying with our mother because she could afford to give us a better time. Our loyalties were split by having to spend two thirds of each holiday with our mother and one third with our father. I screamed at night after each transfer and took to wetting my bed. Hand-overs took place with intermediaries, the most memorable being at the Caledonian Hotel in Edinburgh with Git. On the whole we were shielded from parental battles in a way modern children are not, but we were lucky in our step-parents, which sort of gave us two for the price of one.

Our stepmother, Shish, had a father we never knew, a disagreeable Irish politician, ennobled as Lord Brougshane in 1945. Her mother, Poke, was highly intelligent and lived at 19 Chelsea Park Gardens. At night she left a note for the burglars on the hall chair: 'Silver in the dining room. Please do not disturb!' When she died she instructed her sons to tell the Kensington and Chelsea Council to remove her. They declined. As she didn't want anything religious there were problems, but eventually cremation seemed nearest her wishes with the ashes to be spread on her mother's grave in Highgate Cemetery. This they were unable to find, so they spread them on Karl Marx's grave instead which would have entertained the old lady. Shish had one sister, Joyce Wilson, and two brothers. Patrick, Assistant Military Secretary to the War Cabinet 1942-5, was a lawyer and reputed to have written the Dirge of the Adjutant-General's Secretary.

> The great ones depart at last for their dinner
> Leaving the Secretary growing thinner and thinner
> Racking his brains as to how to report
> What he thinks they will think
> That they ought to have thought.

The other, a famous fighter pilot, DSO, DFC became a distinguished secretary to the Friends of Covent Garden.

Shish was musical and argued incessantly as an intellectual exercise. It was hard to understand how my father, who hated dispute, could have allied himself to such an uncompromising companion. She taught me much for which to be grateful – to speak French at meals, play memory games, read books, quote poetry, and argue logically, which our own children seem incapable of doing, preferring to rule by force of indignation. Uncle Edward was a man of energy, who played football at Harrow once a year until he was fifty five, and had been in the 2nd VI at Cambridge for tennis. He rode horses – of which my mother was terrified – hunted, played polo, was a keen Territorial gunner, and ran a successful small business, Metlex, in Sumner Road, Croydon – the one from which I was saved! His deceased father, Max Mayer, had emigrated from Germany at the end of the nineteenth century and was a diamond merchant in Hatton Garden. His widow, Mummy Mayer, Matilda known as Tilly, always dressed in a large fur coat and lived at 20 Bolton Gardens where we stayed before going to see Edward VIII review his troops in Hyde Park in 1936. An anarchist took a pot-shot at the King on his way back to the Palace. That morning for breakfast we had soft herring roes, which I still detest.

Christmas 1935 was spent with Gang-Gang at Kensington Court where we were spoilt rotten and although she never learnt to cook herself, we were fed like fighting cocks by Sarah Bell who produced wonderful ice cream covered in hundreds and thousands. Always a visit to our grandmother, even after the war when she lived at 57 Palace Court, was a cause for celebration with lobster mousse, roast chicken, and orange jelly shaped like a rabbit. For my birthday in 1936 my present was a complete set of wooden Highland soldiers. The following day there was a brief encounter with education at Wagners in Queensgate where we played football in Kensington Gardens, coloured pictures with crayons, cut out animals, and started to learn to read and write.

A week later George V died. I was taken to see his funeral pass at Hyde Park Corner perched on the shoulders of Jack Simpson, one of my mother's ex-beaux whose father Tommy designed golf courses. In the spring we went by paddle steamer to see Aunt Edith Kindersley at Hamstead Grange on the Isle of Wight where my first tooth came out and the fairies replaced it with a silver threepenny bit under my pillow. That summer my mother rented Ford Place in Sussex where lessons were conducted by a Mr Ashley who took us to HMS *Victory* at Portsmouth and to the beach at Bognor, not presumably to see where the late king was supposed to have uttered his famous phrase! I remember it mostly for the Eldorado water ices in chequered three cornered cases, and for being very cold. Our mother had a passion for the seaside and having endowed us with bad noses and bad chests, had a touching belief, along with many of her contemporaries, that sea air was good for us. This was usually followed by winters inhaling Friars Balsam, head under a bath towel, nose blocked with catarrh, and doses of Syrup of Figs or Milk of Magnesia 'to keep our motions, regular'! Today they would have called it 'prophylactic medicine'.

That year autumn was spent at Hopeman and winter at 94 Eaton Place. My stepfather stood, without success, for London County Council and wore a big blue rosette. At Christmas the butler took me down to the Servants' Hall and gave me beer, which was disgusting but grown-up. There was a governess, Miss Lucas, who walked me to see the Changing of the Guard at Buckingham Palace, or at St James's where the pipers of the Irish Guards wore saffron kilts. One day a German military band played on the Horse Guards Parade and a bandsman fainted which made our morning, after which we watched Admiral Beattie's funeral moving under the arch into Trafalgar Square. Another time Miss Lucas lost me watching the bayonet fighting behind the railings at Wellington Barracks. Sixty years later, as a non-executive director of Booker Countryside, serving under Derek Barber, I watched out of the window from the 27th floor of Portland House and saw where Miss Lucas had wandered off. Her only real entitlement to memory was that she sent me a large collection of Portuguese stamps after she left.

In the spring of 1937 Bellasis House near Dorking, on top of Box Hill, was rented from Lady Ridley, grandmother of Nicholas, Mrs Thatcher's Minister who later took the duck shooting at Muncaster. He told me they thought she would leave them a lot of money when she died, but all they could find was 40,000 Turkish cigarettes and a hundred pairs of shoes.

Father, Geordie Gordon-Duff with PTGD, 1934.

The summer term of 1937 was spent as a day boy at Chinthurst School at Tadworth, but apart from a fairly chaotic start to my education, life began to take on a pattern.

My father needed a job and joined the RAF Volunteer Reserve at Scampton, later home to the Dam Busters, living at Anderson House, South Carleton. We visited the Lincoln Imp in Lincoln Cathedral, and were allowed as a treat to go to watch the planes leaving on night manoeuvres. He taught me the world was round and spun around the sun; how to look for the Plough in the night sky like Galileo. We dug the garden trying to find Australia, but before arriving he was posted to Grantham where we caught ladybirds and kept them in match-boxes. We walked to church at Christmas, bells ringing everywhere through the night. Father lived in a house at Welby Gate and worked at St. Vincents. I did not meet the young Margaret Thatcher.

After that back to Moray to Inchstellie in the Crook of Alves. Between oatfields full of blue chicory, scarlet poppies and creeping thistles we walked to the shop to buy round sweets which changed colour as we sucked them. That was the year the British Prime Minister returned from Munich after meeting Hitler, uttering the greatest lie in history – 'Peace in our time.'

Thirty eight years later I returned to that shop and met John MacIver of Coltfield who showed me his acres of weed free barley, his shed filled with a new tractor and all the latest machinery. 'And do you know,' he said, 'I go everywhere on a bicycle!' That night he rode it seven miles to the NFU meeting in Forres where I was speaking. Somehow it meant there was still hope for humanity.

In September 1937 my mother sent me to school at Southey Hall, Great Bookham as a day boy, and the following summer to board. We turned hay in the grounds with our feet and discovered the agonies of hay fever. Henry Fussell was headmaster and my form mistress, Miss Walsh. Reading their reports it is hard to understand how it was possible to persuade myself to hate the place. One weekend out from school at the far end of the Bellasis gallery whose walls were painted with canvasses of classical deities I shot Aphrodite through the eye with my bow and arrow. Bunce, the chauffeur, drove me back at night in disgrace and somewhere among the litter of this house is my postcard of apology. One winter Saturday I wept all night saying I hated school, probably because it was the only reason that sprang to mind. It was a performance repeated at the start of each term for eight years. My mother would pull me from the bottom of the bed by my hair and tell me to stop 'abandoning myself to grief'. It must be hereditary because our children were capable of virtuoso performances which made my efforts look pallid. As soon as she went school was quite enjoyable, but my poor mother was left shaking with grief. Two other inherited characteristics were hatred of the east wind, and a strong jaw. As children DSTM meant Don't Speak To Mum – the wind is in the east – and years later, after speaking at a meeting in Strontian, a crofter came up and said, 'Well, my boy, we don't know what you can do for us but one thing is sure certain. The chin your mother put on you is the most hopeful sign we've seen for a very long time!'

1938 passed quickly. A visit to the Holborn Empire to see *Where the Rainbow Ends*, the Surrey Union point to point in March, and a daylight performance of the Aldershot Tattoo in June, with the inevitable stay at the seaside at Broadstairs in July. My mother bought an Austin 7, DBY 592, into which she would pile thirteen children to follow the hounds. She bought and sold it three times and it was finally disposed of in 1948 at Strathmashie when she noticed a wheel running down the road beside her! At weekends there were tennis parties and shooting parties, and one day Laeta Lucas-Tooth came with her three children. John we later knew as the Little Red Flea and one of his sisters had elastic bands in her teeth. Their father, a distant cousin, eventually became an MP and their mother was the only person who could put the whole six inch diameter of a cartwheel biscuit into her mouth at once.

In New Year 1939 we were taken by my sister's godmother Annette Bailey to see Jean Forbes-Robertson and Seymour Hicks in *Peter Pan* at the London Palladium and then, wearing Gardie Duff's kilt jacket and plaid, to the Lord Mayor's Party at the Mansion House. I danced the Lambeth Walk with Beryl Howell, the Lord Mayor's daughter, an ex girlfriend of my stepfather and mother of David Howell, Minister of Transport in the 1980s. Then back for my last term at Southey Hall.

On 6 May we lunched in London with the Ellises at 15 Craven Hill before going to my new school. Roger was at St. Peter's Seaford and together we were packed onto a train at Victoria. In the carriage was a ghastly boy called Stephen Bryans – a bully. My tears would have filled the countryside through which we passed, but St. Peter's was a good school, run by Pat Knox Shaw (PKS) and his wife and we were well educated.

War was expected and air raid shelters dug. After lunch in summer we rested on red and blue striped rugs in the sun. There was PT and woodwork with Major Apperley, French with T.D. Pickard Cambridge, later blown up by a mine on an English beach, and Latin, and History, and Geography, and English, and Arithmetic all taught by patient people to whom, in retrospect, we owe much of our later enjoyment of life. Under the dormitory window we watched romance blossom between PKS's stepdaughter, Margaret Buckle, and John Farebrother. His brother Michael fancied her too, and it was he who became the last headmaster before the school was disbanded in the 1980s. Twelve years later shooting at Manydown it came to mind when Pop Fane, chairman of the Boxing Board of Control who wore a rose in his buttonhole summer and winter, stated at lunch that he had the best report ever written from Eton. 'Fane is like Margate – vulgar, but bracing!' His son, known as Buck, also a vicious boxer, kicked me up the backside with a cricket boot at Eton. We learnt to play games with enthusiasm and never to challenge the umpire's decision. How times have changed! In the hall was a drinking fountain which today would no doubt be forbidden by the health police.

That summer holiday by train to Peebles, with Gang-Gang and Bobs Neve, my sister's governess. At Newcastle I fell between the train and the station. Uncle Uel, my grandmother's brother, had taken the shooting at Elibank. He was meant to be stupid when young and had been despatched to the Indian Stock Exchange as a suitable destination. He was, however, so charming that everybody gave him tips on the stock market and he grew seriously rich. He bought a tiger place at Ootacamund and a large estate at Hazelwood in County Sligo, where he shot a 32-stone stag, the record red deer weight for many years. He married an Irish nurse, Aunt Katie, and at the age of 60 got himself a son, Brian Berridge, my contemporary, who was as charming as his father, but died young. At Elibank the two of us gained no brownie points for shooting at the vital parts of a naked statue in the garden with his air gun and trying to shoot a salmon in the Tweed.

We thought Gang-Gang never did anything bad. She had a white wig with a blue ribbon one day and a pink one the next, and sat in the chair with hands folded. She was always sixty-six and spat phlegm into a bowl beside her. When, however, she died my mother found a note in the back of the family bible saying that at the age of nineteen she had run away to the stage in the States with her sister, Aunt Stella, who really was naughty, and had been proposed to by Robert E. Lee, the Confederate general, just before he died. Aunt Stella married a dissolute Irishman, Rupert, Earl of Clonmel, was a good artist, a great beauty, and in the war ran the White Elephant Laundry in London, as well as writing a book – *The Yellow Taxi-Pig*. She would take us to lunch at Claridges, taught us how to listen to three conversations at once, how to walk into a restaurant looking down our noses to left and right, and how to slip the unwanted remains of a meal into a handkerchief for her pedigree Pekingese.

After a week we left for Inchstellie and at 11 a.m. on 3 September we listened to the Prime Minister, Neville Chamberlain, on the wireless. Britain was at war with Germany. Twelve days later we were bundled by train to Stirling, thence to Elibank. South the following day driven along St Mary's Loch by Newman, Gang-Gang's chauffeur, in her Rolls which made me feel sick. We reached Bellasis at 1 a.m. The whole country was blacked out for fear of German bombers. Shortly afterwards the signposts were removed in case of invasion.

It was the start of six dreadful years for a nation still mourning the dead of another war. On 31 August Uncle Edward was called up. As usual, the General Staff, unsupported by a Prime Minister reluctant to rearm, prepared for a previous war with amateur warriors, many still mounted on horses, with few tanks and fewer aeroplanes. War with troops in impregnable positions was expected. People sang: 'Hang out your washing on the Siegfried Line if the Siegfried Line's still there.' Gas masks accompanied us everywhere – and our identity cards. Goodness knows why there is so much hoo-ha now about their reintroduction when every snooper's IT system knows all about us anyhow. Soon there was food rationing and meat was rationed until 1954. On trains notices proclaimed: 'Careless talk costs lives!' and rumours of spies abounded promoted by such stories as *The Thirty Nine Steps*, the film of which we had seen at school on the day its author John Buchan died. Opposed to our men was an air force seasoned by service in the Spanish Civil War and military strategists whose battle plans were based on speed and mobility. Germany still smarted from the injustice of the Versailles Treaty with whose terms it had no hope of financial compliance. Its people were lashed into passionate rage by Hitler, one of the greatest orators of all time. So started the Phoney War. We had a map in which we stuck coloured pins to show how the front lines moved. Nothing happened for six months. On Sunday nights the BBC played the national anthems of the Allies to which we listened before sleep. Twice a day we heard the news on the wireless.

On 22 September back to school, but home three weeks later in quarantine for German measles and in time for my mother's thirty third birthday. Pitprops held up the Gallery ceiling in case of air raids and eight evacuees arrived from London. My mother kept in touch with them until her death. There was still a cook, Mrs Anthony, and a multi-coloured cat called Tippy Scat. Winter, the head gardener, was paid £2 per week and we planted Love-in-the-Mist in our garden. In January Elspeth and I stayed for the statutory ten days with our father at the Lodge Hill Hotel at Pulborough. It was bitter winter. We froze snowballs on window sills, made slides on icy puddles, and knitted mittens for the men in France. We landed in trouble when, on their account, we sold our collection of cigarette cards to the hotel residents. Back to school by car on 8 May although petrol was rationed. The big end went, the final straw for my long suffering mother sitting beside her snivelling child.

The German offensive was in full swing. On 24 May I was collected by car. At the beginning of June the remnants of the British Army escaped dramatically from Dunkirk in an armada of small boats. Roger Ellis, who played an increasing part in our family life, was staying and we laid frustrated plans to stow away in the back of our mothers' cars when they went to serve tea to the troops as they passed through the station. Roger's father died about then and we shared most of our holidays for the next six years.

On 17 June France fell, the first time I saw a kingfisher, flying between shady river banks near Mickleham. On the 19th St. Peter's moved to Veryan, near Truro, where for one term we did lessons in the garages of the Nare Hotel. We collected cowries on the beach and learnt to identify and press the many flowers. The cliff tops were covered with thrifts. At night the Local Defence Volunteers, forerunners of the Home Guard – and Dad's Army – patrolled, rifles slung, outside our windows searching the moonlit sea for enemies. There were occasional puffs of smoke from the anti-aircraft guns at Falmouth. Holidays started on 6 August. The regular summer fires on Headley Heath were still sensational, but above our heads the Battle of Britain had started with young men in Spitfires and Hurricanes harassing the German formations. The sky was often full of falling machines. One day my mother watched a German parachute landing. Cries for help sounded from the other side of the valley where we had picked the primroses and violets for her in spring. Bravely she donned her tin hat and armed with a stick set off to find no more than a cow stuck in the brambles. Beneath this mayhem Roger and I picked the gooseberries.

In September school moved to the Fortescue home at Castlehill in North Devon – an ideal destination for curious children. There were early morning walks, two by two, and everywhere birds. My cousin John Gordon-Duff's mother had been a Fortescue so they were kind to us. (John was the breeder of the Smithfield champion, Even Girl 3rd of Cobairdy.) There was a beautiful portrait of Lady Fortescue – from my memory by Laszlo. The ballroom was used for lessons, Evensong, and boxing. There, after breakfast, our names were ticked when we had done our 'morning duty'. In winters we went beating for the shoots and in return were given a picnic lunch and a Kit-Kat. We played football and rugger with much enthusiasm and cricket with less. One local river featured in Henry Williamson's *Tarka the Otter*. Over another was the Ogley Bridge where grey wagtails nested. In woodland banks we found wrens' nests and somewhere, at the bottom of the garden, the eggs of a linnet and long tailed tits.

The Devon countryside was a wonderful classroom for any child and in the

Bridget Toynbee, the lady 'with the green silk dressing gown with white spots', aged 100.

woods we collected beech mast and acorns for the local pigs. At nights I studied the Bible with the aid of the Bible Reading Fellowship and became quite religious. Helped by a boy called Schoeffler, whose father had been one of the principal singers in *The Flying Dutchman* at the Vienna Opera, we grew mustard and cress on wet blotting paper on the windowsill. Most of this time I slept in Mind Your Head and shared a room with Robin Hooper. In his sleep he threw hairbrushes and once swallowed the door key, which was only reclaimed after a diet of brown bread and porridge. Izal loo rolls contained riddles which we wasted countless sheets attempting to find. At morning we had cold baths, then lined up outside the sick room to have our throats sprayed by Sister with some noxious substance to keep us healthy. Sixty years ago passing in that passage on her way to the bathroom was Bridget Toynbee on a visit to her son Peter. She was dressed in a green silk dressing gown with white spots and seemed the most beautiful person I had ever seen. She is now 99. I never saw her again but last Sunday, prompted by Peter, encountered at a reunion lunch, I called to tell her. She sounded as though she had all her marbles, but hated being so ancient.

My mother comments in her photograph book: 'December 11th, 1940 P.

back in quarantine for measles. December 23rd got it!' She read me *Thy Servant a Dog* and taught me six-pack bezique and pelmanism, still the best remedy for concentration. At nights I listened for the distinctive throb of the German planes on their way to London. Once they dropped a bomb in the woods which were shortly afterwards felled in one drunken night by some Canadian soldiers. Their doctor, also drunk, chased the housemaid round the Christmas tree and petrified my mother by suggesting he was very good at treating children with measles. Later, returning to Eton we used to stay at the Hyde Park Hotel, a terrifying experience with the guns in the park in continuous action interrupted only by the whistle of descending bombs. The people of London were incredibly brave – and humorous. At school we learnt chess. With cockroaches we had caught we played the Beetle Game on the top of a shiny black table on which we split up a chalk circle into segments with different odds. The luckless insect was released from under a box and bets placed with matchsticks on which way it would go. We used the same table on which to deposit the scurf from our heads. It showed up rather well.

In the same room PKS asked me to translate '*Polyphemus oravit*'. 'Polyphemus beseeched.' 'No!' with which I crossly said, 'Well, besooched!' A black metal geometry box flew past my ear. The rebuke was deserved but in modern times, with a litigious parent, the poor headmaster would probably have ended in court. It should have been besought! Later, at Eton, Peter Whiteley, Captain of the House, delivered eight strokes of the cane on my backside for not having a short enough haircut on a Field Day. The only injury was to my dignity. I had cut my own hair with my nail scissors – not badly, just not enough! Usually hair was done on Wednesday nights by a Mr Woodman, who had a wig and a false moustache – a curious advertisement for a barber! The discipline was fair and educational. Contrary to modern thought it has never prejudiced later gentle tendencies. The only quarrel is with PKS's theory of never running with the hare and hunting with the hounds. This bothers me because increasingly active compromise is needed in modern life to escape paralysis by irresistible forces and immovable objects.

For two term ends my mother met me at Taunton station and took me back to Brook House near Oswestry whither she had migrated when Bellasis was requisitioned for important German prisoners in February 1941. To her horror, when crossing a river in South Wales, I asked the man in the corner its name. 'It's the Oosk,' said the man. 'Oh!' said this horrid boy, 'You mean the Usk.' The memory still makes me cringe. Later, with Roger Ellis, we travelled back and forth alone, he losing his ticket and smoking cigarettes which made him sick. This was the man later considered an outstanding headmaster first at Rossall and then at Marlborough. We travelled alone without fear by rail and learnt nothing worse than bad language!

On 19 December 1940 my half-brother, Roderick was born. The following year Father was posted to Abingdon, a parting from Scotland which distressed him until he died in 1966 from smoking aged 70. He rented a house at Cothill. There were rare orchids in the wood and a house nearby owned by the inventor of Nissen huts. Around the garden was a high wall above a brook with many buddleia bushes which attracted butterflies, mostly Cabbage Whites, whose caterpillars persecuted the cabbages. Elspeth and I were paid tuppence per hundred corpses which involved great danger from falling off the wall. I taught my stepmother to play chess and sometimes we went to tea with the elderly mother of Leonard Cheshire VC, the founder of Cheshire Homes. She had contracted sleepy sickness in West Africa and watching her pour tea from the silver teapot was tantalising.

During the Christmas holidays of 1941 we stayed in the Star and Eagle at Goudhurst to visit my stepfather who was with an artillery regiment at Mystole where the adjutant, Pat Talbot-Smith, taught me to cheat at Racing Demon sitting on the floor of his office. At Easter we went to Brook House, Woodhill, home until 1945. Gang-Gang's Rolls, minus Newman, was jacked up on bricks in the garage. She lived with us, teaching us to play bridge or paint in oils each morning. If our cards were bad we learnt to sit on the poker and never to fold our napkins when going away if we wanted to return. She had a devilish sense of humour inherited by her grandson. Also there was Mademoiselle Roy who helped us bird nesting when empty nests in the hedge evoked her usual expression: 'Vieux comme Herod!' Lapwings everywhere nesting in the newly brairded corn and in early mornings my mother took me to a bog beyond the Bath Wood where we watched the reed-buntings at their nest and listened to the drumming of the snipe. There was constant consciousness of nearby hills even then. To church at Trefonen. Uncle Edward's spaniel, Rudolph, used to follow at a distance, sneaking in behind us, slipping up to the altar when my mother took Communion. Returning many years later, pinned to the board outside the church was an extract from Chief Seattle's address to the Commissioners from Washington – 'If all the beasts were gone man would die of a great loneliness of spirit.' Throughout my working life that statement has had a deep resonance, encouraging me to speak publicly in terms which even politicians could not fail to understand.

Our mother ran a YMCA mobile canteen around North Wales as far west as Bala with Patsy Moorhouse (later Lady Cookson), Moira Deacon and Doris Stobart with whose children we played bicycle polo and went on paper chases. In holidays we travelled with her around the army camps learning to love spring in the North Wales valleys and around Lake Vrwny. Otherwise we bicycled, petrol being rationed, and occasionally went by train to Chester to a useless dentist who gave us toothpaste samples which did little for our teeth. As a result we were sent to a beast in Oswestry called Kidner who heated his instruments so hot he burnt our mouths. Living with us were Carmen Roy and Mousie, Miss Anderson, governess to Elspeth and our cousin Romayne, later replaced by Miss Vennard who imposed discipline and thus, by command of our

Sister Elspeth, aged 15.

grandmother, was dismissed. Elspeth and I disposed of one cook by leaving a note in the kitchen saying 'Waste not, want not!' Her successor had never heard of summer pudding so on her day out my mother made one – which failed. Roger and I were sent to dump it in the pond before her return. That pond was a source of endless pleasure with trout we occasionally caught and a boat in which we played hectic games likely now to give the Health and Safety Executive a fit. All of which reveals why the country needed Trade Unions!

We played classical music on a wind-up gramophone and Elspeth collected silver threepenny bits in a whisky bottle which our mother robbed for church collections. We had our own garden where we grew vegetables and dug for victory, criss-crossing the plot with string soaked in Renardine to keep away the cats and mice. Our mother kept hens and bees, and a couple of pigs, and taught herself to cook well although hating it. She had never gone to school, but educated herself continuously by reading. Her generation, used to privilege, must have needed to make terrible adjustments. During the General Strike in 1926 she and her half sister, Sheila Chichester, thought they should volunteer their services at the Labour Exchange. These two innocents – our mother was

19 – were astonished to be offered jobs as midwives, but elected to make soup instead! Driving away, strikers threw bricks through the windscreen of the car which Grandpapa had given her for not becoming engaged to a man of whom he disapproved.

Fathers are strange. Marion Burrell, daughter of the Burrell (of Burrell Collection fame) should have been my godmother but had been forbidden to talk to my mother who had introduced her to two men – not the required dukes – with whom she fell in love. Eventually she met a duke who courted her, but her father's reputation made him run for cover. She died a spinster, a lovely person who spent her whole life caring for her father with one small intermission as matron at Newlands School. He left her nothing, although his trustees tried to make amends. At the age of 76 she inserted an extraordinary notice in *The Times* saying that she wished in future to be known as Sylvia and inspired my respect when she told my redoubtable mother: 'Really, Rosemary, you're the bossiest woman I've ever met!'

September 1941 took us by train to Tenby where my stepfather was on a gunnery course at Manobier. He gave me a 20-bore shotgun which I carried unloaded for a year learning about safety, how to handle it, how to clean it, supervised by old Roberts, the gardener. Today the nation is barmy when young people can no longer have that basic training in firearms and fieldcraft which made us efficient recruits for our National Service. Back to Castlehill with a bottle of raspberry jam which leaked from my case on the rack. The fellow travellers thought it was blood!

We went to Kinloch Rannoch the following August to shoot at Kynachan with Mrs Mackinlay (née Crabbie). I fired my gun and shot my first grouse on Schiehallion with Johnny Fraser. The garrons went to the hill with Mackinlay's whisky in one pannier and Crabbie's Green Ginger in the other. I conceived a passion for the old woman's youngest daughter, Tupenny Chiene, nineteen, married to an accountant taken prisoner in Hong Kong. I kept her photograph next to my bed for years and later used to see her and George in Edinburgh. Thirty five years later at an NFU dinner in Aberfeldy, Major Whitson of Lick, trying to wind me up, was horrified to be told I knew exactly who he was and that I had won the three-legged race with Tupenny, his sister-in-law, at Tummel Bridge sports in 1942.

Common Entrance papers passed me into Eton and Hubert Hartley's house (HHSH) at Baldwins Bec. Despite the big magnolia grandiflora outside the door, it was stated by the Prince Consort to have been the ugliest house he ever saw, but it faced Windsor Castle and was draped in Virginia Creeper which I trained through my window on the third floor. This was May 1943. My first day at Eton must have been a nightmare for my poor mother. We drove around Hyde Park in a taxi, she exhorting me to pull myself together and think of Montrose's second son who refused to be swapped in a prisoner exchange with his father's lieutenant in 1645. It seemed irrelevant! We boarded a train to

Windsor, sharing a carriage with a boy called Huggins who also wept the whole way. Our combined output would have driven a hydro-electric scheme. As soon as my mother left tears ceased and it was only years later when our own children went away to school that it was possible to realise her agonies. My wife is obstinate – in me it's called determined – and our combined genetic output produced a terrifying power of protest in our four daughters! Uncle Edward had written advice from West Africa on his way to command 304 East African Light Anti-Aircraft Regiment in Kenya. My father also wrote, having been promoted to Group Captain, SOA, 1 Bomber Group at Bawtry. Our holidays with him were spent at the Old Bell, Barnby Moor when we helped Angie Farrer, Master of the Grove, exercise her hounds. Later he took a house at Tickhill God-Help-Us whose church bells rang every four hours, a different tune each day of the week. Monday was 'Bluebells of Scotland'.

Hubert was away at the war until 1945, his place temporarily taken by Francis Cruso (FJAC), a serious bachelor who sang. Hubert's wife Grizel remained in residence, large, full of vitality. She called everybody, including the coal man, 'darling', had a heart of gold, and treated us as the children she could never have, having lost her baby after sliding down the banisters. She kept open house and fed us like fighting cocks despite the rationing. I messed (took my tea) with Andrew Forbes-Leith and John Gooch who once had to write an apology for being late for prayers. He wrote, 'Who would have thought/ That I'd be late/ At any rate/ It really doesn't matter/ So let's stop this idle chatter!' which was not appreciated. For tea Mrs Dunne, the 'boys' maid' fried us bread and the Spam and sardines which our mothers sent. Otherwise thirty eight of us ate in the dining room, presided over by the Dame, Olive Hempson, whose cousin Anne Frost eventually became our daughter's mother-in-law. Francis Cruso took prayers at evening before doing his rounds to discuss our individual problems. Today the Nanny state would say this was inappropriate but it prevented many difficulties before they arose. One night, returning from the memorial service in Chapel I fired a cherry pip between finger and thumb through the open window at the poor man's neck as he said house prayers, an act for which I still pay mental penance. Assuredly I shall go to hell. One night, when chairman of the Dumfries Music Club, returning home with Marisa Robles, the Spanish harpist, she said: 'Patrick, you go to heaven?' 'No.' 'Well you and I, we will go to hell together and I will teach you to play zee harp!'

Our rooms were tiny with a folding bed, an ottoman for clothes, a Windsor chair, and a bureau to keep our books and at which to do our extra work which occupied an hour or two each evening. After the War the Provost and Fellows, seeking to offer places to a wider range of students, approached various County Councils. Eventually Leicestershire sent a bus load of parents and boys. On inspecting our quarters the parents' comment was: 'Our little Willie live in accommodation like that – not bloody likely!' We had been reared on tales of Sparta and Leonidas at Thermopylae so hadn't really noticed.

Having learnt to want to learn, Eton education gave enormous advantages in later life – not least an ability to get on with difficult people. Twice lately I have returned, once to address the Agricultural Society where I found myself in the same room where Mr Sladen attempted to teach us about the gold leaf electroscope. I put wet blotting paper in my shoes to make me faint before a test, but lost my nerve before the experiment was concluded. The second time was to an exhibition of pictures by my friend Alasdair McMorrine. The boys were beautifully mannered and nowhere did I find the alleged superiority or snobbishness attributed to Eton pupils by the outside world. It was a large school and we were taught in classes of twenty or thirty by teachers of the highest standard. We learnt to work alone. Our education was very broad and nobody specialised until passing School Certificate. There was compulsory exercise and we enjoyed competition at work and play, learning to stand on our own feet far from home, capable of challenging injustice when we thought we were right. Early school was at half past seven on weekdays, fortified by cocoa and a biscuit and a brisk quarter mile walk to the classroom.

My first Classical Tutor was Oliver John Wellington Hunkin, son of the Bishop of Truro. An unconventional man, he read Damon Runyon to us. D.C. Wilkinson, whose son William became Chairman of the Nature Conservancy Council, introduced me to agriculture by mistake when he gave me five hundred lines of a Virgil Georgic to copy after he found me fighting on the floor with Colin Baillieu – who was bigger than me! Basil Greenup taught me to recite poetry in a loud clear voice for his Saying Lessons. W. Hope-Jones taught us to do long division in our heads and as a hobby was reputed to lie in his bath looking for mistakes in the logarithm tables. G.B. Smith had a bald head, sang alto in the choir, and was a liberal historian under whom I studied with Douglas Hurd. David Graham-Campbell imparted a lifelong appreciation of history and became headmaster of Glenalmond. We learnt to write elegant prose, never to start sentences with 'but' or 'however', and never to use two words where one would do, unlike the modern Civil Service. Our manual was Townsend Warner's *On the Writing of English*. Simon Barrington-Ward, later Bishop of Coventry, whose father was Editor of *The Times*, sat beside me at the back of the class trying to teach me to imitate his beautiful copper-plate writing at a desk where my cousin Robin had carved his name in 1931. The headmaster, Claude Aurelius Elliot, a Cambridge economist and mountaineer, taught Industrial History during which I studied most of Rudyard Kipling under the desk. Lionel Fortescue terrified us and was reputed to own half Iceland, but the one to whom I owe most was Llewellyn Slingsby Bethell whose hobby was collecting stones from the sources of as many rivers in the world as possible. He taught Classics and made us translate slices of the local paper each week into Latin and Greek verse. It was learning that sense of metre which has given me the ability to write poetry with ease. A Scottish lawyer, Fletcher of Saltoun, once wrote: 'If a man be permitted to make a country's songs he need not care who writes the

Country's laws.' Another great influence was Alan Barker, later married to Jean Trumpington, one time Agricultural Minister and a formidable smoker, who livened up debates in the House of Lords. He became headmaster of the Leys School of Cambridge. His teaching of history as a logical sequence of events did more than anything else to get me into Oxford.

At first we wore an Eton jacket, later a black tail coat with stiff collar and white tie. For Sunday chapel, or going up the High Street beyond the parish Church, we had to wear top hats which occasionally earned us an illicit half-crown from photo opportunities with gob-smacked American GIs.

Entering Eton my first mistake was hitting the correct note in the singing test conducted by H.G. Ley, previously organist in Westminster Abbey. I became a probationer in Lower Chapel choir, which astonished my mother who had told me never to sing in public. It was a mistake easily rectified after one half (= term) by instructors not entirely deaf! My mother's money was wasted learning to play the piano with Mr Ogilvy who spent most of the lessons telling me how, until quite recently, the rats would run across the King's Scholars' beds in College. Years later I took lessons in Dumfries with Arthur Riley, a student of Myra Hess whose concerts we had attended in London during the War. By then, aged forty, I began to understand but my fingers would never move as fast as my brain. All the same I loved music and that first summer, in School Hall, Malcolm Sargent conducted an unforgettable performance of Beethoven's Pastoral Symphony, assisted by a violent thunderstorm outside.

Second mistake was being unable to swim, which meant having to play cricket instead of row. Cricket was a game alternating between terror and boredom. At 16 I passed my swimming test when the Captain of Games, Ronald Nall-Cain, unable to swim himself, said he would beat me if I didn't pass in a week. I learnt to swim. We bathed in Cuckoo Weir, a filthy arm of the Thames through which dead bodies sometimes floated. The test consisted of a header into murky depths, so many yards breast stroke, so many yards backstroke, then treading water for a minute. By then I had taken up shooting with a rifle. We travelled to Bisley between miles of ponticum rhododendron once or twice a week under the care of Staff Sergeant Vincent, travelling in the back of an army lorry. It was uncomfortable, but preferable to cricket and we quickly learnt to handle our rifles as an extension to our arms as well as being able to strip them down.

Third mistake was having to fag for James Whitaker. His father was Director of Military Training, but he was the smelliest, untidiest seventeen year old anyone could have encountered. His brother David, afterwards a vicar, produced outrageous excuses when late, such as getting his head stuck in a cannon in Cannon Yard while examining a bird's nest. He was alleged to have been the only officer to get the Colours of the Coldstream Guards stuck up a tree marching down Birdcage Walk. The other brother Ben later became Labour MP for Hampstead. Although frowned out of existence in these politically correct times fagging was a harmless pursuit. Members of Library (prefects) would shout 'Boy!' The last to arrive had to deliver messages to friends in other houses. We made toast for their teas on a toasting fork and lit their fires. My first message was from Robin Farquhar-Oliver to Timmy Smyth-Osbourne who later became my brother-in-law.

As we grew older Eton Chapel became pivotal to our lives. Led by choristers of the Choir School, instructed by Sidney Watson, a friend of Elgar, we sang lustily, and more or less in tune, many of the hymns and all the canticles which we knew by heart. The advent hymn, 'Hills of the North rejoice!' and the lines from one at Evensong: 'And the homesteads and the woodlands/Plead in silence for their peace' remain etched on my memory. After confirmation we found our way through the 1662 Prayer Book, regularly attending Early Communion each Sunday before breakfast, but the most moving moments were the voluntary Saturday evening memorial services for Old Etonians killed during the week. Many had walked along Common Lane among us, rowed on the Thames and played cricket on Agars Plough only months before. Suddenly they were dead. Life and death came close to each other in a way later learnt in fields at lambing time. Death is a reality that townspeople and their representatives never understand in their search for a risk free society which only exists in their imagination.

In the Science School we learnt the facts of life from Wetty Morris, and elements of genetics, studying Abbé Mendl's experiments with the same everlasting peas that had grown at Peggy's gate by the Broom of Moy. Darwin's theory of evolution began to penetrate our skulls and combined with Ethics, taught by Giles St. Aubyn, put me off Science and Philosophy for years. Both were and are boring and dangerous. With Mr Duchesne, Dutch Cheese, we worked with Bunsen burners which petrified me, although creating blue copper sulphate crystals appealed to my artistic senses! Later in life it became clear my ignorance of basic principles of science and machinery had been a serious omission. Attempts to remedy early neglect culminated in sitting on a British Nuclear Fuels committee in London assessing the Public Perception of Risk in the Storage of Low Level Nuclear Waste for the next 10,000 years – a bizarre challenge. In wilder moments a fantasy exists of writing a thesis on the correlation of the date of sighting the first swallow in Dunscore in spring and the rise of the nematodirus worm. For several years there was a gap of exactly twenty one days between the birds' arrival and the veterinary forecast of the worm's rise, information vital for the health and management of our lambs!

Some element of knowledge must, however, have stuck. In 1945, aged 15, climbing Braeriach with Roger Ellis, my stepfather, newly returned from the Burma jungle with such irritating theories as 'It's all a matter of organisation!' 'One man one job!' and 'Any fool can be uncomfortable' – all true – tried to lecture us about the birds and the bees. 'Oh that!!' we said; Wetty Morris had briefed us for life better than my science results could have foretold.

We learnt to discipline our temper playing games. The Field Game was energetic and peculiar to Eton. My position was 'Post' in the middle of the 'bully', a sort of scrum. When the opposition scored a 'rouge', propped up by two or three supporters with the ball between my feet, they faced me with a 'ram' to push the ball over the goal line. It was daunting to hear the chant: 'Left up, right up, left up, right up, one two three ram,' as they aimed for my stomach with lowered heads. People were rarely hurt but I remember one sprig of the nobility hacking my shins in the bully when nobody was looking. He became Professor of Ceramics at the Courtauld Institute!

The Bible we studied in Greek and English but religion has bothered me ever since succumbing to a bout of high church fervour at Trinity, Cardinal Newman's college, at Oxford. Churches have always been peaceful places to avoid the outside world. Claude Elliot lectured us from the pulpit on how lucky we were to have moments of quiet contemplation each day and I remember his words: 'Just as playful pussies turn into cynical cats…!' but observing the awfulness of religious wars it is hard not to doubt. At Oxford I belonged to the Heretics and remember an atheist stating Christianity was only a way for the ruling classes to encourage the poor to endure their poverty in the belief of a better life hereafter. Now I am agnostic and life seems pointless, leaving nothing except to smile at those one meets beside the lonely road. Even so there are occasional chinks of light. One day a young girl, Marcela Koupilova, guided us round the Brevnev Monastery in Prague. Her concern at my lack of faith translated itself into two or three letters about her family and her grandfather's farm making me doubt my unbelief until I remembered Motley's *Rise of the Dutch Republic* studied at school. The horrors inflicted by the Duchess of Alva on the luckless population of the Netherlands, and later the ravages of the Thirty Years War, were stern warning against the dogma of religious fundamentalism. Nevertheless the Papacy's attempts to maintain eternal values compare favourably with the Anglican Church's limp appeal to the loose morals of secular society at a time when thinking people seek some unmoving rock in the shifting sands. Many years later, going to the hill with the Bishop of Norwich, Dougie Langlands, the stalker, explained we felt nearer to God in the hills than the church. At dinner that night the Bishop told my mother-in-law, his cousin, he had spent the day with a couple of 'damned blue domers' – which the two of us remain, not in a state of grace.

Yesterday the new Bishop came to lunch – a very holy man, the Vicar said. He is walking around his diocese as Lenten penance and arrived looking like a drowned rat, covered in mud. He hates walking and seemed more like a Celtic saint than a C of E bishop. No beer added to his discomfort. Could he have lager? None of that either, so he had to make do with grape juice which earned us no gold stars in Heaven. He was nice, and the bishop before. Having completed the restoration of the Church the Vicar arranged a date for him – the one before – to bless it after tea with us. On arrival a note from Malcolm said:

'Sorry, can't be there. Gone to tea with the Dalai Lama in Florence!' Luckily Ian Harland laughed.

The Reverend Malcolm Stonestreet is larger than life and should wear a broad brimmed hat like a Catholic priest. He has done much good for the $5^1/2$ churches in his care, although his wife says he only went into the church because he wanted a title. Revd. seemed much less uncertain than a seat in a vandalised House of Lords! As well as preaching he is good at raising money and is often on the early morning train to London from Oxenholme. He raised funds for the restoration of Muncaster Church and is a good preacher who cannot be guaranteed to take the party line with his eccentric parishioners. His cavalier attitude to money would have made him not a Roundhead in the Civil War and to everybody's astonishment the Lord does seem to provide! He paints with a vivid brush which will be missed when he retires. For thirty years the Central Lobby of the House of Commons has been my middle-class version of 'underneath the arches' when it's cold and wet, and I shall always remember him coming up to me there asking, 'What the hell are you doing here?' The last Vicar had eyes like Rasputin, a musical wife with whom he was not in tune, three children, and a chip on his shoulder. He came out of Africa. Three before was Murray Hodges, a man of prodigious memory, who with his wife in a sidecar rode a motorbike and kept cairns. When we married in 1955 he let us graze ewes in the churchyard and held services at Easter to which we took our dogs, and the halt and the lame and the blind of the sheep world to be blessed. Now there is a dearth of applicants for the priesthood because the Church Commission has hitherto offered miserable contracts of employment and starvation wages. To enter the modern church almost requires a vow of poverty – and the grass in the Churchyard is cut by the Copeland Council, instead of by our sheep. Although I only go to Church when the Vicar wants me to read the lesson I do realise it is needed more than ever as a focus for community life. Without belief days seem aimless and very lonely. It is not academic points which need scoring, but some answer to the cry of the spirit for shelter from ruthless economic forces. I am no socialist, but the message of Thatcherism that people are no good unless they earn more than their neighbours has immensely damaged society.

The first half at Eton passed as a goody-two-shoes, frightened of making mistakes or saying anything to upset the authorities – a state from which I seem to have recovered. Sam Scott, Master of the Beagles, persuaded me to take two puppies home to walk in the holidays. Postcard to mother who sent telegram to say don't. This was suppressed, and sitting on my suitcase in the corridor I travelled, with Courtesy and Countess in a crate, on a very long-winded train. They were thirsty so I slipped my best handkerchief soaked in water from the filthy you-know-where through the slats to give them a drink somewhere about Wolverhampton. They chased the hens, ate the ducks, pestered my mother as she tried to smoke the bees to sleep, but turned into excellent hunters – which did not help my mother who was unwell and had to have a hysterectomy in Edinburgh on her way back from Dulnain Bridge where we went to stay with the Ellises at Wester Finlarig at their Aunt Gwen's. Travelling there was an administrative nightmare repeated for three Augusts. Conducting five rioting children without a sleeper from Brook House, to Crewe, to Aviemore, to Broomhill complete with six bicycles was some undertaking. My mother never travelled light. Pam Ellis joined the circus somewhere and on return journeys to London the two mothers settled on the floor of the guard's van with a bottle of gin while we played chess or cards. The guards were bribed with a box of eggs from the persecuted hens once or twice a year and became family friends. Trains were overcrowded and late, but on them we learnt to talk to people – a habit that has persisted. Lately I have travelled with Youssuf Baikhal, Secretary General of the British Council of Muslims; an environmental student from Lancaster University carrying on an extraordinary conversation with her mother whose fingers were stuck in a mincer some- where in Surrey and she wanted to know how to extract them; a three year old hammering it out on a computer – yes, three; and a student poetess from Bangor University who persuaded me to speak at her wedding! Usually these days it is memorial services!

Summer holidays at Finlarig meant freedom – fishing at Lochindorb; learning to play golf at Grantown, stacking the logs in Aunt Leaf's shed over the road; doing *Macbeth*, or *Julius Caesar*, or Scenes from the Bible for the adults. As boys we always stole the best parts. We suspended Roger's sister Julia from the door by her pigtails as 'Absalom my son!' Later a famous skin specialist, she learnt her trade keeping pigs on the first floor of the Radcliffe Infirmary at Oxford. To Grantown to watch the pipes and drums of the 52nd Lowland Division beating retreat, and to the cinema to see Valerie Hobson who, with her husband Jack Profumo, later became my friends. In the pine trees at Abernethy there were crested tits, as we bicycled to climb Bynack or go up Glen Einich. Our journeys were feats of endurance which probably tested our mothers waiting at home as much as us. When Uncle Edward returned from Burma in 1945 to fight the election in Camberwell as a Conservative, we went one day to stalk at Kinveachy. He missed three stags but while waiting for him under a bank of heather we watched the tops of the horns of thirty stags moving across the horizon twenty yards in front. It was a magical introduction to a world which would come to mean so much in later life.

In 1948 an undistinguished school career ended. I was neither very bright nor particularly stupid, which didn't seem to matter as the Captain of the School, academically brilliant, chewed his pencils and later passed out of the OCTU at Eaton Hall with the highest marks ever awarded. Within a week of being commissioned he lost his whole platoon on the German railways. People with Firsts are often odd. Having studied the chapel lists I could name six or seven hundred boys by sight and the memory game has always helped me. I wish they would stop sending junk mail inviting me to subscribe to a course telling how to do it. We read Ovid and Horace and Virgil in Latin, and Euripides in Greek using Gilbert Murray's cribs to help. The polished vagabonds became citizens with an appreciation of basic values. We studied the development of Government and its conventions in Britain and Europe and were told that entry into the Civil Service was a worthy aspiration. Cabinet responsibility was a central tenet of good rule. We prayed in Church 'that we may be godly and quietly governed'. Service, and using our privileged education to help others was necessary. What on earth has gone wrong?

Much more successfully than Charles I and Strafford, the Executive has usurped the power of Parliament. The Prime Minister and the Lord Chancellor strut their piece. Most of their advisers have never run a business and are busy weaving expensive dreams which will cripple everybody else's. Parliament is full of career politicians with little ideal of service, many of them having become MPs via local government, or as parliamentary assistants, without experience of real life. Thus they are totally irrelevant unless they become Ministers – which they probably won't if they say what they think! The Press rules, causing murder and mayhem in the corridors of power in its search for sensation – and circulation.

So was our education all for nothing? I don't think so. Today I put on my Old Etonian tie, rarely worn, to put two fingers up to the Establishment! My last year at school was spent as Captain of Games at Milligans, a new house. It seemed a funny appointment for someone no good at catching cricket balls, but I was in the Shooting VIII, won a Donegal Badge at Bisley, and with my cousin Brian Berridge used to zero our rifles on the 30 yards range in Windsor Great Park, using as targets the leaving photographs of our friends. Finding something to be good at was a major boost to my self confidence. Wyndham Milligan, charming, ex-Scots Guards, commanded the Corps of which I was a keen member. He owned one of only two pictures I ever coveted, 'Kirkcudbright Landscape' by an art master L. Menzies-Jones. The other was a Munnings, seen at a Sotheby's exhibition, owned by the nice sister of the boy with the buck teeth on the end of the childhood bench. Wilfrid Blunt, a brilliant flower painter, brother of Anthony the Spy, tried unsuccessfully to teach me to draw.

For the last eighteen months of the War we spent uncomfortable nights in the air raid shelter when the Germans sent over the Doodlebugs, VI and V2 rockets. On 6 June 1944 we watched the air armada on its way to D. Day. Ralph Dundas, who had been hit on the head while sitting on a bench in Hyde Park, told me later that on his way to Southampton, as a member of Eisenhower's staff, he suddenly remembered he had left the plans for the invasion (of France) on his desk in London. Eleven months later the European war ended. We celebrated by throwing a senior colleger called Vos into Barnes Pool – a racist act of which I am still ashamed. Sixty years later people question why the Austrians and Czechs never resisted the Nazis, but looking in the faces of young people today one questions how many of them would have resisted the hysteria, the cries of *Sieg Heil*, the marching troops and the military bands in the streets.

The end of hostilities brought the return of many beaks (masters), among them Hubert Hartley and Fred Coleridge, Master in College who taught us appreciation of A.E. Housman's poems, whose simplicity of style and evocation of the countryside still means so much. My mother kept 'A Shropshire Lad' by the loo.

The Captain of Milligans, Sinclair Eustace, left suddenly under a cloud, but not before he had taught me the names of the stars standing in Luxmoore's Garden. Now, looking up at night, man seems so insignificant. Forty years later I read Hoyle's *Nature of the Universe*. His conclusion that man is a tiny grain of sand on a very large beach has depressed me ever since – a fertile seed bed for a bishop on his penitential walk!

Eton greatly enriched my life. Admiring Grey of Fallodon I wished to become Foreign Secretary. Luckily Tony Crosland, my tutor in Economic History at Trinity, took the job instead. I refuse to believe that the Liberal interpretation of history translated by G.B. Smith, at whose feet Douglas Hurd also sat, is irrelevant to the changed world. People fought all their lives for universal suffrage – now half the electorate don't vote. People entered Parliament to serve their constituents – now too many appear to want only the wage and their career. People believed what politicians told them – now they don't. Once they believed the now incredible Press. Someone, somewhere, please give back a modern version of our old ideals.

Chapter 2

The Big boy took me into a lonely corner of the field and
told me the awful things mothers and fathers did together.
It was several years before I discovered he was quite wrong.

Jack House 1906-97

IN MAY 1945 Uncle Edward returned from commanding 304 Anti-tank and
Light Anti-Aircraft Regiment, part of 11 East African Division in Burma, to
fight the Election as Conservative candidate for Camberwell, an east London
constituency he had no hope of winning. As an MP he would have been totally
frustrated. He brought green oranges from Sicily as a gift, the sweetest oranges
anyone tasted. We went to the Hinds Head Hotel at Bray for the weekend and
ate scallops. When my mother took me out we had tea at the Cockpit in Eton
High Street and at Christmas I always shopped for the family from Ma
Browne's antique bookshop. Looking at the library shelves today my good taste
surprises me although almost certainly the books were never read by my
parents! Parents asked sons if they knew sons of their friends and were
invariably told 'He's horrid!' – even if unknown. Meeting many in later life and
finding how charming they are, it was a stupid comment. At Fort George in
1951 my platoon commander was Donald MacLellan. He once went home to
see his father, ex-Seaforth Pipe Major, and said: 'Father I bloody well can't stick
that man,' to which the wise old man replied: 'Well, my boy, perhaps it's just
that you don't know him very well', the most wonderful comment on human
nature.

Mother wore embarrassing hats and sacrificed a great deal to educate me. I
was dressed by Tom Brown (tailors) which still has an Eton shop and another in
London where prices are more reasonable than most. Mr Tom retired, Mr
George took over. He was a good business man who toured Scotland annually
following a postcard enquiring if his past clients would like him to check their
waist measurements in their homes. Orders would be fitted in Edinburgh. One
day in 1980, returning the six miles home at lambing time, I stopped to talk to a
man burying a sheep. A car drove up. It was Mr George. 'Good Lord, sir' – I
always thought I should call him sir – 'It must be you. I made those trousers for
you in 1957.'

That summer we went to Garve travelling by the day on the milk train to
Attadale where the Schroders kept warlike spaniels which needed taming before
going away at evening. At night, watched by Miss Wigglesworth, a beautifully
groomed Bevin Boy with white gloves played Mozart on the hotel piano.

Mother Rosemary, aged 44.

Outside we learnt to Spey cast in the sight of Ben Wyvis and stalked rabbits with the Somali dagger Uncle Edward had sent from East Africa – a lethal weapon in a beautifully worked leather case still in my possession. We walked to Corriemoilzie to tea with the widow of Karamojo Bell, a famous elephant hunter. There were crested tits and hawfinches in the roadside trees and the Japanese war ended with the dropping of the atomic bomb on Hiroshima and Nagasaki. In August my mother left Shropshire for their new home, the Old House, Rotherwick, inhabited pre-war by the Moyes family. Martin was at Hartleys with me and his father was a King's Messenger. They had been succeeded by Alexander Gibb and Partners who left the garden like a hayfield. We travelled by train from Waterloo to inspect. Elspeth's room was twice as large as mine – I measured it and wept with fury the whole way back to London. Contented holidays were spent there until 1955. A nightingale sang in the apple tree outside my window and in summer there were sweet peas and asparagus, and the air filled with the scent of roses and philadelphus. There were apricots on the wall and in spring wallflowers and forget-me-nots below. We played tennis with friends and shot pigeons in the wood. Once, when Uncle Edward was shooting with Lord Rotherwick at Tylney, Roger Ellis and I hid with my gun behind the garden wall to ambush pheasants from one of the drives. It wasn't popular! We learnt to ride at Popley Fields, now a suburb of Basingstoke, and in the dining room sometimes had to eat with a riding crop between our elbows to make us sit up straight.

There was a dour pony called Jester, impossible to budge unless the hounds were near, when he was uncontrollable. We hunted with the Garth occasionally and sometimes with the HH on horses hired from Joan Andrews, hacking to the meets near Alton at cockcrow. We went racing at Sandown and went to horse shows, and in 1946 watched the Victory Parade from a shop on the south side of Oxford Street, cheering as Uncle Edward's Kenyans marched past. He taught us a few words of Swahili and the phrase with the greatest resonance was '*N'taka kwenda nyumbani*' – 'I want to go home'. Even then home meant Scotland. We followed the Farley Hill Beagles hunted by the Hermon-Worsleys. The whipper-in was Colonel James Macnab, married secondly to Pauline who later married someone else who was killed by his Dexter bull. Neighbours were distinguished. Field Marshal Lord Alanbrooke, architect of victory and CIGS in the War, lived five miles away. I went to dances with his daughter Kathleen. She was sadly killed when thrown off her horse on Wimbledon Common shortly after her marriage. Sir Paul Maltby, AOC in the Far East when the Japanese invaded, lived in the village. His son John became chairman of Burma Oil and AEA. Together one night we dug up the newly installed 30 m.p.h. sign, an unnecessary blot on the Rotherwick landscape of 1950. Selena, the daughter, became an architect, married first to the impossible *Times* rowing corres-pondent, and later to a master at Eton. Colonel Cumming had been in the Klondyke Gold Rush, and Sir John Swayne, Adjutant General in the War. He arranged for Roger and me to stay with M. Guiton, a farmer at Paramé near St. Malo.

In 1946 France had not recovered from the German occupation. We worked in the fields; the loo was a long drop to be used accompanied by a bottle of sal volatile. We bicycled to Mont St. Michel and to Rennes and in the evening played chess with the Guiton son. Afterwards by train to Sablé-sur-Sarthe via Chartres Cathedral where a funeral passed with black horses with black plumes on their bridles. La Roche Talbot was home to Madame la Comtesse de Montalembert, a formidable woman with whom we had to play bridge at night. Her grandfather had conquered Algeria, an exploit of which she constantly reminded us. After dinner she played Beethoven sonatas very loudly, sometimes hitting the wrong note. The cast was completed by her nephew with one of those ribbons in his buttonhole which French ex-soldiers wore; his two sons, Philippe and Thibaud, who wore white silk stockings and knicker-bockers, and stole our bicycles; and Stella Binney, a girl from Gloucestershire, never seen before or since. It was hot and there was not enough to eat. I remember being handed what looked like apple snow. As there were never second helpings I took as much as manners allowed to find it was sour cheese. After this gluttony I lay on my bed in the heat of the afternoon reading books about Napoleon in French. We made little allowance for what the French had endured. On a visit to Angers we purchased two bottles of Vouvray for our mothers and the best part of our visit was drinking the top of each bottle out of the soap dish to avoid customs duty on the way home. We returned by Paris where my bicycle brakes failed – a terrifying experience! Having money for only one room in the Hotel de l'Est one slept in the bed, the other in the bath. It was an education on the meaning of insecurity!

Summer of 1947 passed quickly in the harvest field working for Mr Ford at Rooks Farm stooking corn sheaves full of thistles and killing rabbits with sticks as the binder cut the final swathes. At Finlarig we were only allowed to shoot rabbits, but I shot a partridge, watched through a telescope by the keeper, Anderson. Uncle Edward tried to bribe him with a cigarette, but I was hauled in front of the Seafield factor, Gilbert Brown, in Grantown to be dressed down, an interview repeated the following week after blocking the drains by the public road which flooded.

After the Ashburton Shield at Bisley in 1948 Eton became part of my past. We visited the Olympic Games at the White City where Jonquères d'Oriola's wonderful horse Marquis III, who swished his tail, was third. Ruth McWilliam, the agent's daughter from Muncaster, married his relation Philippe who farms on the northern edge of the Pyrenees. In autumn Uncle Edward took the shooting at Strathmashie from Sir John Ramsden. It was the start of a lifelong love affair with Laggan, and that October was filled with memories of countless special people, mostly now dead. We shot grouse and ptarmigan up Glen Markie, and snipe in the bogs around Laggan Bridge, eating our lunch under the Kirk dyke. We flighted duck at the Spey Dam at darkening and went home to bed by moonlight past the Catholic chapel at the foot of the Dun where the priest kept a goat and came once a month. In the Mashie we caught trout, dropping worms dug from John Duncan's midden into the frothing pools under the alders after a spate. We ate everything except for the rabbits which were so plentiful they threatened the sheep's grazing. There was a mad cook who threw a fish at me and left, relying on the fact there were grouse in Surrey and she had shares in Fyffes bananas. We walked up grey partridges in the turnip field at Coull and named one of the deer ponies Clare after Donnie Wilson's sister. At Gaskbeg many hares ran among the thistles, eventually controlled when Ben Coutts borrowed a lorry load of donkeys from a seaside resort in their off season. My first stag was shot in the Big Wood under the eye of John Duncan, my friend for the rest of his life. He gave me cast-off jackets and his tweed cap with a hole in the top, later famous around Dumfries where Joe Benson, the auctioneer, leant from his rostrum after selling my cattle and sold it for a pound to an Irish dealer. He gave it back saying: 'Why boy, here's your bonnet and here's your pound – I was only paying for the hole!' The family burnt it. The

Big Wood had been felled by Newfoundlanders in the War, leaving only a few pines at the top where for three years I listened to the wind before going south and to the roaring of the stags. In 1948 a New Zealander with a horse still dragged remaining logs to the roadside.

At the house John's wife, Isobel – they both came out of Moray – made pancakes and oatcakes for tea to eat with her raspberry jam. John won the hundred yards at Laggan sports, aged 43, and was one of the last real gentlemen in the world. Kirk elder and referee in local disputes he was assisted as headkeeper by Willie Maclean who disliked heights, and Hughie Milne of the piercing blue eyes from out of Ardnamurchan who always said 'Gyess, gyess' and was married to Bella who never stopped talking. Hugh cut my hair in the gunroom at night before fastening himself in his flimsy car and rolling down the hill to Laggan. John would tell how Mrs Eden, a previous tenant, had been stalking in the Black Wood when a swarm of bees got up her knickers. She stripped and took off down the hill leaving him gaping. Another time, returning in bad fettle she fired two barrels at the chauffeur's washing and sent him off to buy new shirts.

On Sundays we walked three miles to the kirk where Rev. Morrison issued it hot and strong from the pulpit. 'The vaast impeerial spaces, and the laingth, and the braidth, and the height o' Goads' domeenion and power!' while Uncle Edward cleaned his nails with his penknife in the gallery. The Lindsays were there with Patsy and Bumpy, sweet smiling daughters who cared for Laggan and its people. Eugenie Lindsay, their mother, parachuted into Belgium in the 1914 War and in 1940 was Secretary to the Director of Military Intelligence, as well as being the first woman to go down the Cresta Run. After Church we walked back to Strathmashie for lunch and then to the top of the Dun, the old Pictish fort.

Colonel Oliver Birkbeck taught me to shoot better, which he was entitled to do having done not much else except shoot and hunt for most of his life. His children were quite wild and Mary, the daughter, eventually trained the winner of the Waterloo Cup. Sir Anselm Guise came, known to us as the Old Cock Ptarmigan; Hugh and Patty Saunders – he was Secretary of Unilever; Barbara Royle and her husband Sir Lancelot, the head of NAAFI, who threw buns across the dinner table as we ate the stuffed pike we had caught in the Dam Loch; Patience and Edward Windley, a distinguished colonial servant from Kenya; Sheila and Kit Burlison, who ran Hennells, the jewellers, and died of meningitis. Arthur Sturge, known as the Crooked Man because he had a crooked gun, and his wife Beryl whom we called the Iron Dominion and was very beautiful; but the best loved of all was Uncle Percy, everybody's friend and an extremely able business man who ran Brixton Estate and masterminded the formation of BUPA. He wrote to his wife, Aunt Cecily, every night. When they married she made him change his name from Mayer to Meighar Lovett. Her father once hired the Albert Hall for her to sing. She had yellow Rolls Royces, yellow pigs, and yellow horses, was highly intelligent, but disliked her brother-in-law, although she was nice to me on the rare occasions we met. There was a constant stream of our young friends, and over it all presided Uncle Edward, reliving a life he had known in the 1920s.

We were young and fit, and I never wanted any of it to end, but in October I went up to Oxford to read Modern History which in those days started at 55 BC. Walking through the gates of Trinity with my bicycle (cost 30/-) a Revelation suitcase, and £20 to put in Barclays Bank as my term's allowance, the future felt strange, but not impossible. My rooms on staircase 4 were serviced by a scout called Spanner who made the bed and brought hot water to shave in a basin every morning. My mother provided a Fullers walnut cake, oatcakes, butter from Kenya, a jar of honey, and a large tin of Nescafé. The bath was 250 yards away through three quadrangles, a disincentive to cleanliness. My neighbour was Neil Burton and over the passage Tony Crosland, later my tutor in Economic History and later still Foreign Secretary, a job to which at that time I aspired. He was a good instructor and with the aid of Adam Smith's *Wealth of Nations* probably gave me enough understanding to question some of the wider lunacies of latter day Governments. Those rooms were my quarters for two years, looking over the tops of the tulip trees – dreaming. 1948 was a good time at Oxford, still full of interesting people returned from War, which spread one's friends over ten extra years. Trinity was presided over by J.R.H. Weaver, an authority on roses, who summoned me to discuss my uncertain future having failed Historical Geography for my prelims. Luckily a prior visit to the College Library to study *The Diseases of Roses* enabled me to turn the conversation to black-spot which saved my bacon, and taught me that a sweet smile and a little ingenuity could extricate me from most minor problems!

Michael Maclagan, the Dean, tutored us on Roman Britain for which we studied an impenetrable book by Collingwood and Miers. The most attractive Roman was Agricola, alleged to have laid waste Scotland as far north as the Dun of Strathmashie. His son-in-law Tacitus wrote: '*Ubi solitudinem faciunt pacem appellant*' – 'where they make a wilderness and call it peace', a quotation later sent to John Silkin, Minister of Agriculture in 1977, when I was Hill Farming convenor of the Scottish NFU, underlining the Government's seemingly total indifference to livestock farming in the Scottish hills. We had to write weekly essays for which I lifted chunks from *Puck of Pooks Hill* which my tutor knew but could never quite identify.

There were many friends from the Commonwealth as well as Britain. I joined the United Europe movement and was an unashamed Imperialist having studied Elton's *Imperial Commonwealth* at school when one fifth of the world was still pink on the map. We argued far into every night after dining in Hall, supervised by Cadman, the Chief Scout. My closest friend was Pierce Carrigan from Co. Tipperary, who had arrived at Oxford on bail having run over a man in Dublin. The judge's reported comment was: 'I regret to tell you, Mr Carrigan, but your many times great grandfather came over with Oliver Cromwell and I have no alternative but to put you into the jail!' He arranged bail on a date there was a race meeting at the Curragh, and the following day at Sandown, and eventually won his appeal.

We were not diligent students but our tutor on the Tudors and Stuarts was Bruce Wernham, a talented scholar, who set all the right essays which we reread for our degree papers – the morning one before breakfast, the afternoon one at lunchtime. Unfortunately Pierce muddled the two one day when Signal Box, who carried our money, was third in the Derby! He left without a degree to work on his uncle's estate in Colombia where he found the situation so volatile he returned to become assistant to Vincent O'Brien, the racehorse trainer. Before Christmas 1949 he took me home to Clonacody to hunt. The crossing from Fishguard was violent and we had to land in the wrong port having been sick all night. By taxi to Clonmel through a romantic landscape untouched by time with donkeys in carts and madness in the air. I have loved Ireland ever since. In a week we hunted five days, shot snipe on one, and had Sunday lunch with two Germans who arrived late at 3 o'clock after walking their cow seven miles to the bull. Across the Golden Vale there was snow on Slievenamon. With hounds in full cry, jumping the banks on Lady Godiva was terrifying but the horse knew more about it than I did. It was an early lesson in the empathy between man and beast which gave me so much pleasure in my farming career. The priest rode a grey which tipped him over the worst obstacles before jumping after him. The vet cut wire and leapt on his mount as it leapt through the hole. Some fields had no gateways. One day with the harriers on a hired horse which had been third at the Clonmel show, we arrived at an enormous hairy bank where the one-armed master assured me, 'Sure it was the only horse in the whole of Ireland could give him a lead.' I fell off jumping into the field to find the only possible exit was the same gap. I fell off on return to find the hounds vanished – and the Master, so went home.

By my bed Ines Carrigan put Lord Dunsany's book, *The Curse of the Wise Woman* written as an autobiography. There was Laura, unable to decide whether she was a good Roman Catholic or believed in Tir-nan-Og. Wanting to meet her if still alive I wrote to the old man and have unfortunately lost his reply written on a small scrap of paper.

'Dear Mr Gordon Duff, Laura was murdered when Mr Heineman (turn over the page) allowed my book to go out of print.'

The whole book was a figment of his imagination.

The Clonacody scenario was lifted direct from *Experiences of an Irish RM*. The roof leaked and everybody was a little bit mad, but it was also very romantic, Conor Carrigan had a study known as the Room of Beautiful Thoughts, on his desk a photograph of Jean Donoughmore, later kidnapped with her husband by the IRA to whom she gave a vigorous response. The hounds met at the gates of

Knocklofty, their family home, Sybie Masters, famous huntswoman in charge and in the field her lodger who had come for a weekend to hunt and stayed thirty three years.

The idyll had to end. By train to Belfast where a herd of runaway cattle almost pushed me into the harbour on the way to the Glasgow boat, and thence to Findhorn, before staying with John Duncan to shoot a hind. The Newtonmore bus was late and missed the last train south. I walked in moonlight ten miles along the old A9 to the Loch Ericht Hotel with a rifle on one shoulder and a haunch of venison over the other, never seeing a car in the deep snow. Oxford seemed a world away – and somewhat irrelevant!

After a year at Trinity Roger Ellis arrived after National Service in the Navy. For my final year we shared rooms under the Trinity clock and I was one of the few lucky enough to live in college throughout my Oxford career. The Grinling Gibbons mantlepiece would have been beyond our means elsewhere and we played classical music on a gramophone. Dvořák's 'Serenade for Strings' and the Brahms Double Concerto remain in my head. One night we entertained Michael Maclagan and his rather ample wife for bridge. Our chair collapsed under her weight. He was a wine snob and when choosing the champagne for the Commem Ball we tricked him by changing the labels. He later became a distinguished Herald, a disguise which suited him well. Colleagues included Jeremy Thorpe, a brilliant violinist at Eton, who forsook his music and joined the Liberal club. I joined the Carlton, the United Europe Movement and the Heretics where we listened to a pacifist, an anarchist, an atheist and a variety of credible anti-establishment figures. We danced at the reel club and I took push-me, pull-you dance lessons above the Cadena café, next to which was a tailor who altered my white breeches when I became Master of the New College and Magdalen Beagles. He commented: 'Very good leg for a bishop.' At Barclays Bank in the High Street an avuncular Mr Davies cashed my cheques, consoling me when my account was overdrawn sixpence, which seemed the end of the world. We drank little, but kept a bottle of sherry in our rooms. The Secretary of the beagles was Spike, Major Escaut Cresswell MC, who lay in bed in his digs lobbing the empty gin bottles into the next room. He was later in the middle of proposing to my sister in her basement flat in the Cromwell Road when he fell asleep. She married instead Gerald Carter of the Rifle Brigade, an ex-Army heavyweight boxing champion. We rioted in the Broad, rallying around a blue silk banner on the three hundredth anniversary of Charles I's execution and knocking off a policeman's helmet. I learnt to slip into College after hours over the high gate below the new Bodleian, then squeezing between the railings by the College library or climbing through a first floor window next to Blackwells on the Broad.

Lectures were low priority, but Alan Bullock on Hitler and, at the Indian Institute, Dr Davies who had been a British spy in Afghanistan in 1919, were both rather racy. My academic work was minimal and my 2nd Class Honours

Degree astonished my family, my instructors and Roger Ellis, who was far more intelligent and worked harder for the same result.

Nancy Astor came to the Union and her unforgettable goodbye was: 'Well goodnight, boys, mind your morals and never ever forget you'll never again be as important as you think you are here!' My politics were genetically right wing, a prejudice there has been no difficulty in diluting over the years. Political extremism is obnoxious but there is a slender margin between that and not minding enough. I remain not a socialist, but Grace Kelly's alleged comment before her death is good enough philosophy for me: 'All I wish to be remembered as is as a decent human being and a caring one.' Although capitalism works along the grain of human greed too many casualties are left in the ditch, unable and uneducated enough to cope. Communism does not work. One crofting committee thought that if every grazier had identical numbers of cattle they would all be equal, until some wag at the back pointed out that one of them would have to own the bull! Sometime, somewhere there will have to be a synthesis. Although Margaret Thatcher herself is very generous her doctrine taught people to believe they were only successful if they possessed more than their neighbours.

At the by-election, after Quentin Hogg had become Lord Hailsham, I canvassed the top of the Iffley Road on behalf of Laurence Turner, under the guidance of Richard Webster, drafted in from Aldershot and later becoming the senior Conservative agent at Central Office. It was great fun knocking on doors. At one house with a Labour poster the householder took me in, gave me tea and agreed to stick my poster in another window. Perhaps that is why foreigners think the British mad. It was to be twenty years before I collided with politics again.

In 1948 the New College and Magdalen Beagles were hunted by John Wells, who had been hit on the head when an aircraft crashed on the playing fields at Downside. His family lived under Wittenham Clumps and his father, Judge Bensley Wells, claimed to be the only judge to kill a man in Court. When accused of lying the man dropped dead at his feet. He had also coxed the Oxford boat on the three consecutive occasions it sank in the Boat Race. The hunt kennels were on top of Cumnor Hill where Joe Webb had been kennel huntsman since 1904. Colin Schwerdt, with a tuft of white hair, who became an eye surgeon, drove the hounds behind his antique car. Other regulars were Pi Fraser from Moniack, the coldest house in Scotland with two fires in separate walls of the drawing room from whose windows we used to shoot bullfinches among the currant bushes as they ravished the buds; Bernard Kelly with whom I hoped to travel to Tibet, assisted by a push and a prod from his father who was Ambassador in Moscow; Pierce Carrigan, Lavinia Jenkinson, John Richardson, Bobby Collins, Richard Boddington and a host of hangers-on, some more serious than others. I became a whipper-in and later carried the horn. Two hounds remain in my mind – Rebel and Joker, the latter a red and white bad tempered dog drafted from Ampleforth. A brilliant hunter, he was lost one night at Cokethorpe after we had crossed the Windrush losing those followers only out for a canoodle. In summer we helped Joe feeding and exercising and my nostrils still twitch at the smell of porridge and cooking meat.

It was difficult to persuade anybody to walk the puppies until they were old enough to hunt so I taught myself to write backwards and wrote to children of likely victims in Looking Glass writing. I am still quite good at it but was severely put down when the lawyer, Rabbi Julia Neuberger, sat next to me at lunch at Hutton-in-the-Forest and wrote just as elegantly with her feet. Mine are flat and won't hold the pen! Priscilla Nicolson, who took me to the Angus Ball and sometimes washed my breeches, lived at Fyfield Manor where Perkin Warbeck had walled up his mistress. It was there I appeared one summer afternoon with a beagle puppy in my bicycle basket to try to persuade her mother, Mignon, to take it. Her father Bunty was terrifying and had been in charge of shipping at Calcutta during the War, but Aunt Mignon became a second mother to me, adored friend and confidante until she died. She kept a light in the window above the mulberry tree in case a traveller was lost and when I was at Eaton Hall in 1952 she would leave my bicycle at Oxford Station to ride at midnight the nine miles to stay for the weekend. One of thirteen Shuttleworth children, in the 1914 War she drove a horse and cart with vegetables from Harrow to Covent Garden. She told me her father was in the Indian Navy in 1882 when her grandfather, Admiral Beetham, on his way to wind it up, was wrecked on the coast south of Bombay where he operated a long-boat rescue service with the later-to-become-Lord Dalhousie. They rescued Beetham and his sailors and on the last load one carried one of the admiral's daughters aged 11, and the other one aged 12. Laying them on the seashore they looked at each other and said: 'Aren't they beautiful? When they grow up we'll marry them' – and they did. Priscilla calls the story a romance. Jamie Dalhousie says it's probably true.

Through the summer of 1949 I rode my bicycle, sometimes a hundred miles a day, visiting farmers within a wide area north and west of Oxford, arranging winter meets. It was my first lesson in the need to communicate with people on the ground. In most places people, particularly Government organisations, no longer take time and it is disastrous for human relations in a countryside which is becoming increasingly resentful. Why do anti-hunting MPs refuse invitations to see what happens in the hunting field, preferring to judge on images carefully selected by PR departments of PETA and the RSPCA? Their urban voters catch litter bin foxes and loose them in a countryside where they are lost and spread disease. They need not be surprised they are hated by many people among whom I move. When I meet them in the House of Commons they listen with courtesy – and closed minds – but too many politicians have never seen life and death in a lambing field and it is essential that their education is extended if the countryside they profess to love is not to vanish under their eyes. I no longer shoot or hunt, but having learnt so much from the pursuit of both, am bitter that those who seek to follow where countless generations have gone before are to be outlawed in the name of human progress. In the BBC in Edinburgh one single reporter has a country upbringing. The Press cry for sensation, not common sense.

When not otherwise engaged my summers were spent on the ranges at Bisley or Blewbury Down where the sky was alive with the flutter of larks' wings and there was the smell of thyme and the sound of bumble bees among the scabious. At dark at Bisley during the summer Meeting we listened to nightingales and the calling of nightjars outside our tents. Gordon King ruled the North London Rifle Club where I had a locker, and there was a steward called Pybus. It was there that we boiled out our rifle barrels in the evening, pulling them through with four by two amid a constant smell of Young's Oil. There were young and old, and a few women, and the old men were good to us, sharing their knowledge of wind and rifles, and faraway places of the world where they had served the Empire. Arthur Whitelock coached the OURC Long Range Team, a very precise little man with a Bentley whose doors one banged shut at one's peril. We lay for hours on our backs with match rifles on the firing point at Stickledown, practising or competing at ranges from nine to twelve hundred yards, learning to judge the wind from the flags, a strange combination of old men and Oxford and Cambridge undergraduates. Once a year we met at Cambridge for the Long Range meeting – the only place I was ever drunk and somebody put me to bed. Drink never played a major part in my life and when I refused sherry at lunchtime at Rotherwick Uncle Edward's comment was 'Only cranks don't drink and I don't like cranks,' even although he bribed me not to smoke. Many people encountered at the time at Bisley, like Ronnie Melville, became distinguished public servants. There were father figures like Hugh Maxwell and Tom Rankin, but the doyen of all was Lord Cottesloe who took a fatherly interest in everybody and gave me his No.4 competition rifle, which I eventually donated to the NRA. One winter he asked me to Sunday lunch at his home. I started to walk from Oxford the night before through a white and silent countryside with frosted trees by roadsides and moonlight reflected in rivers I crossed. By dawn I came to Aylesbury and caught a bus to Swanbourne where he presented me with a book of his poems about Ardkinglas and Purbeck.

In 1949 I was hon. sec. of the Oxford University Rifle Club (OURC) and Captain in 1950, writing a dozen letters a week to old members. In winter when not beagling we spent afternoons at the small-bore range at Parks Road culminating in the University Match under Baker Street Station for which I stayed in my stepfather's flat at 12 Chesham Place. We had scrambled eggs for breakfast, and potted shrimps from Beauchamp Place, under a full length portrait of Aunt Stella by Roberts, now in the National Gallery of Ireland. I featured as 'Man of Muscle' in *Isis* which amazes me now, looking in the mirror at a rundown septuagenarian, and it was only marginally less amazing than being centre spread in Japanese *Playboy* thirty five years later – a fact with which I like to shock audiences of blue rinse Conservative ladies. I was fully clad though not much else in the magazine was! I was a member of Vincent's Club, and when funds allowed, was shaved with a cut-throat razor at a barber next door.

As a member of the OUTC, commanded by Anthony Taylor, there was a month's attachment in 1949 to the Highland Brigade Training Centre at Fort George, then commanded by Colonel Neilson. My platoon commander was an idiot called McRitchie from the HLI who had won the MC in Palestine and fired a two inch mortar down a tunnel behind us to let us know what it felt like.

Social life was uninterrupted by scholarship. Augusts and Septembers were at Strathmashie and one July rushing through France in a train with Malcolm Fraser from Reelig where we had spent happy hours among the stooked corn waiting for pigeons or ducks. We meant to go to Tours, but arrived at Lyons, before moving to the Hôtel de Gare at Culoz, where we were fed by a charming girl called Jeannine, and bitten by fleas, but couldn't escape for three days, having no money because of Bank Holiday. At Geneva the clean beds and the deep toll of the bells of St. Pierre were wonderful. In Paris we attended the Parlement where two sides of a semi-circle argued at the top of their voices across the centre while the chairman protested she was normally a patient woman, but things had gone too far. As usual, returning to Scotland was a miracle.

At Oxford Bobby Gates took me to tea at Elsfield with Susan Tweedsmuir, John Buchan's widow, and Bill, his brother, to lunch at the Bear at Woodstock with nephews of Emperor Haile Selassie who had presented the Order of Abyssinia (Third Class) to my future father-in-law when he was thirteen for teaching him to work the lawnmower at Bulstrode. The countryside was continually criss-crossed by bicycle – dinner at Hinton Waldrist with Clifford Cameron and Sunday lunch at the Bay Tree at Burford with Henry Noel and Alan Barr. One evening on the edge of the Cotswolds dusk was full of the scent of red roses seen across a wall at the Freunds' house at Wilcote Grange. I watched cricket in the Parks where Kardar bowled his left arm googlies and the wicket-keeper, I.P. Campbell, carted the bowling, while I tested Jean Hopkins on Medical Mnemonics before walking her to dinner at the Trout at Godstow. Each year the family attended the Varsity Match at Twickenham in early December exhilarated by the sight of Clive van Ryneveldt scything through the opposition. International days still pass slumped in front of the television. Occasionally there were lectures and weekly essays to write for Bruce Wernham who once asked if I was making it up as I read or whether my writing really was illegible. On Sunday a hat was always worn to Church, and a bowler and blue suit to go to London. Once John Wells took me to the Catholic Service where it shocked me to see buttons in the collection.

Our life was privileged, but taught an early duty to help others, not in a patronising way but out of genuine concern and later from the pure pleasure of knowing someone able to redress an injustice. Our mother did charity work at Stepney where she had one client with eight children who dreaded her husband's annual release from prison. She lived in a permanent state of pregnancy. No doubt our mother provided practical advice on family planning – probably ignored. We attended dances, expected to take care of sisters or what our parents considered 'suitable' prospective wives. I was not good at it, but knew to leave a tip by the bed for the housemaid and to write by return to my hostess after staying away. My sister boarded across two rivers and two fields at North Foreland Lodge whose headmistress was The Gam, Miss Gammell, the sister of a Cameron General. One report said: 'Elspeth is not a good bed maker.' Her response to Uncle Edward was: 'I'm just not made that way!' – which caused a storm. She lives at Nether Wallop now and though we rarely meet she remains a wonderfully solid presence in my life. In spring we went to point-to-points with the O'Briens or racing at Sandown, and one winter weekend to Uncle Percy and his daughter Maxine at Bruton to shoot snipe in the Langport withybeds. She married Charles Wingfield of Onslow near Shrewsbury who held gliding records and, after taking up fishing later in life, used to take the temperature of the water at Balnacoil before choosing his flies.

Through this intense activity my mind was centred not on the Venerable Bede nor on Paléologue who was by this time demanding my attention as I studied Foreign Office telegrams 1870-1914, but on Strathmashie, rented by Uncle Edward for three years from Sir John Ramsden, my future wife's grandfather. It was there that the family golden retriever chewed my accounts the night before Uncle Edward's audit. As usual they had been concocted on the last night of term with a wet towel around my head, and as usual they didn't balance. The precision of double column book-keeping has been one of the most important lessons my stepfather taught.

I attended the Northern Meeting Balls staying at Raddery with Aunt Katharine, the Frasers at Reelig, or the Mackintoshes at Rebeg, and twice was sent to Bettine Gough, my mother's friend, at Inshes. Viscount Gough had one arm, shot brilliantly, and commanded the Irish Guards in Turkey after the 1914 War. On exercise the umpire pronounced the battalion dead, but their colonel, thereafter known as Lord Go, sat on his charger shouting: 'Irish Guards, ch, ch, ch...ch...ch...charge,' in face of which the opposition fled. I trumped the old man's ace playing bridge as his partner which didn't amuse him, but he kept good books in the gents. Also at Inshes was Phyllis MacRae who kept her hankie up her knickers and whose husband Duncan had flown under the Forth Bridge with my father when they were at Leuchars at the RFC flying training school – an exploit for which they were carpeted. They took me to the Skye Balls with Gina Fox and Flora Fraser, now Lady Saltoun and a force to be reckoned with in the House of Lords. Her son-in-law, Mark Nicolson, is Aunt Mignon's grandson and relieved me as chairman of the British Deer Society in 2001. Also in the party were Gina's parents, Pam, a Conservative MP and his wife Myra who insisted on taking the Rolls to Dunvegan on totally unsuitable roads. We stayed in a hotel where the salt air tarnished the silver mountings on my hair sporran, bought for half a crown from a junk shop in Inverness. My wife says it still stinks of goat. I walked for miles and miles in the rain listening to wind in telephone wires, and at night danced with someone twenty years older than me – and fell in love with her. She taught me all the tenderness of loving in those early days of my life and fifty three years later we are still friends. Her son telephoned this morning to say she's in a nursing home with a broken hip. It is strange because yesterday was her cousin's funeral and as I listened to the pipers marching through Westminster playing 'My Home', 'The Mist Covered Mountains', and 'Oft in the Stilly Night', it brought back the far-off evenings by her fireside where she taught me to listen to Gaelic songs. Afterwards at night we would wander arm in arm past the nets along the shores of the Moray Firth watching the moonpath across the waters. Her name was Pam.

Back at Oxford it was necessary to work and I began to spend time in the Bodleian trying to correct my mental attitude to the Wars of the Roses, but even now, living in a house where Henry VI took shelter, it remains hard to sort out that messy part of English History. The history of Scotland, too, was a grievous gap and it was only forty years later on meeting T.C. Smout from St. Andrew's, who gave me some of his books, that I could begin to correct years of neglect of a subject regarded by most English schools as irrelevant to the teaching of British history. Wallace, Bruce, Mary Queen of Scots, the Stuarts, the Act of Union, and the Battle of Culloden were the sum of our scholastic knowledge. We knew more about European history than about the flowering of a separate Scottish culture which entitled Scots to be proud of their place and able to identify with it, not in a narrow nationalistic way, but as a fact of life of which to be certain. The election of Winnie Ewing as MP for Hamilton in 1967, described by my unappreciative stepfather as a disaster, was a first step towards Scottish devolution despite the continued diffidence of Scottish people.

In spring Pam and I had seen the arrowheads of geese fly north and sat among the blaeberry plants watching the blossoming of the geans at Randolph's Leap. The Moray countryside remains a magnet calling me back to childhood even if the main threads of my affection are woven into the Highland hills and the Islands. At Finals I felt guilty seeing others, to whom a good degree was a serious matter, taking Benzadrine when my sole shelter was a photographic memory and a nimble mind which enabled me to invent an answer to: 'Describe the effects of the silting up of the River Scheldt on European history.' Years later out of a book at Muncaster a letter fell written by her brother from the Netherlands campaign in 1799 to my wife's great-great grandmother. 'Dearest Isabella, The Russians came today. They were all dressed in leather and they stunk. The smell of them reminded me of the books at home in Granny's library.' For my viva I could not answer the questions, but the results, sent by telegram, equipped me with a 2nd Class Honours Degree in Modern History which made me ever after deeply suspicious of people with paper qualifications!

Having finished the written papers Pam collected me and we sat among the bluebells under the hazels in Wytham Woods where we had no business to be, as we listened to the clump of the keeper's boots on the path, not knowing that Wytham Woods would return as a major irritant during two frustrating years as chairman of the British Deer Society.

Chapter 3

'Join a Highland regiment, my boy. The kilt is an
unrivalled garment for fornication and diarrhoea.'

John Masters, *Bugles and a Tiger*

IN AUGUST 1951 I joined up as a National Serviceman at the Highland Brigade
Training Centre at Fort George for six weeks basic training in the Potential
Leader's Squad. The weather was brilliant each morning when Lance Corporal
Ochterlonie shouted 'Wakey, wakey. Feet on the floor!' There were no bath
plugs so we used our socks. Weekly barrack room inspections were rigorous and
we early learnt a good officer ran his finger along the tops of the lockers to
ensure there was no dust. On arrival we collected our kit and were given our
TAB and tetanus jags. That night everybody felt miserable and I was surrounded
by delirious men from the Islands who had never left home before, all speaking
Gaelic. The platoon commander was Donald Maclellan, later to command the
Queen's Own Highlanders. In immediate charge was Corporal Maclean, an ex-
butcher from Coatbridge, one of the finest leaders of men I have ever met who
at first was very hard on us. The man in the next bed, Bremner from Forres, was
saving up to go to the loo on his first weekend home and became ill. On the
other side was a miner from Fife who deserted, and beyond him a man who
painted pink ducks on the barrack room walls and threw them bread. He was
released within a week. In the cookhouse we had soup from pots in which the
ATS cooks washed their stockings. Many from less well-off homes turned up
their noses at the disgusting food, but I was so hungry I would have eaten
anything, and supplemented meagre rations with Empire biscuits from the
NAAFI. Each evening the pipe band beat retreat and the sound of the Battle of
the Somme rising above the ramparts of the Fort made one proud to belong to a
Highland Regiment.

After a week a runner from the CO summoned me. Outside the Orderly
Room the sergeant major barked: 'Halt there, you horrible little man! Right
turn. Now salute!' In front was the second in command, Major Powell of
the Seaforths who stuttered, 'G-g-g-Gordon Duff, your m-m-mother was a
g-g-great friend of mine. I have a l-l-l-letter from her here, w-w-wanting to
know if you-you can have a w-w-week's leave to sh-sh-shoot g-g-grouse in
W-W-Wester Ross. I'm afraid you can't!' – to my relief.

We drilled, and fired rifles and Bren guns, and Sten guns and mortars. We ran
and jumped and scrubbed the floor of the gym where Corporal Petrie of the
Army Physical Training Corps forced us to do things we never knew we could.

Eventually we were despatched to our selection board (WOSB) at Barton Stacey. In the evening some of us went to Winchester where the singing of the choir swept up the pillars of the darkened cathedral. We performed tasks in teams to surmount impossible obstacles and had to give five minute lecturettes. I spoke on the Pleasures of Being Alone – despite which I became an officer.

There was a month's delay before entering OCTU at Eaton Hall during which Farquhar Sutherland, whose mother kept a hotel at Halkirk, and I went to stay with John Duncan at Strathmashie. We tramped across the Corrieyarrack in bare feet to Fort Augustus and were collected by Charles Ian Fraser who drove us home to Reelig. Later he went yellow from drinking too much orange juice and died. On days out I went to the Station Hotel in Inverness where my mother's ex-housemaid took me to the stores and fed me McVitie's wholemeal chocolate biscuits, or else to Slackbuie where Nanny produced chocolate cake. Whenever we left the Fort we had to stand over a mirror in the Guardroom floor – to ensure we were properly dressed. When we moved to Muncaster I remember the Cumbrian Women's Institute Annual rally. Two and a half thousand women ate all the food, used all the water, and blocked the loos. I had to judge forty nine limericks. The head woman, strong Chapel from Alston, was scandalised by my winning choice:

> The kilt Patrick wears is well chosen
> But it tickles me pink that supposing
> If caught in a gale
> Would ladies turn pale
> And Patrick's assets be frozen?

Next morning it was on Radio Cumbria – what I call the wireless!

In November I went for sixteen weeks to Eaton Hall, home of the Duke of Westminster who we occasionally met in the grounds. In my barrack room in the house only three of the seven inmates completed the course, and I admired the determination of those without the advantage of physical fitness we had acquired at school and university. Early morning parades were avoided by running around the Obelisk which resulted in being an undistinguished member of the Cross Country team. We competed on Saturdays and if I wasn't last it was a success. Major Woodruffe (Sussex Regiment), Roy Rutherford (Loyals) and CSM Clegg (Coldstream Guards) were in charge of us, but the vast bulk of RSM Copp, also of the Coldstream, filled our horizons. Once I arranged for all cadets from Highland regiments to parade in kilt and spats which offended him. 'Mr Gordon Duff – Sir – what would you say if all those from the Guards Brigade appeared in cheesecutters [hats] because that's what you're in danger of forcing them to do!' I felt like part of an HM Bateman cartoon.

We competed with full packs, rifles, and tin hats over the assault course, faster and faster as the weeks passed. One man, Allison of the Rifle Brigade, fell off a

Eaton Hall OCTU, March 1952. PTGD fifth from left, front row.

rope and fractured his skull. Weekly we went to the cinema in Chester and fell asleep long before the end of the film, afterwards visiting Cunningham's Oyster Bar. We fired on the ranges at Sealand and went for two days and a night to battle camp at Bickerton digging trenches, afterwards filled in, before marching back. Having inspected the feet of our squad there was weekend leave. I staggered to the train and slept the whole way to Oxford. Halfway through the course we went to Trawsfynydd where St. Andrew's Day was spent up to my waist with a Bren gun in the middle of a freezing river and a snowstorm. At evening we dried our clothes in the Nissen hut and I walked with a schoolmaster from South Wales through a landscape with clouds streaming across the moon to visit the statue of Hedd Wynn, killed in France in the 1914 War the night before he was due to return to receive the Bardic Crown. It was very moving.

After the King's death in February 1952 we travelled by train to battle camp at Okehampton. Dartmoor was snowy and they fired at us with live ammunition. Back at Eaton Hall I was Senior Under Officer and commanded the passing out parade of several hundred cadets. The band of the Worcestershire Regiment didn't know the Cameron March Past, 'Pibroch of Donuil Dhu', and we had to make do with 'Hielan Laddie' as we marched past General Gale. The experience taught me to throw my voice so that a microphone is rarely necessary to address a meeting. I passed out, commissioned into the Queen's Own Cameron Highlanders, marching before a proud father who had served in the same regiment, self confident and believing nothing impossible. Suddenly the nights of ironing the box pleats of my Jock's kilt and the tucks in the back of my battle dress, of shining boots with a hot spoon, and polishing my father's cap badge seemed worthwhile. The proudest emblem of all was the blue hackle worn in my bonnet. Meantime there were two weeks leave before posting to the depot at Inverness and thence to Redford Barracks in Edinburgh as part of the advance party awaiting the battalion's return from the Canal Zone. I had to remind myself from time to time of Lady Astor's farewell to the Oxford Union!

At Redford the newly commissioned subaltern considered himself God's gift to the nation, but was returned to earth with a bump. My first night as orderly officer the guard was inspected at ten o'clock – officiously! The piper played, the bugler sounded the Last Post, the flag was lowered, and the prisoners visited, before drawing a chit telling me to turn out the guard at 2 a.m. Ten minutes after sinking into an armchair in the Mess, the telephone rang. 'Oh! Sir, come quick, come quick, there's a ruddy nutter o' a woman here.' Dressed in blues and trews and my father's greatcoat, a Glengarry on my head, black cane with silver regimental mounting under my arm, I strode off with an air of invincibility. Sergeant Benton was shaking like a leaf with the Jocks in the background making rude gestures, and a woman laying her nightie and her silver hairbrushes on the Guard Room floor. 'Young man,' she said, 'I'm Lady Constance Comyns-Comyns. The communists are watching my house at Leith and the police said you'd give me protection.' Her accent was nearer Morningside than Leith. I called Sylvia Dunne, the ATS officer in the next door barracks, to suggest the problem was more in her line than mine. She sweetly removed the old lady leaving me to regain my armchair thinking what a fine fellow I was. Minutes later the telephone rang again. 'Oh, sir, that ruddy woman's back.' We called the police and an intelligent constable told her if she caught the next tram there would be a man standing under the Tollcross clock which would be the signal the Communists had stopped watching her house. It had to be the five minutes in the twenty four hours no man was under the clock and one hour later the poor lady returned to be taken away in a Black Maria. I never had the heart to look in the telephone book to see if she really existed.

The battalion returned from Suez marching up Princes Street, pipes playing and crowds on the pavement. I was proud to belong. Donald Macbrayne, nice but liked a dram or two, was left in charge while most people had leave. For some illogical reason he made me acting MTO (Transport Officer). I irritated the drivers by taking the distributors out of their lorries at night when they forgot to immobilize them. I had passed no driving test, but having been instructed by a terrified mother, and a rather cooler Pam, felt competent enough to ask the colonel, Twizzel Grant-Peterkin, to sign a certificate telling the Edinburgh City Council to give me a licence. For years I felt guilty answering 'Edinburgh' to the form asking 'Which Council holds your certificate of competence to drive?' Years later my mother-in-law was stopped in Brackley High Street while a constable pointed out her car licence was fourteen years out of date. She purchased a new one and nobody complained. Nowadays the authorities are not so pragmatic!

One morning Donald Macbrayne summoned me, still several sizes too big for my size 10 boots. 'Gordon Duff, I'm aware you could run this battalion better than me. Unfortunately it's my job not yours!' – after which I went off to buy a packet of custard creams and a bar of Terry's Devon Milk Chocolate wrapped in pale blue paper with dark blue bands across the corners.

My first job, decreed by Jock Crichton, was teaching Privates Andrews from Lossiemouth and Robertson from Brora to read. I bought a book saying 'A' is for Apple which was neither useful nor interesting, but eventually they were able to translate battalion orders and are now probably tycoons. Monday mornings were spent at the Law Courts bailing out Jocks who had celebrated returning from Suez by lobbing bricks through shop windows at the top of Leith Walk on Saturday nights. They later repaid by volunteering to carry heavy equipment on route marches. James McGuigan was my special friend and before his posting to the Black Watch in Korea where he was killed we saw *Viva Zapata* at the cinema. Mexicans have style. I read of one community returning a Government official to Mexico City, tied to his saddle with a label round his neck, saying 'Mind your own business', an action with resonance in days of Government interference in the minutest details of everybody's lives. Tommy Lamb, who had lain wounded in the middle of the artillery barrage at El Alamein, became my company commander.

We drilled and went on route marches and two months later at 4 a.m. on a Sunday morning we marched to Gorgie Station with pipes playing to the disgust of the housewives of Craiglockhart. Years later they were further disgusted during the visit of the King and Queen of Norway. The horses of the Household Cavalry trotted down the same road lifting their tails as they went, depositing a supply of manure for the roses. Unfortunately they were disappointed because the Council lorry cleared up the mess before they had even fetched their shovels.

We travelled for thirty six hours sleeping the night on a bench at Newcastle Station, crossing from Harwich to the Hook of Holland, and then endlessly through Holland and Germany until reaching Spittal beside the River Drau in Carinthia, near where Austria borders Slovenia and Italy. From there the Cossacks had been disgracefully returned to their deaths in Russia after the War. Some of the NCOs had also been prisoners in what had become a DP camp ruled over by Marius, a delightful and distinguished Yugoslavian who gave us slivovic when we had dealings. We marched from the station in our kilts to the horror of the inhabitants whose last unhappy encounter with a Highland regiment had been with the 8th Argylls. My room in the Mess at the old Posthaus Hotel overlooked the Catholic church whose bells tolled each morning for services I sometimes attended. Next door we drank *Kaffee mit schlag* at night with the Adjutant, Tony Findlay's dog sitting drinking on the chair beside us. We started work at 5 a.m. each morning and rested in the very hot heat of the day. Along the road was a *schloss* belonging to Count Norman and in the fields women worked while men appeared only to watch.

At first I was in charge of the drafts coming from Inverness – a wonderful job for a conceited young subaltern of independent mind. We marched to the ranges always accompanied by a piper, Mackenzie 92, later a bank manager before retiring to Portree where his widow Christine still lives. In the August grass were bugs that bit and we marched back itching with the men singing 'Keep right on to the end of the road'. For three weeks at a time we took to the hills, always with our piper, going wherever the map took us, practising elementary tactics. When we camped at evening the Jocks too often picked the autumn apples for which I had to apologise. At Eaton Hall we had learnt the Principles of War – Surprise, Concentration, Offensive Action, Mobility, Economy of Effort, Speed, and Cooperation – and tried to translate them into the everyday life of a private soldier. We had also learnt a defensive position should be 'easy to move from'. Now I watch friends ignore these basic principles – and often ignore them myself – which makes life more difficult than it need be! We shaved in the rivers and were supplied with food at faraway rendezvous by some angel in a lorry. The first week the Jocks loathed, the second they enjoyed, and by the end of the third they disliked returning to barracks as much as I did. As we marched past the Guard Room RSM Agnew mouthed, 'Only another National Serviceman.' Tony Findlay didn't like the way I dressed either. For Burns Night in the Sergeant's Mess I was expected to sing a song and dance with Mrs Agnew, who kissed me, an experience neither of us enjoyed – or forgot.

Ronnie Borradaile became C Company Commander. He and Audrey were endlessly kind and I used to chase their two young sons around the floor with a wastepaper basket on my head. Managing children seemed so simple until encountering our own! He had been a prisoner-of-war but escaped and for many years visited the Italian families who sheltered him. A relaxed man, I once encountered him in a clearing in a wood during an exercise, sitting on a log reading the newspaper while the Colonel dashed around like a man demented. On the same exercise – we were supposed to be defending Western Europe from Russia – two men and I shivered in the snow under the bridge at Villach with inadequate instructions to blow it up if the enemy arrived. The only person who came was the GOC, General Urquhart, famous airborne commander from Arnhem, who asked: 'What are you doing, my boy?' I didn't know and have remembered ever since to be frightened of explosives and that communication must be a principle of life.

The other subalterns in C company, later commanded by David Murray – a brilliant and knowledgeable piper of whom the CO was rather frightened – were Neil Macpherson and Rory MacDonald from Blarour. Second in command was Alan MacDonald who had a black and tan dog, Bonny, and eloped with a local lady married to a Swede who claimed to be my cousin – Baron Rosenberg de la Mar. The Rosenberg de la Mars fed me on coffee and cakes and took me to farms in the back of the hills unchanged since the fifteenth century, with corn cobs hanging from the ceilings, places I would never have seen as an ordinary soldier. Neil Macpherson was a good skier and remains one of the most quietly conscientious friends one could have. I hated ski-ing and confidence wasn't reinforced when Hubert, the guide, ex-instructor of an Austrian Mountain Division, hit a tree fracturing his skull shortly after undertaking our training. We climbed for days on end without skins followed by terrifying descents on narrow icy tracks between the trees. We did langlauf races at which I was no good, but in the end my skis saved me from the battalion boxing when I fell on them and broke my coccyx. Neil was brilliant and emerged from the ring covered in blood.

We did terrible things but were always saved by Rory MacDonald having done something worse. In the autumn we climbed at Lienz in the Dolomites where B Company was stationed, staying in the Kirschbaum Hut sleeping on benches, like hounds, with lots of Austrians. Visions of heroically conquering Everest evaporated rapidly and I seemed much more likely to fall down a crevasse on the Gross Glockner glacier. We travelled by train to Salzburg for a long exercise in the snow with the Americans who did things in style. British army cooking equipment was too small for their turkeys. They evacuated their 'wounded' by helicopter to Naples and presented medals to their soldiers for gallantry in face of the 'enemy'. We crossed a river with fixed bayonets, a piper playing, to the horror of the opposition who turned and fled. Their umpire commented: 'Shitkovsky – if the US had infantry like that we'd sweep the world.' The Jocks infuriated our allies, speaking Gaelic on radios which seldom worked while the air was alive with 'Hello Snake-Eye-Easy One One. Are you receiving me?' from a lost American tank. Two nights I slept in a shed of damp beech leaves and when it was time to return to Salzburg managed to hitch a lift with the leading tank of a long column on whose engine my frozen backside was thawed. Having the squitters I had to dismount and watch the end of the column disappear down a very long road. Back at their billets the Jocks were shocked when the American top-sergeant, failing to find anyone to obey his orders, did guard duty himself.

Winter passed with guest nights at which the four junior subalterns had to dance a foursome on the table. The pipe-major, Evan MacRae, who tried to teach me the chanter and had written the tune 'Over the Chindwin', played. In my mind's eye the shadow of his bearded figure can still be seen marching around that table in the candlelight. The Borradailes had daughters of friends to stay – Jill Herrick, Susan Knight, and Diana Evelegh with whom we tobogganed in the moonlight. As spring approached I walked with Susan one Sunday above the Weissensee watching for the *Schneerosen* and the daphne flowering through the snow, but every week I wrote to Pam. In spring they sent me by train to umpire an exercise at Trieste. On the first day an American APC overturned on the road to Opicina killing its occupants. At night, bored, I took off my white armband and climbed in the rear of a lorry, pushing my skean dhu with its Cairngorm top (in its scabbard!) into the driver's back, telling him to drive. Horrified, he drove me into Jugoslavia and we were lucky to return without being arrested. On the third day I was kneeling looking at a flower as General Winterton, Jill Herrick's future father-in-law was passing. 'What are you doing, my boy?' '*Anenome pulsatilla*, sir', with which his ADC, Stacey of the Rifle Brigade, stuck his nose in the air saying 'Ugh, flowers!' I only saw him once again, marching in front of me at the Coronation. The exercise finished in four days instead of fourteen so there were ten days leave which included visiting Venice where the canals were full of orange peel and stank.

At Spittal it was time to say farewell to friends before returning to the Depot at Inverness in preparation for the Coronation at which I was to carry the Regimental Colours. Hamish Logan was in charge, a colourless officer who eventually became a brigadier but I don't know how. The Queen's Colours were to be carried by Ian Mackinnon, a Regular, later CLA Director in East Anglia. We marched for miles and miles along the roads and one day were marooned at lunchtime in a ploughed field near Daviot because no one had looked at the map. Had life been going to last forever as a subaltern in Austria I might have stayed in the army, but the Coronation killed it stone dead. We returned without a batman and I was never clean and tidy. My laundry was jammed under the bed until there was no more space when it was carted to Aunt Katharine's washing machine at Platcock, a house to which she had moved on the edge of Fortrose with a beautiful hedge of old yellow highland roses and a fierce gander she taught me to repulse by showing the flat of my hand. My cousin Priscilla – her sister called her the spoilt one – used to drive me back to the Kessock Ferry on Monday mornings. For our final preparations we moved to Redford before travelling to London where we were billeted at Earl's Court. The 2 June 1953 was ghastly.

The day the Queen was crowned should have been filled with sun. Hillary and Tensing had climbed Everest, but in London it rained incessantly. Edith Evans, asked at night by the BBC what she thought of the spectacle, replied: 'Clean fed up with the Almighty, but terribly proud of us.' I wore a new green jacket, white gloves, Cameron officer's kilt, red and green diced hose, and my father's claymore at my side, but our black hair sporrans with their white tassels had been replaced by white blancoed pouches which ran all over our kilts in the pouring rain. We marched to Knightsbridge, and then what seemed like forever. The contingent from the Parachute Regiment fainted in front of us one by one when we halted on Constitution Hill at midday while the guns fired their salute. In Piccadilly a guardsman lining the route fell on his bayonet. Despite our training, carrying the Colours the length of the Mall, right elbow raised, forearm parallel to the ground, was painful but one stirring moment came as we marched into Parliament Square from Parliament Street with the music of the pipes playing 'Blue Bonnets are Over the Border' swept up to the sky between the height of the buildings. Queen Salote of Tonga, a large lady, travelled in a coach with Haile Selassie. Asked who the funny little man was Noel Coward replied: ' That's her lunch!' They never gave me a Coronation medal – which rankles still.

At Inverness increasing pressure was put on me by Douglas Wimberley, the Colonel of the Regiment, by parents and step-parents to stop seeing Pam. In the end I buckled and we parted in autumn in a biting wind on the slopes above Glenmazeran. I hurt her dreadfully, but she remains my friend who taught me so much about the joy of loving and living. As she lived until her mid nineties, the argument she would be dead long before me was wrong. For a final two months at the Depot, where Neil Baird commanded, I was attached to the Brigade Major, Donald Callander, to help organise the Inverness Tattoo and work with Brigadier Alastair Maclean who ran the one in Edinburgh. He had me to stay in Moray Place and drank whisky for breakfast, although his new wife, Lady Strathspey, was gradually weaning him onto gin. He was interesting company and devised a scene where a girl was rescued from the jaws of the Loch Ness Monster. My job was to organise the creation of the Monster by a joiner called Lowrie to whom time meant nothing. The tattoo was a success, despite two unexploded mortar bombs which had to be blown up by Jock Macleod and me. We botched the job and had to go to Raigmore hospital to have the phosphorus removed from our skins. The holes in my father's greatcoat from the 1914 War remain as evidence. My reputation was further dented when leaving the Depot wages in an unlocked safe at lunch time. They disappeared. There was a Court of Enquiry, one of whose members, later father-in-law to Madonna, had made the same mistake elsewhere. They asked me to repay two hundred pounds and it was mortifying to read 'an inexperienced young officer should never have been left in a position of such responsibility'. It taught me to be careful with money.

Chapter 4

The Rose of all the World is not for me.
I want for my part
Only the little white rose of Scotland
That smells sharp and sweet – and breaks the heart.

Hugh McDiarmid

M Y FINAL DAY in the army there was a garden party for the Queen Mother at
Cameron Barracks to which Aunt Katharine came. She pointed me
towards Dorothy McCall, widow of a Cameron general whose son Robin, ex-
airman shot down in North Africa during the war, had a farm in Glenlyon and
needed a student. Her other son, Alan, ex-POW, was a major in the Regiment,
serving at the depot at the time. He suffered from stomach ulcers. It was a day
which changed my life. I knew nothing of cattle or sheep but loved the hills and
was certain working among them would be a more suitable habitat than a
Croydon factory making bathroom fittings. Some weeks later I went to Ruskich
to meet Robbie, and his wife Peggie, originally from Eigg, and they agreed to
employ me for £1 a week and my keep after the stalking season at Strathmashie
which Uncle Edward had leased for what proved to be a final time. He and my
mother were never going to agree to help me to an agricultural future they
regarded as precarious. Strathmashie was for sale and they seriously considered
buying it, but were so cross with my decision that he failed to purchase what
was a beautiful estate of 11,000 acres, including the arable land at Laggan Bridge,
for an asking price of £11,000. It was bought instead by Captain Anderson who
re-sold half for more than he paid for the whole before parting with a penny. In
1950 I had met my future wife, Phyllida Pennington, when calling at Aberarder
to collect rowlocks for the boat on Loch Laggan. All day I sulked because Uncle
Edward used my spinning rod, once my father's, to catch a 30lb pike, but at
night I persuaded my mother to ask the Penningtons to dinner. In 1953 we
renewed our acquaintance. John Duncan warned me whoever married 'that one'
would be saddled with responsibility for Muncaster where he had been keeper
on the sand hills at Drigg. Uncle Edward said, 'Look at the mother and see what
you'll see across the breakfast table in twenty years time.' Looking around, some
of my friends didn't!

Phyllida's mother, Veronica Morley, was incredibly beautiful but a social snob
which hid her shyness and spoilt so much of her enjoyment of people she
considered beneath her. She was kind to children and animals and a marvellous
mother, but poor at feeding visitors, a fact so well known that when staying at

Mother-in-law, Veronica, Lady Pennington-Ramsden from painting by Riddell.

Brackley for dances my mother sent me with a box of biscuits to keep under the bed in case of hunger in the night. She was a rotten housekeeper and her husband ordered cakes from the newspaper. Prunella, our eldest daughter, once told her I hated visiting Muncaster because she never provided potatoes. Thereafter I was given one, but nobody else was – which was sad because my father-in-law loved them. She told Prunella she must realise she was one of the great heiresses of the country, which was untrue and cut no ice with her grand-daughter. She never resented me giving the cook stags' balls to serve for dinner to test the system. She had a fabulous collection of jewellery, but wore psychedelic earrings from Woolworths. She used being late as a weapon, but when she died in 1987 I missed her despite never having found a meeting of minds. Her mother, Molly Sandeman, known as Biddy because she lived at Biddestone, was married firstly to Fred Morley, a lawyer involved with the Crippen case, and secondly to Hoël Llewellyn, Chief Constable of Wiltshire who trained a pack of bloodhounds by hunting his younger son. Biddy had character, but when we had drawn lines in the sand we got on well. The last time she visited we drove her to the Stranraer ferry and shared a bottle of hock in a ditch near Newton Stewart. Her sister, Aunt Sylvia, was married to Hugh Rathcavan who shot out Dennis Stucley's eye shooting grouse at Dinnet and compounded the awfulness by demanding the shoot continue as he'd paid for it.

Phyllida's father, Bobby Pennington, was delightful company but not intellectual. He had a charming smile, was generous to his family and friends but fairly mean to others. I heard him say about an employee: 'She's wonderful, and do you know I pay her very little!' So little, in fact, that we sent her a cheque each Christmas. Father-in-law was born in 1904, Geoffrey William, known as Bobby, second son of Sir John Frecheville Ramsden 6th Bart who, until he died in 1958, treated him as a small boy, returning letters with spelling mistakes underlined. He served in the 11th Hussars until marrying his 19 year old bride in 1927, when he had to transfer to the Life Guards. A fearless horseman, he was second in the 1927 Grand National on Bovril, a horse with one eye. The year he married he was stalking at Ardverikie, accompanied by his wife. Having shot one stag, he heard another roaring in the mist and told her to wait behind a rock until he returned. On coming down to dinner his mother asked: 'Where's Veronica?' She had caught the next train to London. Trained for horses and the army he knew little of land or money until his elder brother was reputedly murdered by his cook in Malaya in 1948, after which he found himself responsible for a great deal of both. Having changed his name from Ramsden to Pennington to inherit Muncaster, when his father died in 1958 he had to add back Ramsden. By that time Pennington was added to my perfectly adequate name which years later caused someone unknown from Fort William to telephone: 'Phit the hell makes you think you're entitled to three names?' Thereafter reverse charge calls were never accepted, even from the children.

Bobby had a wry and sometimes slightly malicious sense of humour, and

Donald MacDonald in the stackyard at Ruskich, 1954.

liked brandy which misled him. Arriving late for a dinner in Kenya after a sip, he sat next to his hostess and announced, 'I think I'd like to go to bed with you!' after which his wife removed him and thereafter kept a close eye on the brandy bottle. He was unfailingly kind to me, as was Veronica, despite a mutual disapproval confirmed when old Nanny Cage found a handful of oats from the Glenlyon harvest in my dressing gown pocket. It reinforced their fears that their ewe lamb might be condemned to a life of penury with a hill shepherd in a Highland bog. Two years later their hopes of deliverance were temporarily raised when Adam, the family Labrador, absconded with one diamond and sapphire engagement ring.

In mid-October 1953 I drove what was then a two day journey south from Strathmashie to Rotherwick in a sand coloured Austin A30 donated by my mother, returning three weeks later to Glenlyon. That August I had accompanied Jock Campbell and Alec Livingstone to a gathering. The hill gatherings were magic with ribbons of sheep flowing down the hillsides in front of the dogs through the cool of early morning to arrive in the fank by breakfast. Ruskich was a small farm with three hundred Blackface ewes, twenty assorted cows, one horse, Dora, aged 40, and a grey TVO Ferguson tractor which started reluctantly. There was no electricity and the oil lamps were lit for the hens in the deep litter house after dark, often wading through snow to reach them. My wages were £1 a week which Robbie could ill afford, but it left enough to buy a bar of chocolate from the vans. We sowed seed and fertiliser out of a sheet learning painfully slowly to coordinate arms and legs, but years later in Tynron it entertained me to see the trippers watch over the dyke how the peasants worked. We scaled dung and lime and basic slag with a shovel behind Dora, also used to cart swedes to the stackyard in autumn where they were covered with straw, later to be fed into the hopper of the hand-driven turnip cutter for the cattle. The limited in-bye land along the floor of the glen was worked on a strict rotation of oats, turnips, oats undersown, and four years leys. We used no spray and cleaned the ground as we singled and hoed the turnips, and the two or three drills of potatoes grown for the house. Some of the harvest was done with a binder, but much had to be cut with a scythe and bound by hand in sheaves with wisps of straw before stooking. Eventually it was carted to the stackyard for threshing in winter, before being put through the bruiser for the cattle. Hay was cut by tractor and reaper with a man sitting on it to raise the blade at the corners or on encountering obstacles.

There was one other person on the farm, Jimmy Christie who had arrived off the road shortly before me, with nothing much except a razor and the clothes he stood in. He lived in the bothy and taught me, besides other things, to build a ruck of hay with a fork after gathering it behind the Tumbling Tom. Jimmy was restless though. Eight months later he suddenly stalked out of the hayfield and took to the road again, only to be run over by a woman with a guilty conscience who took him home to Killin to look after her place. His successor, Donald John MacDonald, had worked as a ghillie at Corrivarkie on the south side of Loch Ericht. He drank a bit and one day, after a jaunt to Aberfeldy, I found him, drunk as a lord, lying smiling in the waters of the burn smoking his pipe. From him I learnt to build a stack.

Only let out for exercise the cows were tied by the neck in the byre in winter and their calves let out of boxes to suckle night and morning. Their simple diet of hay, turnips, and bruised oats was perfectly satisfactory. The house cow was milked by hand, a task at which I was bad, being sometimes rewarded with a kick in the face as I sat on the stool beside the long suffering beast. The spring born calves were sold as yearling stirks at Aberfeldy, where the lambs were also marketed. Never having driven a tractor I couldn't back a cart to save myself. On arrival my first task was to go to market sixteen miles away, picking up sheep from Angus Macaulay at Fortingall. To my relief it was possible to turn the tractor in a wide circle without backing. We chopped logs endlessly having sawn the fallen trees with a crosscut. I washed up and took the children to school in a monstrous old shooting brake, one day picking up beehives from the keeper at Chesthill who was moving to Berwickshire where he could see England across the river – which upset him, but not as much as the bees which escaped in the car. I evacuated and only returned after dark to retrieve them. The farm was rented from Major Fuller, Invervar.

The keeper was Glendinning, ex Dragoon Guards, and the schoolteacher Mrs Gillespie whose husband had been an unsuccessful farmer at Dalreoch near

Amulree. Dorothy McCall also lived at Invervar, and at Craigianie John and Wendy McHugh who used me as baby sitter for their daughter Morag and whose son Robin became our student in Dumfriesshire, a fate also suffered by Malcolm McCall, now of Inverbrora, and an active protagonist of tenants' rights. At that time the thought of my ignorant youth later instructing anyone about agriculture seemed highly improbable. The first lambing Phyllida and I conducted by ourselves was a vivid lesson. We had wild Blackface ewes, and went to the field with a dog which couldn't run and a cat which could. Catching a ewe was accomplished with difficulty and although I had worked on farms for six years and watched my employers do the job I had never physically lambed a sheep with a problem. Phyllida sat on the animal's head with a book called *Home Doctoring of Animals* while I attended to the back end, discovering there are more ways of a lamb mispresenting itself than illustrated in any book. It was a sharp lesson that there is no substitute for experience, and later when we had students they were always made to do the job themselves under supervision.

After that horrible experience spring became the happiest season of the year. There is nothing so wonderful as watching a mother one has helped through a difficult birth licking her offspring. The animals repaid with trust time and again. Modern society alleges farmers keep animals solely for financial gain and seems incapable of understanding farming is not only about economics and politics – although of course farmers have to make a living to keep a roof over their families' heads – but more about the bond between man, the animals, and the fertility of the land. Having inspected from behind the elegant legs of the Minister for Rural Affairs with her stiletto heels and strapback shoes at a Select Committee meeting it depresses me that a Government Minister and officials in London can be so clueless and unrealistic about the realities of life in a countryside they claim to represent. The vast majority of farmers treat their livestock as members of the family.

In 1953 my ignorance was total. Uncle Edward suggested I only thought I wanted to be a sheep farmer to walk the hills of Scotland and watch the sunset. He couldn't understand what farmers did and took until fifteen years later, staying at Kirkland, when he, a business man, was spellbound watching the birth of calves, lambs, and piglets. The thought of dosing or injecting a sheep was appalling. Clostridial vaccines were recent introductions which greatly increased the survival rate of lambs, and little did I know how many would pass through my hands during the next thirty years. Dosing the tups with large carbon tetrachloride capsules for fluke they bit me. The dose guns later introduced greatly speeded operations.

We lived hard, lifting huge weights. Over the river at Inverinain Sandy Macpherson, a shepherd from Skye, could only reach home by ferrying himself across the Lyon, often carting twelve stone sacks of corn to the steading on his back. He was employed by the Walkers of Slatich with whom we maintained an uneasy relationship over the march. For gatherings and handlings we neighboured, clipping by hand at which I was never good, mainly from inability to sharpen shears properly. At summer gatherings we met the other shepherds on top of the hill at 3 a.m. climbing the almost perpendicular side of the Ruskich march. Once a grouse rushed past followed by a peregrine which struck it above the middle of the glen. Other times on our way to meet Duncan Robertson from Innerhadden and the MacIntyres from Braes of Foss we heard the golden plovers above the Sgubach and in autumn the rutting stags, before winter set in with endless shovelling of snow to reach the road end. We ate rabbits Robbie taught me to catch with a line of snares on the fences at the edge of the wood which in springtime was full of primroses. The foxes caused trouble at lambing and one unforgettable night we sat with old Glendinning and Andrew Mackintosh at a den on the face above the house. They trapped the vixen and two cubs. At dawn we watched the dog fox, out of gunshot, with two other cubs in his mouth, disappearing over the hill. It was impossible not to weep a little inside at such a vivid demonstration of nature's cruelty, the destruction of one hardworking family's livelihood, and the difficulty of finding humane balance in the management of the countryside. Shepherds and keepers, farmers and landowners are mostly keen and knowledgeable conservationists and people forget it is their care which has created today's landscape. Tom Renwick saw a woman to whom he had let a house near Innerleithen watching the sunset over the gate. 'What a wonderful view,' said she, 'and to think that the farmers are trying to wreck it!' 'Excuse me, madam, but who do you think made it?'

Peggie worked too hard bringing our piece to the field morning and afternoon, and Robbie and I were so tired at night we sat either side of the fire snoring while she did her knitting between us. Ruskich was no palace, and it was difficult for them with two young children and a tiresome student. My room was eight foot by five with a skylight the only ventilation which let in midges in summer and snow in winter, so was usually closed. The stink of dip, or dung, or sweat must have been overpowering, but I never noticed. Sometimes the tinkers came, but that ended when one party arrived in a car and threw away sandwiches Peggie gave them because they were made with margarine. One particularly nice man came on a red bicycle. Eddie McMahon wintered at Queensferry, but spent his summers moving around the hills, sharpening scissors and knives, and doing jobs on the farms in return for his keep.

We bought tups in Stirling and walnut whirls in a sweetshop at Crieff on the way home.

The seasons passed with heavy snow in winter, poor weather at lambing, endless rain at hay and harvest when we had to hang the sheaves on the fences to dry, and perpetual mud while we shawed the turnips. At nights we read by oil lamps – books from the Times Book Club and the *Scottish Farmer*, learning the names of farms and farmers and prices paid for their stock, information which stood in good stead later. I played cricket for the Glenlyon Farmers against Aberfeldy, scored no runs and bowled underarm. There were parties at Christmas with Sonia and Watty Yellowless, the doctor who briefly persuaded Aberfeldy to dig for victory. He later became President of the McCarrison Society and his articles on healthy eating are worth rereading. Tom Finlayson, chartered surveyor, and his wife were often there, with the McDiarmid brothers from Mains of Murthly who have maintained a constant presence in my life. In January 1954 they acutely embarrassed me when having to act changing a baby's nappy for a game of dumb crambo – an innocent bachelor with a mouth full of safety pins. At New Year 1954 we watched TV for the first time at the Coshieville Hotel, next to where the Runcimans kept pigs and grew raspberries. Occasionally we attended church at Bridge of Balgie, but mostly memories persist of that incredibly beautiful glen with the brilliant hue of the trees by the river in autumn and the kindness of the family who took me in, sight unseen, on the strength of his mother knowing my aunt. Although we seldom meet, the McCalls, now living in Sutherland, have been constant friends for fifty intervening years. Kirsty, married to Robin Pilcher, was our bridesmaid, and Malcolm our student for a year. To be asked to speak at Peggie's funeral in Dornoch Cathedral, and for her to ask Robbie to put one of my poems on her gravestone, was a great honour and small repayment for that year when they sheltered me as one of their own. Their greatest gift was teaching me to work – and to wash up.

Ruskich was a poor farm whose turnover provided bare subsistence, so it must have been a relief when Robbie went to manage Camusavie at The Mound for the Abel-Smiths, before eventually taking the tenancy of Inverbrora and Uppat. I was a liability – particularly with dogs. They had three collies, a mongrel Jomo Kenyatta, the Unwanted Black, a dachshund, and Bella, a Siamese cat with a piercing voice. They found me a wild animal, Rough, who had to be given away as nobody could handle him, but one Sunday Robbie came with me to Loch Katrine where we bought June, who understood. She was beautiful and would gather from far places, but had one terrible fault. She loved hunting rabbits. In the nick of time myxamotosis intervened and although living in a kennel she accompanied me everywhere, leaning on the front seat of the car wherever we went, squeaking because she couldn't bark. Unfortunately she had an eye for the boys and was served by Jomo. One puppy went to my future wife. Emma had a mouth like a rat with which she was rather free and was stopped just in time before she bit Prince Phillip in the bottom as he was poised over a map in the Sandringham office at York Cottage. June became part of family life when I married and was perfectly house trained. On moving to Sandringham in 1957 we thought she would dislike Norfolk so took her to the Greaves's at Blackchub in Dumfriesshire from whom I had bought some Highland cattle, but I was so miserable the next day I drove the hundred miles from Muncaster to bring her home. In Norfolk we tried unsuccessfully to mate her with a dog

Robin McCall with Kirstie at Ruskich, 1954.

belonging to a shepherd called Elijah Rout who was so embarrassed he insisted Phyllida remain out of sight. Poor June was run over soon afterwards hunting a hare. At Ruskich I bought a second dog, Croy, from Sandy Grant, under shepherd at Aberarder Farm who rode a motorbike, hadn't slept for twenty five years, and found the nights lonely. Croy was a good dog but rough with sheep and had to be dismissed when I succeeded Sandy as Neil Usher's very-under-shepherd.

In summer 1954 there was a 4/5 Cameron TA weekend at Achnacarry. The battalion was commanded by Lochiel. Rory MacDonald put me up at Tirindrish. It was time to think of finding another job and I contemplated offering my services to Lochiel at Glendessary at the far end of Loch Arkaig. The area remained full of the echoes of the '45 and being reared on D.K. Broster's *The Flight of the Heron*, and *The Dark Mile*, it had enormous appeal to a young man still not grown up – a state in which I remain at the age of seventy four. Robbie encouraged me to apply to Braid Aitken, of Auch, a seriously steep place where the enormous owner was reputed to knock down his shepherds if they disagreed in the fank. Events intervened. The Penningtons invited me to stalk at Aberarder. It was there in Coire Chriochairain, having missed every stag presented to me by Murdie Maclean, stalker, raconteur, smoker, fox killer, Highlander, that I asked my wife to marry me. Having relieved my mind of that problem it was possible to resume killing deer. She said neither 'yes' nor 'no'.

In November my time at Ruskich ended but Phyllida was to return with me for the Aberfeldy Ball. The situation was unsatisfactory. I got jaundice which was dreadful. Detained in bed by my mother on an endless diet of steamed fish I embroidered a tapestry to put on top of a sewing box for the beloved and crocheted her a blue and white bonnet long since eaten by moths. At the beginning of January 1955 we set off together for Perthshire. Near Scotch Corner it snowed like there was no tomorrow. I stopped the car and told her she must say 'yes' or 'no' or she'd have to walk. She said 'yes' and luckily it was only a short way to her cousin Anne Buxton at Newsham Grange where, anxious to impress, I churned the butter by hand. On return from Perthshire I went shooting at Bagnor with Neil Macpherson's family and damaged my car on a kerbstone on top of Boar's Hill going to Versions Farm at Brackley, where Phyllida lived, for a day's hunting with the Grafton. Her father was joint-master, as had been her grandfather, and later her sister, and nephew, Charles Smyth-Osbourne. At night, I hacked home with Dick Agnew, snow dripping off our noses, scenting the impending death of an old familiar world. I never hunted on a horse again. While the car was mended we killed the rats with sticks, bolted by terriers from the stacks in the field as the corn was threshed.

By the end of January it was back to Kinlochlaggan as Neil Usher's under shepherd on £5 per week living more or less as family in the bothy at Aberarder Farm which had a stock of 1,000 Blackface ewes with 500 wethers at the west end on Creag Meagaidh. The head shepherd was Duncan Macnaughton and there was a cook, Rosa MacRae. She made the best porridge in the world and was the daughter of the assistant housekeeper at Ardverikie, who worked with Miss Cameron. It was touching going to the big house to be given the best tea service while those two good women insisted on using the kitchen crockery themselves. Mrs Duncan at Strathmashie, begged by my mother, did my washing and kept me fairly clean.

Neil Usher, adopted Highlander, ex-student like me of Eton and Trinity College, Oxford was deeply knowledgeable about countryside matters and Scottish history. A member of the Church and Nation Committee of the Kirk he was a wonderful story teller, married first to Betty Murray-Usher of Gatehouse, a formidable character. They had one son, James, who attended seven different schools, a feat challenged but unbeaten by our daughters. I first saw him from the top of the hill through the end of a telescope, his car rolling gently towards the waters of Loch Laggan. The marriage was not a success although Betty relied on Neil's advice until he died. He went to work in forestry in New Zealand, before returning to marry Dorothy Scott-Moncrieff and taking the tenancy of Breakachy in Laggan from Glentruim. Long ago the land had belonged to the MacNivens who fell out with the Macphersons, cut out their bull's tongue, and cut the petticoats from Cluny's daughter, after which the Macphersons took the pragmatic step of crossing the Spey and massacred the MacNivens. Neil went to war in 1939 leaving Dorothy, often ill, to run the farm, but returned when the Department of Agriculture demanded maximum land under the plough. In 1946 he became tenant of Aberarder Farm. Dorothy's brother George, a widower, had a hair lip and wrote books and she more or less brought up his three children whose mother Ann, an Orcadian poet, had drowned herself with postnatal depression in the burn at the Halfway House between Dalwhinnie and Laggan.

It was a winter with snow drifted to the top of the ground floor windows of the house. We tramped ways through drifts for stranded sheep. At weekends I climbed to the high tops blown bare by the wind and could see range on range of hills to the west, little realising the part they and their inhabitants were to play in my future life. Morning and night I milked Betty, the house cow, an accommodating creature until she choked herself with a small turnip she had stolen from the pit, but there was a less accommodating Highlander who died. I had to dig an enormous hole with a spade. Each day, wrapped in my old Gordon plaid, dressed in army boots with a bonnet on my head, I walked four miles across the foot of the hill to the western march, making sure no sheep were stranded in the crags. In spring I ploughed the field by the loch in my kilt and had chilblains on my knees. We planted Kerrs Pink potatoes, with two drills for Murdie, the stalker, who took the job seriously, regaling us with tales of how he had won the battle of El Alamein single-handed. Once thoughtlessly I set a match to the dead grass above the Moy woods and was rewarded with a noisy fire brigade. The stalker at Moy, old Ewen Mackintosh, kept a sheep called Peggie, which lived in the house, but always disappeared on clipping days. He supported twenty two cattle in the byre only one of which he milked, believing it was cruel to put them in calf again. One cow lost its tail on a barbed wire fence causing him spectacular grief and a bicycle ride seven miles to the hotel for whisky. At midday before walking home along the silent snowy road beside Loch Laggan I would call for coffee with the Dundases at Moy, an Ardverikie lodge with cardboard stuck across the broken drawing room window. The stalker at Luiblea was Jockey Gibson married to the Rambling Rose.

One weekend I travelled by train to Muncaster to meet Phyllida and her parents to see about working there when we married. It was the end of January with Suffolk lambs in the fields south of Carlisle. We inspected the Chase, destined briefly to be our home, then inhabited by the vicar and his wife who kept a parrot and a cairn. We met the agent, Ian McWilliam, a Fleet Air Arm pilot in the war who had worked for the BA (British Aluminium) at Fort William, and was not well liked for having to put screws on the unsatisfactory financial situation. Muncaster until 1951 was an estate of 23,000 acres, comprised mostly of small let farms whose milk was collected in churns from

PTGD 1955 (aged 25).

the road end, a few Herdwick sheep on the common grazings, and a bed and breakfast business. The farm of Brotherilkeld had a substantial sheep flock and the Home Farm was in-hand. There were 77 acres of garden reputed to contain the largest collection of species rhododendrons in Europe, and approximately 500 acres of trees. Much of the countryside resembled a snipe bog. Before 1939 the grouse yielded bags of over 100 brace a day on Birker Moor. In 1951 the estate was reduced to 6,000 and in the late 1960s to 2,000 acres. McWilliam had been installed by Curtis and Henson to restore the situation. He had a reputation for being difficult which seemed no problem to my innocence of twenty five years. He returned me to Whitehaven to catch a train to Carlisle. In Scotland there were no trains on Sundays and I walked with my case, ten long miles to Gretna before hitching a lift with a lorry to Perth, staying in the Station Hotel and catching the early train to Newtonmore on Monday morning. Phyllida was due at Inverpattack but was injured when her aunt drove her into the back of a lorry near Carlisle.

At Kinlochlaggan there was a social life with the hotel, Martha at the Post Office, whist drives, dances, and once a week the Highlands and Islands Cinema in the Hall. The people at the roadside were a fund of information, the best stories being told, as only Highlanders tell them, by Jimmy MacRae, the roadman. Communication was swift by what was known as the drum, and at night, when dialling via the telephone exchange, Robertina and Walterina, forty five miles away in Grantown, usually knew where people had gone out to dinner and connected us. Fifty years on that care and concern for neighbours seems to have vanished with the rush of modern life, but when it is found, out of the blue in unexpected places, sometimes among complete strangers, it restores faith in human nature. The hills of Laggan are still a place where the rocks, and the sky, and the wind through the grass stop my life spinning out of control in a senseless world. In 1986 we made a film at Ardverikie with the BBC about rural depopulation. At the finish they asked me to write something to go across the end of the programme and I wrote:

Leaving Loch Laggan

Will it be there
That I must find my destiny
Among those crowded city streets
Where men no longer smile
Learning their lust for gold
Or here –
Where in my youth I lambed the ewes
Finding the harmony of wind, and sky and hills?

Should it be there –
Among those cultures of an alien race,
Where men forget the poems of the Island seas,
And sunset on the silver sand –

Should it be there I am condemned to die
I would fear death,
But here,
Among the timeless Highland hills
I learned to love so long ago,
My hair brushed by the breeze,
My eyes alight with sky,
This is the Scotland that my fathers fought to keep,
For which, I, too, am quite prepared to die.

If I could have one single wish,
It is to lie eventually among the tartan moss
Where first I crawled
Under the shadow of the eagle's wings
Among the herds of autumn deer,
Watching the woods below
The banks of yellow tormentil.

There I would wish to stay
At rest
Above the diamond waters of the sleeping loch,
Nursed by the memories
Of all the people who have taught me how to love this place
As part of me, as part of life,
Far and away beyond
All greed for gold.
For this is home, and these,
These are the people and the land for which I fight,
And here among these hills
For them,
I would not be afraid to die.

Phyllida reappeared having been patched up and stayed with her aunt at Inverpattack. We wandered the hills with the dogs and were treated with great kindness. On the farm hoggs returned from wintering to be dipped and dosed. I learnt never to drag sheep by the wool on their backs which bruised the meat. The three year old wethers were strong and wild, but their meat made money and the heavy fleeces were valuable. Sadly, changing tastes have made them unacceptable, because their ability to utilise the poorest grazings, unsuitable for breeding ewes, made better use of the hills. My watch fell in the dipper to be rediscovered when I drained it two weeks later – still working. It was suggested the makers use it as an advertisement and give me a new one. They thought not. The watch stopped. The ewes were gathered and the gimmers kept in-bye for lambing which started on 22 April. In the woodshed lived a litter of half-wild cats which spat, outside a long line of empty Ribena bottles – my staple drink. In one park was a badger sett. Deer wandered at will. The little daffodils under the pine trees in front of the farm came out. We watched arrowhead after arrowhead of geese flying north across the farm, changing direction above Creag Meagaidh. Each morning after porridge at 5 a.m. we went to the hill to make sure lambs were sucking, had enough milk and were not stranded the wrong side of a burn from their mothers. Twins were walked back to the farm. Our round took us up the Cripes where there was a fox den, across the top of Coire Chrannaig above the birches, until we came to the Coire of the Lost with its steep cliffs, a place where the cattle from the sheilings above Glenshero were supposed to have been lost in the mist and never seen again, stolen by the fairies. There one day I watched an eagle, wings spread across the rock face unable to move while two ravens attacked it. By nine o'clock we descended the Piper's Burn in time for breakfast and to milk Betty, where it was warm sitting on the stool beside her, my head rested on her flank with the rhythmic sound of milk running into the bucket. On 19 May came a dreadful blizzard with a level six inches of snow, as we drove ewes and lambs to shelter. My clothes were tattered, and my boots holed, though I mended my socks. My mother had written to say she must have me for six weeks to clean me up in time for our wedding. Six turned to three. At the end of May it was sad to leave the Ushers, who gave us silver candlesticks. Shortly afterwards he surrendered the tenancy and bought Cullachy above Fort Augustus.

Chapter 5

Did movement threaten from behind scrubbed hedges,
The spring of winter coiled in frosted mould,
Mock at their privilege and seem to trap them
Nearer the thicket of their growing old.

Maurice Lindsay, *Picture of the Caledonian Hunt*

PHYLLIDA AND I drove south on Election Day 1955, by way of Muncaster to meet her grandparents. On the doorstep Smith, the butler, was grinning, having been telephoned by Aunt Joyce to look in the boot of the car, where he found the remains of my lambing clothes, stinking of sheep. It was not an auspicious start to a regime where everybody changed for dinner. Each night Smith put cufflinks and studs in my shirt, laid out my dinner jacket, and put beautifully ironed pyjamas on the bed. Eventually Phyllida was deposited at Brackley. At Rotherwick my mother ensured I was ready for the wedding on 21 June 1955 at Holy Trinity, Brompton. Phyllida looked beautiful, Roger Ellis was best man, and I wore shoes which everybody could see were not a pair when I said my prayers. We were married by Arthur Fuller, a cousin of Phyllida's, formerly Vicar of Sandringham, and spent the first night of our honeymoon in the Savoy Hotel, much too tired to enjoy it.

Next day by air to Geneva seeking the memory of the bells of St. Pierre, and thence to Talloires where we nearly drowned ourselves in a rowing boat in a storm on Lake Annecy, walked a little, drank citron pressé lying on the bed, trying to keep cool in the suffocating heat. A second week was spent at Vevey on Lake Geneva. The Tour de France passed through, oddly dressed men on bicycles, and for the only time in my life I read *The Times* from cover to cover – a poor advertisement for a honeymoon.

Home spelt relief. A new Morris Oxford Traveller with gears on the steering wheel was waiting. For the next eight years XPF632 carted everything – children, pigs, Herdwick tups, Blackface lambs, silage, hay scraped from the roadside where the Council had cut it, mothers and mothers-in-law for whose attitudes the whole operation was designed to shock! The Chase wasn't ready so we lived for six weeks with Phyllida's grandparents eating in the Great Hall at Muncaster with Grandaddy selectively deaf, his ear trumpet beside him. Each night we dressed for dinner, a habit persisting until 1970. At early morning I used to climb through the garden to the Deer Park to count the sheep, sometimes picking mushrooms on the way. The view over the sea to the Isle of Man and the Galloway coast, with its continually shifting blues, still moves me and returning down the footpath in spring, seeing so much to do and so little time to do it, Housman's poem about the cherry tree returns again and again. 'And since to look at things in bloom/Fifty years is little room/About the woodlands I must go/And see the cherry hung with snow.' There was a proper shepherd, Les Greenhow, and together we shifted ewes and lambs down the road, with the reek of sheep strong in those hot August afternoons. Handling facilities were minimal and the flies dreadful. At lambing time the black-backed gulls did terrible execution and were difficult to approach with a gun. Most afternoons we worked among the rhododendrons, Grandaddy lethal in his electric chair, commanding his seventy four year old wife to heave enormous branches he taught us to prune by undercutting with a bushman saw. We pulled up ponticum and brambles, learnt the names of plants, and watched him make hybrids he never expected to flower for twenty five years. One particularly fine late flowering sweet scented auriculatum hybrid he named after his wife, Joan Ramsden, and it is her picture, painted by Laszlo, in a black dress which dominates the drawing room. Her brother lost an arm to a lion in Africa and Granny lost her diamond brooch in a clump of ponticum. Before the War there had been thirty two gardeners, reduced to twelve in 1940, one of whom found the brooch two days later. In 1958 numbers were cut to six. In 1955 they were supervised by MacMillan. He returned to Ardverikie a year later when his place was taken by Andrew Kennedy who came from Logan, and was previously in charge of students at Wisley. There was still a chauffeur, Percy Matterson; a Clerk of Works, MacErlane; a building contractor's business; a joiner, Maclaurin; a plumber, Dan Lewthwaite; a painter; a head forester, Dunne; two Postlethwaite brothers, with Alan Mounsey, later Chairman of Seascale Parish Council on the farm; along with at least twelve tenant farmers, plus Derek Hartley and Sawrey Hodgson, two livestock dealers who rented Walls Meadows. Jimmy Bell was the keeper, married to a champion peppermint maker from Norfolk. Into this maelstrom of his wife's highly unprofitable inheritance fell one ignorant man.

After two years the situation became impossible. The estate belonged to my father-in-law who was rarely there because his wife didn't hit it off with her parents-in-law who were always in residence at rhododendron time when she wanted to come. I, with no official position, believed people should be led, McWilliam that they should be driven. Rumour still has it Jimmy Bell chased him round the Estate Office desk in a rage and one secretary was so cross when she left she burnt a lot of estate papers. The natives drove wedges between us. At evenings I visited the tenants, and took two painful lessons in Cumberland wrestling from the Todds at Hinning House on the way to Jack Matterson at Howbank and the Todds at Low Eskholme, both of whom gave us a calf as a wedding present which they could ill afford. The McWilliams gave us Teal, a beautiful springer spaniel. Old Farren at Brighouse, descended from one of the Spanish sailors shipwrecked at Ravenglass after the Armada, taught me business

Father-in-law, Sir William Pennington-Ramsden, from painting by Halliday.

Some of my friends, Aberarder Farm, 1955.

Aberarder Farm, 1955.

philosophy: 'Be like the Jews – a little profit and a quick turnover,' and when Lord Rothschild was asked how he made his money he replied: 'By selling too early, my boy.' There was little profit as we forked the sheaves onto the cart that harvest time. Pennies still counted and the traditional wisdom in the London clubs was 'Farming always loses money, old boy!' It was regarded as a fact of life.

At the end of that fiery summer of 1955 we went to Aberarder to stalk. Bobby was constantly bombarded with investment advice which seemed to involve him in putting up money and the adviser taking the profit. One day a man appeared with slicked back ginger brown hair, a gin soaked moustache, a wife with bangles round her ankles, and 'crook' clearly written in his eyes, suggesting investing money in Northern Rhodesia when it was about to become Zambia. Thank goodness, for once father-in-law said no and the man was sunk without trace being sent to prison for selling a boatload of left hand boots to the Pakistan army.

Each year in autumn we spent two or three weeks shooting or stalking at Ardverikie or with my stepfather who rented at various times Dunbeath, Balnacoil, and Glenfiddich where the Blackwater Lodge had the most picturesque view from any outside loo in the country, looking across a half door listening to the grouse calling and the roaring stags – and bitten by midges. It was, however, always Ardverikie where my heart lived among people I understood and with whose troubles I could identify. Within the wider family there was a collision of cultures about what a Highland estate should mean – ownership, employment, enterprise, enjoyment, investment, public access – and the conflict within and between individuals remains. Even as Convenor of the Scottish Landowners Federation time and again the American Indian saying came back to me: 'We do not own the land, the land owns us.' Without that basic instinct there seems little point in farming or owning land.

In 1957 shortly before Grandaddy's death he managed to retrieve the money from the sale of his Malayan property and bought Treasury Bonds in the West Indies which matured the following day, enabling him to send tax free cheques to eleven family members to purchase shares in Loch Laggan Estates Ltd. That fund of invested income has enabled the estate to withstand the financial switchbacks of ensuing years when at least one of the enterprises – farming, forestry, deer, holiday houses, and a hydro-electric scheme on which the maintenance of the estate has relied – has come under pressure. His grand-daughter Carola was excluded. Her mother, Katinka Willoughby, having divorced Uncle John in 1946, married an American and Grandaddy not wishing to include someone likely to spend a lot of time in America, paid her out. Carola feels bitter, believing she was disinherited, but her mother was always thought to have spent the money. Eventually Carola married George Miller III who was on Wall Street and had a son, Sebastian. People liked George, but he drank. When seventeen Sebastian was sent to New York where his father was dating an unsuitable floozy. One night, the story goes, when they went out to dinner he telephoned the police complaining his car had been stolen. He gave his father's car number and the police arrested the couple in the restaurant, jailing them for the night – which took care of that. Later Carola married Robert Philippi, born in Patagonia, son of a well-known polo player. He has a good brain which he has wasted.

Winter came with afternoons spent with Jimmy Bell and his Border terrier, Towser, combing the woods and bramble patches for pheasants and an odd woodcock for the pot. In the evening we flighted mallard and teal on the duck ponds at High Eskholme, where there was also a snipe bog – which in 1955 might have described much of West Cumberland. Returning at dark to Phyllida and the fireside was a peaceful time filled with an elementary correspondence course on agriculture whose simplicity would have confounded the latter day sophists of DEFRA. The pheasants were fleet of foot, able to run four miles from the sea to the far end of Muncaster Fell, unless Towser caught up with them when they flew into the high trees. The dog barked until we came and flushed them by clapping our hands. We didn't kill many, but Hugh Falkus did. The ultimate poacher, a fine television presenter and naturalist, an excellent writer of fishing books, he was a rogue. He had been a prisoner-of-war, escaped, but was caught again. When the Germans were about to shoot him they asked if he had anything to say. 'Bugger off!' was the retort, turning his back on his persecutors. At that moment the Allies broke into the camp, which saved him. A drunkard, he never recovered from the death of one of his wives, and now he has gone I am sad not to have known him better. His last wife, Kathleen, daughter of Armstrong of Cragg, the farm where much of the original tick research was conducted in the 1940s, must have been a saint, She, too, sought solace in the bottle. Hugh was the enemy of Jimmy Bell, who was the enemy of all foxes. One winter he snared fifty two, and when we returned to live at Muncaster in 1982 he caught sixteen in the garden between mid-October and Christmas. Jimmy rode a bicycle until he was 103, and died at 106. Life should have been idyllic.

It wasn't. Relations with McWilliam were uncivilised. Sometimes he sent me to sell pigs in Millom market when Stephen, son of Jack Roberts of Muncaster Head, was a great support, but at lambing time there was a crossing of swords. The Northern Dairy Shorthorns, for which he was responsible. took priority as the first blade of grass appeared. In an attempt at reconciliation he asked me to be godfather to his son, who now farms at Ulpha. Jeremy has become a good farmer and a thoughtful man. At Easter we took the pet lambs and the dogs to be blessed in Church, and grazed ewes in the churchyard.

Our eldest daughter, Prunella was born on 20 June 1956 at a nursing home in Queensgate. The gynaecologist was Mr Snyder. Meanwhile McWilliam found an excellent way to divert me. Ian Scott, a distinguished diplomat, married to Drusilla, daughter of Lord Lindsay of Birker, Master of Balliol, had been posted to Beirut. They owned 'a very fertile little farm' on the top of Birker Moor.

Wife, Phyllida Pennington, 1955.

McWilliam could get me the lease at a reasonable rent which would provide a chance to start farming on our own. It was a swift and violent introduction to business. Whincop and Low Ground was a thirty two acre rock in the middle of a bog with every disease in the book. There was an outrun on the common grazing for 66 Herdwick ewes, and a dipper into which they were plunged by lifting them up to shoulder height and sliding them over the edge. I knocked the sump off the oil three times in the first month driving along the far-from-public track which passed through a steading with two gates between which lay in wait a collie that bit, and its owner, Jack Boow, who was equally unfriendly. I imagined it was possible to make a fortune and employ a man! Billy Sanderson was lame and gentle, and his character summed up all the virtues of a West Cumbrian. The first Monday we attended Cockermouth market and bought from Slack of Mealo, a respectable man in knickerbockers, four black stirks as well as a white heifer from a less respectable dealer, Alan Ritson, once a vet in the Indian Army. In the street outside we bought a horse from another crooked man with a cap pulled down over his eyes and a red scarf with white spots knotted around his neck. As he had backed my father-in-law in the National when he was second on the horse with one eye it seemed all right to buy the animal. Within a week the stirks had eaten the tail off the horse which had broken every gate on the place.

There were no hefted sheep, so we bought good Herdwick hoggs from Seatoller and Watendlath. Herdwicks are born black and supposed to have one more rib than any other sheep, which means one more chop but also entitles them to jump better than others. These ones wrecked the dykes, hoovered up ticks, and died of louping ill. The lambs had gid, which meant they turned in circles. The supposed cure was to crack their foreheads with a knuckle or burn a hole in their skull with a red hot penny to extract the worm which caused the trouble. The breed has survived where others didn't. They aborted if the weather was bad, which meant pathetic lambing percentages. The lambs were small and the fleeces light. The National Trust owns more than eighty farms in the Lake District and because Beatrix Potter was head of the Breed Society she insisted a clause be written into leases of the farms she donated, stating Herdwicks must always be kept, which was a liability to tenants but ensured the survival of the breed. Their fleeces pale with age and they have romantic appeal. When lambs are away at wintering on low ground they resemble a swarm of black bumble bees. In character they resemble their breeders and are more attractive than the Swaledales which have increasingly usurped them on the hills.

We purchased three skinny red cows from a displenishing sale at Low Place in Eskdale and four or five Galloways from Alston which has the highest public loos in Britain. Later twelve Highlanders came from Ron Greaves of Blackchub in Dumfriesshire whose wife kept a miniature Shetland pony in the house. The bull was a Galloway, Augustus of Mallabay, bought from Jack Porter, the huntsman, whose daughter Mary Brown remembers us driving cattle past on our way from the Chase to Whincop. In 1957 the lambs made 30/- in Broughton market. We only kept the tenancy of the farm for four years at a rent of £50 p.a. It was the cheapest, most violent introduction to profit and loss anyone could have acquired and for that, if nothing else, Ian McWilliam deserves thanks. In 1957 Windscale caught fire. By dusk the dust was over London, but it was four days before Billy Sanderson was told not to drink the milk from the house cow by a letter delivered by the postman, Alan Bailey, the previous tenant's son, doing his daily round on foot. Twenty nine years later the fall-out from the Chernobyl nuclear disaster hit West Cumbria again. Forty five years later, Trevor, Billy's grandson, with baseball cap, a Russian beard, a pony tail, and a degree in fine arts, is the master strimmer of Muncaster.

The removal of my appendix at Sister Agnes coincided with Prunella's arrival. In the next bed Simon Galway, a friend from school whose sister had an eleven pound baby in a taxi on the way to hospital, spent time trying to fill his pot with pee at one go while at the far end of the ward Colonel Cherry constantly rang the bell for the nurses saying he had subscribed to the place for years and wanted his money's worth. The only time I returned to hospital was for removal of polypoi from my nose at the Moat Brae in Dumfries where the matron was shocked to find me reading André Voisin's *Soil, Grass, and Cancer* which she considered dangerous for her patients' morale. His other book *Grass Productivity* was my bible. Prunella was eventually retrieved together with Nanny Cage, who came from Norfolk to deal with a third generation of Phyllida's family, but she was really too old and was replaced by Nanny Carnie, an excellent lady from Edinburgh. Driving north she refused to spend a penny in the relative peace of a roadside ditch preferring the insanitary surroundings of the ladies' loo on Preston station. She became ill. Her place was taken by Nanny Campbell from Carlisle who remained with the family until they were all grown up. The previous baby she had looked after had been killed in a car accident and in many ways she needed our children more than they needed her. A kind woman, ignorant of the world, she never stopped talking.

We employed a couple from Barcelona. Conrado worked in the garden, Manuela cooked. One day, on return from Ardverikie, he had a pain like a thousand devils in his right eye and she in her tummy. As they spoke no English our sole weapon was a smattering of Spanish picked up from the teaching of Bud Hill at Eton. We attended Dr Erskine who cured Conrado and suggested Manuela was pregnant. She said no. After three visits my Spanish improved and I knew every correct gynaecological question in Spanish and English. Eventually Dr Erskine said she needed to visit the specialist in Whitehaven who found nothing and told me to ask why she said she wasn't having a baby. 'Because I haven't the blessing of the Holy Ghost,' which was too much for the six Indian students. I was embarrassed when the doctor sent us to try the man who did tonsils – which increased my vocabulary somewhat. He found nothing. She

PTGDP with eldest daughter Prunella and Dearg, 1956.

returned to Spain where she was given pills she had always needed and within a week she was back.

Outside we grew garlic and there was a weeping wych-elm with aconites underneath, while on the wall poison-ivy grew which caused my sister-in-law Annabel bad skin problems. The Chase was home. On Sundays we cleaned the silver and swept the house. We went to bed at dark most days, rose at dawn, and sometimes watched the moon above Black Combe. The house was later divided and saw a succession of tenants but is now occupied by Arthur Wilson, a knowledgeable forester and a brilliant wood turner who once looked after my mother-in-law's bears. One tenant in the annexe was round the twist and grew sweet peas up the thistles. There have been a few eccentrics in the parish and the real clue to their character was Annie Preston, church warden, who died aged ninety two. The vicar said he never understood her till he took her to a meeting where she proposed a terrible motion against him. To her horror, realising she was going to win, she rose to her feet in a rage and said: 'I have never ever voted with the majority in my life. Please may I change my vote?' There was, too, the letter I discovered in the files twenty five years later from a tenant at Chapels to Charley Carlisle, McWilliam's successor as agent. 'Dear Lord Carlisle, Many years ago you promised you would mend my coal shed roof. You have failed to do so. In the meantime the walls of my house have become electrified. I have done my best to sort the matter by pinning tinfoil to them, but it does not seem to have worked. If you are not prepared to mend my coal shed roof, will you at least insure my life.' Charley lived at Naworth in a real castle overlooking the Debatable Lands, where he and his wife kept separate bottles of gin behind different books in the Library. He had the MC, and a wooden leg, a sense of humour and a lot of pain. The middle of his long obituary in *The Times* stated apropos of nothing: 'In 1929 he was bitten by a monkey at the London Zoo.'

The first winter after we married Phyllida slipped outside the back door and broke her leg. It was badly set in Whitehaven and now causes her trouble. Although she never complains I feel guilty because it should have been rebroken and reset and it wasn't, which somehow seems my fault. By Christmas 1956 when my parents-in-law held the annual party for the local children it had become obvious we needed to move. It was suggested I go as a pupil to Billy (later Sir William) Fellowes at Sandringham where he had been agent since 1936. His first traumatic job had been to cut costs and lay off staff. His son Robert later became the Queen's Private Secretary at an equally difficult time. Norfolk looked just outside London on a small scale map and it was appalling to find myself sitting for four hours in the train on the way to be inspected. Billy agreed to take me on in the summer for two years at a tuition fee of £200 p.a. Shortly before the 1957 Royal Show at Norwich, we moved to Cole Green Cottage at Sedgeford, six miles from Sandringham, rented from Bernard Campbell through Cruso and Wilkin. Our large bed was coaxed up the narrow staircase, but on leaving two years later it took a whole day to get it down and in the end we had to cut it in half. The kitchen was alive with cockroaches and mice. Nanny Campbell, temperamentally unsuited to be so far from Carlisle, left but returned. Mrs Sewell and Mrs Bush helped in the house cooking and cleaning. In the village people's water came from a pump in the street and it was unsurprising the National Union of Agricultural Workers was so strong in that prosperous countryside. Even at Sandringham the cottages were only beginning to be fitted with bathrooms.

We purchased another car, an old Austin, whose gears needed sympathetic handling, but which got me to work and was well maintained by Bushell, the mechanic at Sandringham. Bill Fox, the other student, lived at York Cottage, and when he left, John and Lavinia Mowbray. Billy Fellowes gave an impression of complete idleness and had a large cartridge bill, but knew everything that happened on the 23,000 acre estate, and was kind to dogs. One day a week he spent with a Head of Department listening to problems and examining work in progress. He had a Victorian attitude to life, severely tested when a letter from Prince Philip landed on the desk suggesting they should try inducing the cows to have twins on lines promoted by Professor Hammond, the famous geneticist. When the family were there around Christmas they were generous and invited us to shoot. As a result we often shot four days a week in winter which cured me from ever wanting to shoot much again. There were also invitations to shoot partridges at Congham where Lionel Cecil came. When young he was supposed to have masqueraded as an important maharajah and had the Home Fleet turned out at Spithead for him to review. Another time, en route for Norfolk, coming across a shooting party at Six Mile Bottom he got out of the car with his gun and his dog, and joined the end of the line, shouting to his neighbour he was sorry he was late. Having taken part in the drive he picked up his birds and continued on his journey. At the end of the season there were horrendous hare drives when over a thousand were shot in a day. Once Catherine Peebles, governess to the Royal children, stood beside me and I hated her seeing it. She was sweet and died too young. It posed the persistent questions of people's livelihoods, the survival of the fittest and the balance of life and death with which anyone on the land has to contend, and which is so little understood in urban Britain. Later I wrote a poem really addressing my brother-in-law and stepfather and once recited it to the AGM of the British Field Sports Society in Scotland. At the end they clapped!

Hen Pheasant in a Hampshire Syndicate

Hazel on hazel,
The tap of the beaters' sticks in the rides;
Rustle of leaves
As the slavering mouths of the dogs
Follow the scent where the pheasants fed
On the acorns under the trees;

And the eight men waiting,
Sitting on hickory sticks,
Or standing with twenty six inches of steel
Tucked under their arms,
Taking their Saturday ease in the field
At the edge of the woods on a Hampshire farm.

Surely just one of them,
Purging his week's pursuits in the city street,
Must have felt a small fractional part
Of the fear in the heart
Of the bird, crouched low in the briars,
Not understanding.

Not understanding
How the hand of the man who had fed it from birth,
Fed it even the morning before,
Could suddenly tip up the world,
Making it fly for life,
High, high into the sun, over the trees,
Out of the arms of shelter and over the guns,
For the pattern of pellets to sever
The flesh from the bone, and fracture the tendons,
And horribly maim.

Is there not one of the eight who can feel
A little of pain himself,
As he watches reproach in the terrified amber eye
In the stalks of the stubble;
Watches the blood matted feathers,
And the bare white tendons,
And the set of the fluttering wings?
Is there not one of the eight
Who can feel
Just the tiniest tremor of fear
As he sits on his hickory stick
With his twenty six inches of steel
Tucked under his arm?

At first Teal came with me, tied to my waist by a long laundry line. One terrible day, standing at a peg next to Prince Philip, there was a drive out of a field of Brussels sprouts, with pheasants flying everywhere. Teal managed to wrap the full length of rope around every stalk. It took an embarrassing ten minutes to untangle myself, but at lunch time John Mowbray managed worse. Around the end of the buildings, while eating lunch, his labrador appeared with one of the farmer's turkeys in its mouth. Dodds, the headkeeper, sadly died when gassing rabbits and is forgiven for asking at the start of a shoot: 'Where's Mr Gordon-Duff's second gun?'

Pillar ran the office with Margaret upstairs. I never understood why she recorded the names of people to whom she sent letters. Now it seems easy to forget if one has replied or only meant to write. Munslow ran the building work and Parsons, the garden. The daughter of a later head gardener asked me to write an article on the Ulverston Belly Dancing Troupe which she instructed. Ever eager to accept a challenge I agreed, but lost my nerve when it became necessary to attend a training session. There were two studs where Aureole and Doutelle stood. Brown, ex-forester from Glamis, ran the forestry, taught me to mark trees, and encouraged me to high prune a young larch plantation in my lunch hour. Occasionally I walked home along dusty tracks lined with chicory and poppies under a wide sky full of the song of larks. Sandwiches were sometimes eaten at Park House where Johnny and Frances Althorp were kind to me, and at other times I visited old Lady Willans, widow of the royal doctor, accounted a dragon, but my friend who only needed company. Her garden had a lovely alley of pleached hazels under planted with aconites.

The man to whom I owed most was Roger Mutimer, the farm manager, who taught me new ways to look at agriculture. I bought an excellent book, *Farming for Profit* by Barber and Dexter, which led to progressive thinking, little imagining I would later sit at Derek Barber's feet as a non-executive Director of Booker Countryside, where our meetings were conducted on the 27th floor of Portland House overlooking the railings of Wellington Barracks where Miss Lucas had lost me. At Wolferton Harry Robins took me under his wing, teaching me to handle cattle without fear. We exercised them along roads on a halter, brushing and shampooing them to prepare for the Christmas Shows. Harry had a wife but preferred to sleep above the cattle, and was sometimes seen by moonlight walking across the marshes with his lantern and his father's pole-axe. Mr Tingle from the Ministry taught me about drains. He had supervised the draining of much of the Fens and would have a fit if he knew of English Nature's black intentions to restore the wetlands he had taken so much trouble to reclaim. There was a contractor, Clarke, skilled with a drag line, who gave me four hundred cigarettes at Christmas. I didn't know they should have been refused and they lasted us ten years, by which time smoking them must have been a strange experience for our guests. Pat Ashton, married to Mavis, a New Zealander, was Vicar of Sandringham. He and John Mowbray had both hunted packs of university beagles. Frances Althorp (Shand Kydd), in the pew behind us, sang like a lintie at church, for which men wore bowler hats. She and John Mowbray are godparents to our second daughter Anthea who arrived on 8 March 1958. At Wolferton I arranged the construction of a long carr-stone road, still known as the Pennington Way.

Each morning, before going to work, I started at 6 a.m. on my corres-pondence course with the College of Estate Management preparing for the Land Agents Society exams. The Married Woman's Property Act and Restriction of Ribbon Development are still lodged in remote recesses of my brain, but law and building were difficult. Exams were sat at Oxford in March. I failed the building paper, but passed Part 2 the following year. By perverse logic a degree in Modern History exempted me from Part 1 which dealt with surveying, and my life has suffered from not knowing!

Chapter 6

Fame is rot; daughters are the thing.

J.M. Barrie, *Dear Brutus*

AT LAST MY TRUSTEES understood agriculture was my preferred destination and in April 1959, with the aid of a £20k Trust Fund and a mortgage of £6,000 @ 5 per cent we purchased for £4,000 from Willie Wilson-Walker, ex-private secretary to Lord Asquith, Kirkland of Tynron, a substantial Georgian house with forty acres. Six miles away in the Dalwhat Glen, above Moniaive, we also bought the hill farm of Benbuie – 1800 acres, now under trees – for £3.10s.0d. an acre, together with a Blackface stock of 940 ewes and 220 hoggs. The Highland cows were moved from Whincop. Willie Doak was head shepherd married to Peggy whose daughter Margaret eventually wed Stewart Watson, the single shepherd. When the farm was sold they moved to Selcoth, between Moffat and St. Mary's Loch. It was a time when sheep in Southern Scotland were still herded twice a day, out of the lower ground at night, transferring the benefit of their dung to the top of the hill, and down in the morning. The process had become second nature to the sheep and a whistle to the dogs did much of the work. Communications were difficult as Benbuie lay up a long narrow gated road and there was no telephone. Sometimes I had to leave a message for Willie written with my stick dipped in dung from his house cow.

At Kirkland we had good neighbours. Jim Gourlay remained friend and adviser until his death. His uncle, a Scottish lawyer, Lord Norman, told him when young: 'Just remember, my boy, it's better to submit to any indignity than to go to litigation.' Jim terrified people, who always expected to be bettered in any deal. He answered the telephone with an unwelcoming 'Yes?' Often he rang saying, 'Come over, Duff, and let's swap lies' – usually about lambing percentages, which can be interpreted in various ways to impress the listener. His family, famous Galloway breeders, had lived at Kirkland before the Wilson-Walkers. Jim drove himself hard. One morning at half past seven I was hoeing turnips in the front field when he stopped and asked me to accompany him to Argyll to look at a farm for the Campbells for whom he managed a lot of land. Phyllida expected me home for breakfast, but we drove sixty miles to Wemyss Bay, caught the ferry to Bute, a taxi northwards, and a small boat to Cala in Cowal. We walked the farm all day, bought it, and returned to Tynron at half past eight having eaten nothing. This he frequently did. Phyllida wasn't pleased and I don't suppose his wife Alison was either.

Kirkland of Tynron (home 1959-82).

The Parish was a community still full of memories of the Tynron Martyrs, two children shot by the dragoons at the top of the glen three centuries before, and the Covenanters with their preaching stones on top of the Keir Hills above the blackcock lek at Low Lann. If we weren't about to die for our faith at least we went to kirk each Sunday. The Minister, Reverend McWilliam – my heart sank at the name – was from Northern Ireland and wore a hat like a priest's. Chaplain to the Argylls in the Great War, he came from Rothesay, and was a snob, whose brothers had all played hockey for Ireland, a fact he never tired of telling. He wrote bird books and once, browsing through Hugh Gladstone's famous bird library at Capenoch, was mortified to see the old man had written inside the cover of his *Birds of the Scaur Rocks* that it wasn't very good. His wife was Alice Mackenzie who, having asked us to dinner at eight o'clock was not unknown to say at ten, 'I think I'll just go and pluck the duck!' They lived mostly on biscuits, went to bed at 2 a.m., and rose at leisure. He called regularly at half past seven, wouldn't have dinner, wouldn't go, and wiped the black leaded heels of his boots up and down the chair covers. His predecessor, Sammy Carmichael, son of a coal merchant from Crieff, dressed like a tramp, and used to bicycle over the hill to Moniaive at lunchtime for a drink. On return one day he discovered a tinker's donkey dead, and wrote to the Sanitary Inspector, an acquaintance. The ensuing correspondence remains in the County Buildings in Dumfries.

'Dear Mr Robb, A public nuisance is being committed. There's a tinker's donkey dead at the foot of the hill at Dalmakerran. Please do something about it.'

'Dear Mr Carmichael. It is the duty of a Minister of religion to bury the dead.'

'Dear Mr Robb. Please do not inform me of my duties. First of all it was my duty to inform the next of kin!'

Tynron Kirk whisky went to the House of Commons in W.E. Gladstone's time when it was stored in our old farmhouse where John Burns lived. In those days a man called Lawrie owned the village store and post office, but since 1892 Willie Wilson had been postmaster. He was the local oracle, thin as a rake, straight out of Robbie Burns, who had tied his horse under the bridge over the Shinnel Water when he was the excise man. Willie said he didn't approve of whisky so closed the operation, but it was widely believed his licence was removed for diluting the Scotch with the Irish. The shop was presided over by his niece, Mrs Pollock, whose son Ronald, aged nine, organised his colleagues to help me pick stones from the field – for a fee. Jean Carson cooked, and later her sister about whom John Burns said he had never needed an indigestion pill until Nancy came to Kirkland. A later helper was Mrs Weekes, thrice widowed. The last husband had been a master saddler at Petworth. She was a vile cook and one wondered whether three deaths were a coincidence. She was potty about cats, and hammered a hole in the back kitchen chimney to let the cat come and go. She bought more meat for Kitty than for the family. We had two other cats in our time at Kirkland – Dawson, black, named after Granny's lady's maid, who got stuck up a tree, and Tattenham, because it went round corners fast. The pillar of our establishment was John Burns who informed my comparative ignorance of so many basic farm jobs. That first year we needed to be careful. There was no money to buy a tractor and we relied on Willie Scott's endless good nature when in need. Eventually we purchased a second-hand grey Ferguson TE 20 for £100 which did all the work for fifteen years after I had discovered I needed to press a small button with my heel to make it start. It had a gruesome collection of seven or eight wires which one day caught fire. They were replaced with one, which made it work far better. Our first harrows were a thorn bush cut from the hedge. Mole hills were a problem for the reaper, although Bob Thorburn, a dedicated trapper, kept moles under control even when almost blind. Talking to him one day by the roadside he said he felt a mole under his feet. Setting a trap, at the end of our conversation he pulled up the mole. Such men taught sensitivity about the countryside and the animals with which we worked.

That first season's grazing at Kirkland was let to Davie Wilson of Marwhirn, a renowned producer of dairy heifers. Early morning and night I checked them for udder clap and learnt the feel of the land and grass under my feet. In the top field was a whaup's nest and each season we heard the first oyster catchers calling in the night. Old McWilliam told us the cross on their breasts was supposed to be the mark of Christ given for covering him with seaweed when his enemies were searching for him. One season there was a corncrake in the bottom field. Post came at seven and was answered by breakfast. Turnips were sown with an old machine guided along the drills by John Burns behind Bert Dykes's tractor, two fields of oats being cut by the same contractor's binder. Machinery was difficult, gates were narrow, and backing trailers or buckraking silage into the barn severely tested my limited mechanical ability. Most of the farm was steep. At haytime we worked with neighbours, rucking hay on tripods, later carting it on a ruck lifter to the steading where it had to be forked into the barn. Being afflicted with hay fever and asthma I had chosen an odd profession! At first we used little fertiliser. Lime and basic slag corrected deficiencies after checks by the West of Scotland Agricultural College (WSAC) at Auchincruive, whose Dumfries office was run by Alastair Campbell from Tiree, and later by John Thorburn. The free service was only beginning to be widely appreciated. Later, following the work of Peter Maclaren, ICI Manager at the Leaths at Castle Douglas, and prompted by Idris Hunt at Auchincruive, we became interested in applying increasing doses of artificial nitrogen, but looking back the dung from grazing animals and nitrogen from white clover was a far more harmonious regime. Often I walked the four hirsels at Benbuie, and was always there for the handlings when the neighbours assisted – Jack Edgar, Ken McCall's shepherd from Cairnhead, Harry Spears and his son Bill from Dalwhat, and the Bleazards from Glenjaan. Hoggs returned from wintering at Sessionfield and Lochfergus in Ayrshire on 1 April. Forty years on in Harrods I sometimes meet Mr Hutton in charge of the meat department, a cousin of Lochfergus. The hoggs were vaccinated for louping ill on return and clipped at the end of May when lambs were tailed and castrated.

At the start of July the ewes were clipped by hand, a job at which I was slow, so rolled the fleeces, and tramped wool bags hung from a gallows. Frequently we were stopped by rain. The clip was marketed in 1959 through MacTaggarts at Hawick and later through Woolgrowers in Dumfries where for years Mr Yule and Jack Bryden supplied most of our needs – medicine, dip, and marking fluid made from Bradford sewage. We always went to see the wool graded. On Saturdays in August Thomson, Roddick, and Lawrie started their store sheep sales at Thornhill and in 1959 the market was disastrous. The English had a drought. The usual farmers and dealers from the north of England were reluctant buyers, and to rub salt in the wounds were always waiting in the alley for a luck penny – a tax free tip for bidding for the sheep. Some said they had bought lots when they hadn't and before long I learnt to leave my thank you with the auctioneers.

That first year Benbuie top lambs made 50/- and the cast ewes, sold to Lyle of Palace How at Cockermouth, the same. From then until 1964 the sheep market was disastrous. Having little in-bye land we were weak sellers and only later discovered that by taking grazing from John Marshall at Hardgrove or Ross

Freeman at Clarencefield, could we better our situation. Ross, an ardent Scottish Nationalist from Liverpool, and his family became close friends, and not only was he one of the top dairy farmers, but he was straight as a die. He had a fancy sharpening machine for razor blades and hadn't used a new one for twenty years. When we left Kirkland twenty three years later we gave Pushkin to his daughter Heather, married to Bruce Smith of Threapmuir, Cleish, thinking she would not appreciate Muncaster. Pushkin was a Suffolk Cross ewe with a scar on her nose, originally a pet lamb who annually produced two lambs or three from the time she was one until she was fourteen. Unlike most pets she wasn't pushy but led a gang of five which used to levy tribute from the village. Returning home one afternoon we found her leading them into the Post Office for food. If it rained, no matter how secure the fences, she was always found sheltering her lambs in the garage and we never knew how she did it. Heather made a trailer to cart her behind the motor bike to inspect the other sheep, and I think she lived in the house, dying at the age of eighteen.

In 1964, thanks to assistance from my father-in-law who put up half the money on which we paid rent, we bought Carnsalloch from Johnny Macphail, a noted dealer and finisher of cattle. It was a 200 acre farm beside the River Nith at Kirmahoe and for fifteen years we fattened 200 cattle a year, very often topping the weekly market in Dumfries and finishing most of our lambs and old ewes. Johnny taught me, when selling cattle at home, to stand them on a hill against the setting sun when they appeared twice the size; to clip their heads and tails before taking them to market; and always to give the buyer luck money as it more than paid for an extra bidder. As a result of his advice I still like to sit with my back to the sun when chairing meetings. At first we bought motley collections of cattle from the Huntingdon Road market where the buyers' step was lower than the ring which made judging weights of store cattle difficult, but eventually we bred most ourselves, using Beevbilde bulls, hybrids of Polled Lincoln Red, Red Angus, and Polled Beef Shorthorn, bred by Eric Pentecost of Cropwell Butler, crossed with our black Irish cows. Eamon MacGill from Pointzpass 229 near Newry, sent us ten bulling heifers each year from the west of Ireland.

For five years we did everything right at Benbuie. Six Irishmen with scythes cut 100 acres of bracken twice a year for three years for which we received a grant, and latterly John Burns' son took over the job with an Allenscythe. Jimmy went away to war in 1942 in a horrible snowstorm and was left, a Royal Marine, dabbling his toes on an island in the Indian Ocean whence he returned disillusioned. It was hard to know what he was thinking, but he still looks after the grounds at Kirkland. Hoggs went to sound winterings. We bought sensible tups at Newton Stewart where the short coated Blackfaces were milkier and more prolific than the Lanark sheep, and suited our land. I had delusions about breeding tups but was saved by Walter Ross-Taylor of Wandel, a successful breeder who told me never to pay more for a ram than we expected to get for his son. I went to the Belfast show with him and David Ker of Craigdarroch who lent us Blackface tup lambs and a Kerry Hill for crossing with 40 cast ewes at Kirkland. The Kerry cross was successful, with lambs sold to Sainsburys whose buyer was extremely fussy. We put on 200 chains of hill drains each year by hand and did a lot of fencing, but the only thing which went up was the overdraft.

Life depends on luck and timing. For five years the sheep market was disastrous. Only the overdraft increased. Mr McCalman, manager at the Bank of Scotland in Dumfries, which still holds my account, didn't protest but died of indigestion. His successor, John Walker, who commanded a landing craft on the beaches at Salerno where the Germans had advance warning, appeared equally unconcerned, but I was worried when out of the bushes emerged a lawyer, Gerald Sadler, wondering if we knew of a hill farm for sale. His brother-in-law's brother, Christian Henty, needed one in a hurry. We asked £20 an acre for Benbuie, which produced enough money to repay the overdraft, pay off the mortgage and then to buy another farm, the Snade, 180 acres of hard land near Dunscore which was known as the 'parish of durrt and stanes'. From then until now we have been lucky never to have needed to borrow money. For several years everybody laughed at this lack of business acumen, but when the oil crisis came in 1972 and people were paying up to 22 per cent on their overdrafts instead of the 5 per cent to which they were accustomed, our quixotic approach seemed justified. My children have been brought up with Uncle Edward's dictums 'Lend your money, lose your friend' and 'Neither a borrower nor a lender be'. We may appear wrong to Gerry Robinson who is making a 'Trouble Shooter' programme about the business at Muncaster, who asserts it is easier to make money than give it away, but although we shall never be very wealthy we are free to express views without fear of reprisal which has often been beneficial for the people we have tried to represent. In the late 1990s the Natwest tellers at Seascale were told not to talk to customers as it wasted the Bank's time, which caused me to write to Lord Alexander, the Bank's chairman, pointing out that Muncaster only used their facilities because of the human contact with real people – after which those behind the counter were permitted to return to being our friends!

We bought, in the autumn of 1959, for £300 twenty four six-month-old suckled calves straight off their mothers at the Kingussie sale taking them by train for £1 a head to Thornhill station and thence by Alec Wood's lorry the six miles to Kirkland. Only five years later, when the Beeching axe was falling, the service remained but a man wishing to move twenty Border Leicester ewes from Perth to Windsor had to pay the equivalent of a 1st Class ticket and a sleeper for each sheep. Nobody told us not to put the cattle in a field straight off their mothers and by morning they had vanished. We eventually recovered them, but thereafter always shut cattle in the court until the roar was off them. For winter they were tied by the neck in the byre and became part of the family, even handing on their ringworm which, advised by John Burns, we tried to cure with veterinary iodine, before discovering a mixture of tractor oil and sulphur was much better. In 1962/3 the ground froze solid to a depth of a metre from the end of November until March. All pipes were frozen and it was only then, having to carry water from the burn in buckets, that I discovered how much cattle can drink. When it snowed we sledged with the children on a tea tray down the hill above the house. Feeding hours were regular and one year we fed them seven times a day, sometimes giving the last feed in a dinner jacket after dining out. At half past six each morning I chopped turnips (swedes) carrying them in a swill to the feeding troughs. They had hay and bruised oats, and those early hours with the warm smell of cattle in the byre were moments of special wonder. We mucked out with broom and shovel and wheeled the dung in a barrow up a sleeper onto the midden. After tea we brushed them and combed them before listening to the farming programme on the wireless which sometimes misled us. Colin Preston was pioneering barley beef and my clumsy efforts at imitation almost killed eight beautiful blue grey bullocks – from which I learnt that changes, whether in feeding regimes or political philosophy, were only likely to succeed if introduced gradually! It may not have been the most efficient enterprise, but there was a correctness about it and an essential harmony between man and beast since lost with the high speed of modern agriculture. Even then men had started to patrol farms with stop-watches doing time and motion studies. From that time Government invented the efficiency factor with grant systems calculated by what was needed minus a few percent which resulted fatally in ever fewer people having to work harder and harder to stand still.

Things had started to go wrong with the Repeal of the Corn Laws in 1846 when, as well as poking a finger in the eyes of landowners, Parliament decided food must be as cheap as possible for Britain to maintain its advantage through the Industrial Revolution with low wages and cheap imported raw materials from its empire, to produce manufactured goods with which no other country could compete. Since then consumers have rarely paid the cost of production for food and all Governments clung to centralised control of agriculture, giving just enough in grant and subsidy to prevent the industry's total collapse, using as their motto 'Live horse and you'll get corn.' For livestock, deficiency payment systems adjusted by seasonal scales gave a base price, negotiated annually by the NFU, which provided rough balance, but eventually the Treasury balked at the cost. There followed the Common Agricultural Policy and the Treaty of Rome, one of whose laudable aims was providing incomes to those on the land equivalent to urban workers. Unfortunately initial structures which set the wheat price high enough to pay for small over-capitalised German farms were flawed. In 1976 the Sheepmeat Regime was negotiated with headage payments, whereby many hill farmers have received up to three quarters of their pathetic income, forcing them to overstock to ensure financial survival. For a decade and more those who think have realised the situation is unsustainable. Even more desert the land – and worse still their families – until now there are insufficient experienced people to maintain the environment for whose destruction they are unfairly blamed. At meetings I have to remind environmental organisations, whose attitude is both patronising and damnably pious, that nearly all farmers and landowners are at heart conservationists. I tell the story of Evelyn Waugh's conversion to Catholicism in 1943 related to me by his godson, John Hollis, at Oxford. Three years later, with all the fervour of a new convert, he visited Rome for an interview with the Pope to whom he gave a long lecture on Roman Catholicism until poor Pius XII could bear it no longer and said with a sweet smile; 'Excuse me, Mr Waugh, but please remember I, too, am a Roman Catholic.'

Government organisations such as Scottish Natural Heritage, with strongly centralised administration, say they could do nothing about reforming those policies as Government's hands are tied by European Directives and Regulations to which they have subscribed on the advice of the self same organisations who are blaming those on the land for wrecking the countryside. The system has locked farmers in offices filling in forms whose accuracy is vital. One small slip can disqualify them from schemes designed for their support. Such time should have been spent on the land and among their livestock. As a result vital links between man, the animals, and the soil are broken. Centralisation it appears is for the convenience of Government and its servants. Many years ago Emrys Jones, an excellent public servant, ran MAFF for the benefit of farmers and agriculture, and not for politicians, nor as an enclave of their centralised authority.

Willie Doak found me a dog. Bess was two and had been beaten and he doubted she would work. She sat in the car, seemed pleased with attention, and when we reached home jumped into the office chair choosing a book off the shelf, *Competitive Farming* by Mac Cooper, which she tore to shreds. After that we understood each other perfectly and were inseparable companions for twelve years, even if sometimes she suffered selective deafness. Willie also supplied his uncle Bert to help at Carnsalloch. He told me Doak was an Ayrshire name meaning 'The hole you make in a feather bed if you don't dunch it out quick the Devil gets in!' Bert was a delightful conscientious man, ten years older than me, with a wife Sheila, twenty years his junior, who played football for the Dumfries Post Office. The worst he ever said, when dosing newly speaned calves in the stable as they kicked him, was 'dash it,' until he met our children and graduated to something more expressive. He was gentle with dogs, with people and his two daughters, one of whom dresses poodles. A good fisherman, a brilliant stick maker, he never raised his voice, as well as being an excellent stockman. When Carnsalloch was sold in the late 1970s we gave him his house which is greatly improved and he remains a family friend. James Taylor at the Snade was different. His brothers were successful farmers, hard as the stones of their native Gatehouse. A conscientious stockman, who had farmed at Waterbeck, he was bad at business and had gone bust. His wife, Grace Sloan, was quiet and greatly respected but suffered from diabetes, and although almost completely blind, never complained. She eventually died in the middle of lambing which was a tiresome sense of timing. James was not a romantic, but one spring night at Killyleoch we watched the Aurora which bowled him over so much he had to go into the house to wake his daughter, Mary Grace. That year, among the jackdaws in the field was a pure white one. James' predecessor at the Snade was Willie Marshall, married to Agnes, whose family farmed at Breconside, Kirkgunzeon. There had been some dispute and he had to leave. He was a hardy man, who never stuck. His hands were permanently filthy, but sheep he lambed never ailed, while those of us who washed invariably had trouble. Willie soon went to a farm of his own near Dalry and died suddenly, which was a waste of a brilliant stockman. He is buried under the sycamore in the kirkyard at Carsphairn.

In 1959 Andrew Feilden, Phyllida's cousin, came for a month, before going into the Army. He spent his days carting turnips and on leaving asked if he could have one. He gave it to his mother to take to Garrards, the silversmiths in Regent Street, who must have had a shock. Eventually we were asked to fetch the replica – a small silver turnip engraved with 'In Memory of All Turnips 1959'. Joyce Grenfell barged the queue when I collected it but was so lovely and apologetic it was impossible to complain. There was a sheriff in Ayr, hard on motorists, and Andrew in his mini insisted on navigating the roundabouts anti-clockwise. Years after he gave me lunch in his club when Richard Crichton, his CO in the Coldstream, said he had last seen him chased by an elephant down the high street of Zanzibar. Andrew later – so much later we had almost given up in desperation – married Rowena Brassey, lady-in-waiting to Princess Anne and can be a little excitable.

The Snade was a run down farm with an old castle surrounded by yew trees – an atmospheric place. There were two good neighbours: Billy Irvine of Borland, a farm I coveted, and Joe Johnstone of Garrieston, a well kent doggy man. The third at Gilmerston was a desperately casual farmer, Tommy Thomson, tenant of Dalgonar, who never mended his dykes and allowed his sheep to wander. Jim Gourlay told me how to sort him out by impounding them at milking time without food or water until he collected them – usually quite soon! The previous tenant had been a builder who kept pigs and erected jerry built red brick walls which collapsed if you pushed them. These we demolished and put up a large shed for a hundred cows. The stoney land dried quickly after rain so didn't poach badly. One autumn when at Ardverikie for the hinds a telephone call came saying James had been haying the cattle in a way we were all guilty of doing, putting the tractor in first gear and pulling the cut bales out behind the trailer. He had left Mary Grace, then ten, in the cab and as he was remounting his overalls caught in the tractor wheels pulling him underneath onto a large slab of rock before running over his shoulders and chest. He was off all winter and should have been dead.

At the same time my brother-in-law Gerald Carter became fed up commuting from Hazeley Bottom to London as military assistant to the deputy Chief of the Defence Staff. He swept out of the Army with no redundancy and went to work for Uncle Edward at Metlex, the job from which Aunt Katharine had saved me. It was not a meeting of minds as anyone could have predicted and in the middle of one night the doorbell rang. There was Gerald saying he wanted to be a farmer. His arrival was opportune and for six months he lived with us, working hard, helping me cut the silage at the pit at the Snade, and a great deal else besides. He shot the cockerel in its comb with an airgun which made it shake its head and he ate more salt with his meals than anybody ate before. In spring he wanted to start farming on his own. We told him not to buy a house without a farm, but one afternoon he did, returning for tea saying he had agreed to purchase Townhead of Glencairn, a nice property on the other side of the hill, owned by the Gillespies. Elspeth arrived with Nicholas and Rosebie, the same age as our two younger children, but he had no farm and eventually we agreed to let him the Snade and sell him our hundred beautiful Irish cows, many of them so quiet you could hand milk them in the field – together with the liability of James who had never said 'Good morning' let alone 'Sir' to anybody in his life. Gerald had never met a rifleman like that without jailing him. After some months it was sad. Gerald said he wasn't prepared to cart silage for the rest of his life and give his family our standard of living. He was never born to be a farmer. He left his family at Townhead while he raised money for a hospital in Aberdeen, before buying a house at Ascot and becoming a successful insurance broker in London, later moving to Nether Wallop. I bought back the cows plus James Taylor, but it was a difficult time for my sister. Their son Nicholas has become a highly successful army officer, married to Louise, and daughter Rosebie, married to Matthew Morton, who farms at Bramdean, is a well known grower of roses.

At Kirkland we won third prize at the FMC Christmas carcase competition and met John Auld from Auchinleck, their buyer, who became trusted adviser on all matters to do with finished cattle. We bought a cattle crush with a weighing machine which limited Bert's 'dash its'. The regime at Carnsalloch was regular for two or three years. Monday drew cattle, Tuesday clipped ten for sale, Wednesday took them to market on the Whitesands where Joe Benson sold them. Thursday we looked at the *Dumfries and Galloway Standard* to see what fine fellows we were. It was a time wasting regime, and we changed to selling them, without the time consuming beauty treatment, to FMC, kissing them goodbye at the stable door, usually seeing them graded at the abattoir. The vanity wasn't so flattered, but it made time for other things. Sometimes Kenneth Kelly of Barncleugh, who, with his wife Barbara have been friends for over thirty years, came to shoot ducks by the Nith at dawn. Once we had a particularly good pheasant shoot at the Snade where I had planted twelve acres of trees by myself. Seeing them after thirty five years and the shelter they provide I am quite proud, but the Whartons, to whom we sold the Snade in 1970, would benefit by thinning them!

Chapter 7

She was so good, he was so bad,
A very pretty time they had.

James Thomson (1834-82), *Virtues and Vices*

ONE DAY Bobby suggested a friend who had got themselves into a muddle with a farm in the Stewartry should seek my help. It was the first of three hair-raising rescue jobs which at that time I undertook without payment. This woman had a small farm near Brackley and had gone to Castle Douglas to buy Ayrshire heifers. As she sat by the ring, immaculately dressed in a sheepskin jacket between two wicked Galloway farmers, they turned to her – she was attractive and stole her daughter's boyfriends – 'Oh,' said they, 'You could teach us how to farm'! After lunch they took her to Slogarie, a lump of rock in a bog, surrounded by trees with a fairly sound hill. She was the daughter of a well-known pedigree cattle breeder in Strathdon who had died in the lift at the Perth bull sales and had a brother, Dandy Wallace, who could take five grouse out of a covey in front of him with one gun. She had married one man she divorced, another who died with a tumour on the brain, and was currently living with a London stockbroker who had asthma to which he ultimately succumbed. She bought the farm and went back to persuade the husband-who-wasn't that he was going to be quicker getting to his office in London from Kirkcudbright than from Banbury. She ploughed up the stone drains, sold the hill to the Forestry Commission, and was left with 100 cows, two employees who hated each other, and three tractors, in case one by one they stuck in the bog. The ground was so wet the cattle had to be dosed once a month for fluke.

On my first day I had to tell the two men one would have to go. They couldn't stick each other. In the end it was the gardener, Colombo, who went to Blairgowrie. Mossop was a Cumbrian, not smart, but a worker, and Mrs Mossop was kind. It was an awful assignment and several times I sat at Slogarie until 2 a.m. trying to persuade Him to go to the bank with Her on Monday morning. It was twenty three miles home across twisty hill roads with black Galloway cows lying in the middle. Eventually I would stagger to bed at 3 a.m. to be woken by Her at seven in floods of tears telling me He wouldn't go to the bank with Her as agreed. Eventually the situation was stabilised, but He died. Appeared on the scene an MP who had been Naval Attaché in Moscow, had an affair with a Russian ballerina, was ten years younger than Her, and was after her money. They became engaged. At this time Malcolm McCall came as our student. One day as we were taking soil samples the fiancé appeared with a loaded .38 revolver looking for Russian spies behind the bushes. He was sure they were after him.

Months later I met Her again in floods of tears outside the market saying she had given him his marching orders because he said he wanted the names of her lawyer and accountant to ensure he could live there if she dropped dead in the bog. Sighs of relief. She then took up with a nice man who bred dogs in Jersey and had a farm in South Africa. By now she owned a farm in Portugal. She married him. Once a racing driver, he was tied together with string, became tipsy with a drink, and was nice – but died. By this time I had withdrawn and she insisted on giving me eight New Forest ponies which I didn't want, saying, 'So nice for the children, dear boy.' They looked beautiful galloping across the hill in the moonlight, but picked up young lambs in their mouths and shook them besides wrecking the beautiful pasture we had just perfected for the ewes and twins. Canterbury Bell's ancestor, the Hermit, had won the Derby in 1879, the only year it was run in a snowstorm. He had bad nose bleeds, and was a rank outsider, but it was so cold his nose didn't bleed. We sold them one by one to the calf subsidy man, Crawford, whose daughter was a show jumper, and luckily the last one went before he retired. I think She had one more beau aged forty something but lost her leg and died.

Slogarie was responsible for my first contact with Ian Lang, and afterwards Peter Hutchison. They were partners in the firm of Hutchison and Craft in Glasgow, who handled our insurance business for many years. Ian was later an MP before becoming a Scottish Office Minister, President of the Board of Trade, Secretary of State for Scotland, a member of the Cabinet and ultimately a Life Peer. His quiet approach was never given sufficient credit and it was through his recommendation I became Chairman of the Red Deer Commission in 1993, a job giving six of the happiest and most effective years of my life. He was also helpful with the Ardverikie hydro electric scheme. In 1988 after a feasibility study by Harvey Gudge and extensive work by Geordie Chalmer, Loch Laggan Estates spent almost £1m, a major part of its investments, on a 1Mw hydro-electric scheme to underpin the jobs of eight foresters, who with their families were a large part of the local community. The awful Nigel Lawson's budget had taken forestry out of taxation, a fatal blow to Ardverikie. Much of the mature timber had been sold, most of the planting completed, and we were no longer able to put forestry wages against taxation. We were denied any grant support for the hydro scheme and in the end, one of the worst days of my life, we had to make six foresters redundant.

The hydro scheme was constructed on a predicted electricity price of 2.5p per unit. In the event it was squeezed disastrously to 1.8p. Without grant support it wasn't viable. In the street in Perth I met Michael Joughin, ex-President of SNFU, chairman of Scottish Hydro-Electric, a robust man with origins in Cornwall. 'They tell me, old boy, you think you need more for your electricity. You'll probably get it in fifteen years, but we're such big producers we don't need you.' They and Scottish Power had the private producers over a barrel, their case reinforced by the restricted capacity of the interconnector to England, assisted by the supreme indifference of Edinburgh civil servants. Eventually I banged on the Scottish Office door at Dover House, where Lady Caroline Lamb had chased her lovers round the marble pillars, and demanded to see the Minister. 'Do you have an appointment, Sir?' 'No, but please remind him he was my insurance man before he became an MP, and my MP before he became a Minister, and I'm sure he'll see me.' I told him, as he represented the Scottish Conservative and Unionist Party, it was a funny sort of union when the English were getting 6p and we were being paid 1.86p. He was supportive and our price rose to 5.4p geared to inflation for ten years, but the story of my exchange with the doorman reached Edinburgh before me!

The next rescue job – unpaid – was at Glencrosh. Peggie MacMillan-Fox had been a good farmer but her attention to business had become increasingly eccentric. She called at Kirkland when we first arrived with her daughter Jane, later married to Antony Heald who had been my fag at school. They left old fashioned calling cards and recommended a dentist in Edinburgh, Doctor Finlayson of 21 Manor Place. He had large hands and was bitten by our youngest daughter, Rowena, whose next dentist said he had never had to shoot at a moving target before. Prunella, meantime, transferred her custom to Mr Thomson who made false teeth for sheep. Aunt Fox farmed Corlae at the top of the Water of Ken, next to her brother, Jock MacMillan, but had just sold it to reduce the overdraft. I felt sorry for the grieve, John Irving, who had a difficult time. His father had been grieve for the Evans family in Wigtownshire. John related how the boss hitched up his horse and trap, dressed in old clothes to deceive the workers and drove off to the station en route for Glasgow where he was head of a big insurance company leaving John and his son Fraser, later president of the Scottish NFU, hoeing turnips. As soon as the old man's back was turned Fraser lay in the drill and slept in the sun. He's still a lovely man and a good hearted rascal.

My baptism of fire was hunting for a £10,000 cheque for the hill cow subsidy, eventually found under the bed. I kept simple accounts and made her put all paperwork in a drawer which was sorted once a week. Her business was conducted in Glasgow and we eventually tidied up her finances. I asked the stockbroker what to do with certificates for Chinese Government Gold Reorganisation Loan (1913) found in a bottom drawer to be told most people used them for lampshades. It was, however, the eccentricity of the challenge which appealed. Aunt Fox was acquisitive and when relations died, although only the middle of five children, she fought off all comers for the remains. Cousin Octavia Rowe of 8 Royal Crescent, Bath of blessed memory, snuffed it, leaving her fabulous collection of furniture. Aunt Fox visited an antique dealer in Bath who enquired if she would be selling. 'No,' said she, 'but I'll take this and give you first refusal,' walking out of the shop with a Japanese ivory, Rats in

Confusion, worth £1500. Each time I saw it I shook. At the end those she had diddled all her life, not least her sisters, tried to get their own back. She would say 'Do have it' when they admired something I knew I had made her transfer to her daughter years before. She gave Mrs Irving a tea service which Jessie very honestly returned. I remained her trustee until the Trust wound up and am still an unpaid Director of the family farming company. Her grandson James is my godson. When not looking after his other grandmother, Lady Heald, at Chilworth, he is supposed to be writing a thesis on the Theory of Chaos. Daphne Heald, aged over 90, asked by a young guest at a dinner party if being old was very boring replied in her rich voice, 'I find a filthy mind a perpetual consolation!'

Life was sociable. North and west of Auldgirth Bridge were the hill tribes. South and East lived Jardines, Jardine-Patersons, Cunningham-Jardines. Buchanan-Jardines, Landales and Keswicks, many of who had made their money in the east and none of whom were exactly poor. Then there were the Buccleuchs whose estates stretched from Drumlanrig to Dalkeith via Langholm and Bowhill, with a long tradition of good management. Duke Walter, married to Midnight Moll, was an example of everything we would all have liked to be if our ancestors hadn't had holes in their pockets. His knowledge and courtesy were something to which we all aspired. He had an excellent Secretary, Lorna MacEachern, and capable factors – Peter Fox at Drumlanrig, Jamie Galbraith at Bowhill, and Jock Milne-Home at Langholm. Peter's son, aged 17, appeared one day to shoot and was appalled to be asked by Prunella if his name was really Fox because her father shot foxes. Jock's wife Rosemary, an Elwes from Congham, known as the Border Bitch, infuriated me by saying, 'Of course the Duke wouldn't lend anything for a Unionist Antique Exhibition.' I had just become chairman and telephoned the next day to be told that if we called he and the Duchess would be delighted to see us. It was Phyllida's birthday, 11 February. On the doorstep – it must have been brilliant staff work – he said 'Many happy returns of the day, my dear. I have sent down for a bottle of champagne.' And he lent four or five priceless items. The next encounter with the Duchess was sitting alongside her at lunch when her earring, the biggest pearl ever seen, shot into my soup. I met it again at the Caledonian Hotel in Edinburgh. Her face was hidden behind a pillar, but the pearl was unmistakeable. Despite being in a wheelchair because of a hunting accident in 1971 their son Johnny has inherited all his father's wisdom, commonsense, and integrity.

Iona was born on 9 April 1961 and our youngest daughter Rowena on 1 October 1963. We worked hard, but had time to play. On winter evenings we attended the reel club at Maxwelton, Annie Laurie's married home where Lauries still lived – Sir John Laurie a Seaforth general and son, Bay, who had been at school with me. Tom Dickson, ex-Argyll with huge hands, famous for stopping a runaway Clydesdale in Princes Street, arranged it. Hugh Stenhouse bought Maxwelton when the Lauries' finances became distressed. Having

Daughters, 1964. Iona b.1961, Rowena b.1963, Prunella b.1956 and Anthea b.1958.

restored the house and improved the farms he told someone the house was finished but the lift wasn't big enough for his coffin. Within a week he was killed in a car crash near Leicester returning from London after negotiating a rescue package for Upper Clyde Shipbuilders. His widow, Rosamund, daughter of Haig of Bemerside, was kind to me, but always taut. People were kind and asked me to shoot. Willie Forbes, almost blind, invited me to Earlston where I was embarrassed by shooting a blackcock straight in front of Robin Muir; David Ker, as well as lending us tups, asked us to dinner to give away bantams, which took to the rafters in the Craigdarroch tup shed at 1.00am, when it was time to leave; Tommy Kennedy at Blackwood was kind, but squandered money modernising his steadings and immediately ripping out the improvements. He had a deer park with a stag called Willy of which he was immensely proud. One day he summoned me as chairman of the Dumfriesshire Conservatives. He produced a cheque for £500 on condition twelve other rich members were asked to donate the same so that the Association would never have to work raising money again. He was scandalised when I tore it up, saying it was not what the Conservative Party should be about and that it should be a party for all the people.

David Ker's bantams never went to bed and roosted in trees. We bought thirty pullets from Robin Thompson of Lannhall, which lived in a hen house. We shut them up at night, but gave up when, having opened the pop hole one morning, we returned after breakfast to find the fox had killed the lot. As often

as not they laid in the top of the bales in the hayshed where I once found
Phyllida marooned by two black pigs which considered the bucket was for
them. We also kept difficult pheasants. One silver hen taught a clutch of
bantams she reared to whistle like her, but the cock was vicious and chased
Nanny and the postman round and round the car in the garage. Eventually he
went to Muncaster and was last seen jumping up and down on the gravestones
attacking the congregation on their way to church. After that he disappeared. I
liked the hens and talked to them, but the pigs were not a success. They were
meant to do reclamation work, but departed when Ajax the boar was tossed over
the dyke by a Highland cow, hitting the ground prepared for revenge. Otherwise
those pastoral days now seem a land of lost content where children learnt the
facts of life among animals of which they were unafraid, and with whom they
formed genuine bonds.

For the next rescue job, Joe Benson, the auctioneer, telephoned, asking me to
help Jim and Mary Johnstone of Amisfield Tower. They employed two men and
she fiddled around with farming. His family had once owned a grain business in
Angus and she had been a well known rider of hacks at the horse shows in the
1930s. The remedy was simple and the land was seasonally let by auction for
grass parks each spring. Jim was ill at the end, a shadow of his portrait in the
dining room by James Gunn. They dropped his coffin lowering it into the grave
at Tinwald kirk and I'm sure I heard him saying 'Dammit, Mary!' – which he
often did – as it hit the bottom. She eventually gave me a silver teapot and
insisted my portrait was painted by Paul Gunn, James' son. Having it painted in
his London studio was fun sitting under the eye of his father's famous portrait
of Hilaire Belloc and occasionally being given a brush to paint a few strokes.
Mary and I parted on bad terms when she told me a gentleman should always
take the word of the employer against her men. She was wrong!

There followed a long and happy association with the Crawford family of
Dalgonar. The monks had drained the bogs by the Cairn and at the time of the
Covenanters Grierson of Lagg was based there, in charge of the dragoons. He
took his captives to the top of the Lagg Hill, put them in a barrel with spikes,
and rolled them to the bottom – an unpleasant man. Colonel Crawford came
from a military family and had been an officer in the Middlesex Regiment. His
forebears were born in faraway places and served the Empire around the world.
His mother had dropped him in a hurry on an island in Cork Harbour so when
he forgot to renew his passport he was most upset to be told he wasn't British.
Martha maintained the standards of 1900 and was an incredibly generous
hostess. Employed on the farms were Jimmy Ross, a gentle unambitious
stockman, and Billy Dempster, fiery, married to a woman who was a brilliant
foster mother. There was a pedigree Aberdeen Angus herd which fully justified
Billy Fellowes' comments when I left Sandringham, particularly when one of
them failed the TB test and we were unable to sell anything for months on end.
Each time the test was clear, the follow up proved positive. The farm was

paralysed for a year and badger fanciers should realise the havoc a total ban on control is currently causing the dairy industry in south west England. Neither side may be absolutely correct and it is an example of the need for compromise, because single interest groups are wrecking the balanced management of the countryside. When Simon and Elspeth Fraser came to stay they watched a family of eight playing outside the window – a delightful sight – but a woman in Somerset fell down a fourteen foot hole badgers had dug under her garden, breaking her neck. They dig the lawn at Muncaster and are even messier than archaeologists currently looking for Romans.

The Crawfords were wonderful hosts and frequently held parties for duplicate bridge. Phyllida sat out, never having recovered from being asked by Uncle Edward if she played. 'Yes,' she had said, but followed it up with: 'I can't remember if aces are high or low.' A few who fancied themselves made unpleasant partners, conducting endless post-mortems, but a husband and wife who played for Scotland were delightful. One night driving home they were flagged down by two men. While one talked they suddenly realised the other was opening the back. They drove off and on reaching home found a finger in the boot.

The Crawfords kept Dandy Dinmonts. One, belonging to their daughter Cecilia Neal, a lady of style, irritated under the dinner table by another dog, drew buckets of blood from its owner's leg. Cecilia's children were also involved with our children's guinea pigs with which they had undertaken some fancy breeding programme, far more successful than Professor Hammond and the twin calves at Sandringham. The animals originated from Rosemary Wilson-Walker's birthday party when her exasperated mother issued one to each child as they left – and they bred and bred. Our daughters rapidly accumulated a surplus and donated one to the Neal children who, with their keeper, were returning by train to Sarratt. While Nanny slept, guinea pig on knee, the fascinated children watched it reproduce and eat the babies one by one – a better biology lesson than Wetty Morris' lectures on the birds and bees at Eton. Attending the weddings of William and Marilyn's children in Dunscore Church, and his parents' funerals, I remember how one day Mrs Crawford sent for Alan Hardy, the factor, wanting him to go to Dumfries for concrete and broken glass to line the top of the garden dyke as she was fed up with the courting couples of Dunscore sitting on it. A mild man, he was horrified: 'Oh! Mrs Crawford, you can't do that!' So swifter than the wind she went to Dumfries for an enormous barrel of black treacle to smear the top. A temporary remedy! Behind the scenes were Christine, a Dutch woman who did everything and hated the Germans; Mrs Campbell, Billy Dempster's sister, ace baker, married to Jimmy who kept pigs, reared calves, and drove the van for Mr Young, the Thornhill grocer; and Davie Fraser the gardener. It was a strange haven from a bygone age.

In so many ways the Crawfords were relics of Victorian times with their kindness, hospitality and natural good manners, qualities handed down to their three children – William, a judge, married to Marilyn Colville, who shot for Britain in the Commonwealth Games in 1966; Cecilia, married to Morton Neal, has a soft furnishing business in Bruton Street; and Guy, an investment manager with Peter Buckley at Caledonian Investments, married to Maud. The train was late going to Guy's wedding and I had to change in the stinking loo of a BR train on its way past Rugby. Mrs Carson, a dentist's wife, was part time secretary at Dalgonar. One day walking up Bank Street in Dumfries a man threw an empty cigarette packet out of his car onto the pavement at my feet. I tossed it through the window saying: 'What a filthy habit!' Three weeks later the tale was retold by Mrs Carson to the Crawfords how a lawyer he didn't know, smartly dressed with a briefcase, had attacked her husband for dropping litter. As I usually dressed like a tramp everyone laughed, and his wife's comment was: 'Thank you, he never listens to me!'

Chapter 8

Scotland's an attitude of mind.

Maurice Lindsay

One afternoon in the mid 1960s George Thomson, secretary of the Dumfries NFU, came as I was pruning bushes to persuade me to join the Union, which was the start of a long association with rural politics and the many friends it has brought me from all over Britain. Meetings in the old Station Hotel at Dumfries were dominated by Jack Blackley, Berscar, a former Scottish President, David Ker of Craigdarroch, John Marshall of Hardgrove, later president of the World Simmental Society, married to the charming Doris (a name I can't stick!) and Jack Gass, Townhead of Mouswald, canny beyond belief, assisted by Robbie Shearlaw, the belligerent Buccleuch farm manager who spent a lot of the Duke's money. Resolutions went to Edinburgh and gradually I began to express opinions challenging the conventional wisdoms of central authority. At the same time I became involved with the Dumfriesshire Conservative and Unionist Association and wrote a piece to dispel any doubts in my mind about the need to support the local Party.

Doubting Thomas

Like the country mouse coming to the town I felt a little lost in the undergrowth of politics. Are politicians really rogues, living by their wits at our expense, and do they really care? A lot of them say they didn't mean what they said before, and some of them don't appear to have anything to say at all. Some of them seem to want power, some fame and some nothing but a safe seat to rest their weary bones. This applies to both parties and as to parties they seemed so alike that I couldn't tell the wood from the trees and I wondered if either could tell the truth. This is what I thought. I decided to make home for my burrow and abandon the Power Game to a more sophisticated mind.

Alas it was a wasted journey and at home I had just as many doubts about whether what I had done was right, as I had before about whether politics were any good. Maybe you will think me simple, but this is what I suddenly thought! Do I believe in Freedom? Freedom to scuttle home to my burrow when I want, and even to opt out of a journey on Whizz Kid Benn's big dipper with all its frights and thrills? Freedom to disagree with Government, even if this means the right of everybody else to strike when I believe they are wrong? Freedom to arrange my business without paying a forced levy for an army of expensive bureaucrats to stamp on my government surplus toes? Freedom to help my neighbour, this privilege of which Socialism appears to be increasingly jealous and wishes to make impossible? Freedom even – and above all – to live in a state where anybody, from our beloved Prime Minister to the meanest citizen in the land, can say and believe what they think, without men coming by night to take them away? Add to those liberties the freedom from economic theories produced by economic theorists. Most of us want to see the people of our country better housed and in better jobs, but this can only be done by work and by people who know that $2 + 2 = 4$ not 6 (the conclusion about theorists is not stated but should be obvious!).

Having thought these not very original thoughts there did seem to be a path through the political jungle. It was drawn with shattering clarity. If I turned to my right I should have the freedoms in which I believed, and if I turned to my left I should find the restrictions which I hated. There must be many others who have this same dilemma. There must be many of them who know that Dumfries has an able and conscientious MP. I realise now that he needs my help just as much as I need his. I would prefer to remain among my cattle and work my fields, but I understand at last that if I am not prepared to make some small sacrifice for the liberties which we have, these liberties will not be there.

With this I scuttled back to town and if you believe, as I believe, perhaps we will meet because only by fighting together can we overcome the forces of socialism who wish to destroy the freedoms which for too long we have accepted as our right.

The agent, Gordon Murray, had experienced difficulties after the retirement of Niall Macpherson, later Lord Drumalbyn, the MP, for many years. An Edinburgh lawyer became candidate, but after messy revelations in the Press about his private life he resigned to be replaced by Hector Monro. Hector had served in the War with the RAF, farmed at Williamwood, Kirtlebridge, and was well known in Scottish Rugby circles, as well as having been a County Councillor and chairman of the Dumfriesshire Association. Married to Anne Welch, who in her youth played golf with my father and was Derbyshire Ladies Champion, they had two sons, Seymour and Hugh, now high in the Army, who called their mother when their parents were going to Amsterdam telling her to take great care of father as he had led such a sheltered existence! After Anne died Hector married Doris Kaestner, a widow from Maryland who laughs at him, owns two or three houses in the States, and yanks him from pillar to post which is good for him after Anne's health problems which made his political career difficult for both of them. Hector has been a friend for almost forty years as MP, Minister, and ultimately as a member of the House of Lords. With the death of Alick Buchanan-Smith he is the last old fashioned Conservative in Scottish politics with whom I can identify. Nothing was too much trouble and it was that concern which ensured his return to Westminster election after election, often supported by what might have been considered his natural opponents, the mining families of Sanquhar and Kirkconnel.

In 1986 I wrote for the Love of Winnie – an affair of the heart.

All of us who live in Scotland are to some extent patriots! Which one of us, on the morning after the Hamilton by-election, was not a little in love with Winnie Ewing and delighted at the prospect of the established parties having a jolt? And which one of us felt no pity for Winnie in Westminster as her flimsy attack was torn to shreds by the debating skills of men who had studied their subject in depth?

She told the SNP conference that between her election and the end of May 1986 she had asked 800 questions and made 9 speeches. You might think she was a regular attender, but from 16 November 1967 to 27 May 1968 there were 157 divisions in the House of Commons. From 131 of these, the 'exclusive' voice of Scotland was absent. Of the 800 questions, most of which were written, I give you two samples.

27/2/68 Mrs Ewing asked the Secretary of State for Scotland on how many occasions corporal punishment has been inflicted in penal institutions in Scotland since it was abolished in England (Criminal Justice Act). Mr Ross: Corporal punishment in Scottish penal establishments was abolished in 1949.

– and to think Mrs Ewing is a practising solicitor!

11/3/68 Mrs Ewing asked the Chancellor of the Exchequer:

What was the total in the latest convenient year, of the import duties on tea, at London, at other English ports, and at Scottish ports respectively.

Mr Harold Lever: There has been no import duty on tea since 1 January 1964.

Contrast these antics with the work of our own MP, Hector Monro. He is now the Scottish whip. He holds weekly briefings at which the twenty-one Scottish Tories plan the week's attacks in the Commons. As a result the Scottish Office ministers are finding that they have to face the facts of life (which means our problems) and the ill-informed naiveté of Mrs Ewing becomes for them a little light, if expensive, relief. Hector Monro attended over 100 of the 157 divisions already mentioned. He does this in the interests of *all* the people of Dumfriesshire. We should be grateful.

Socialist government has sapped our will to do anything for ourselves with its indiscriminate aspirins of social security. At times it has even appeared to dope the leaders of the Conservative party. Nobody said what they believed, but only what they thought the public wished to hear. On to this cynical scene wanders the glamorous figure of Mrs Ewing. Her appeal is unashamedly to the heart. She paints a picture of a united Scotland, spiritually and economically free. She flaunts her womanhood as a political banner in a way that poor old Arthur Donaldson could never emulate. She becomes the spirit of Scotland itself and she will give us freedom!

But freedom from what? Freedom from apathy, I grant you. Freedom from Socialism? Never. Scottish nationalism would mean the creation of a mini socialist state, governed by the mini-skirted figure of Solicitor Ewing. When Scotland needs free enterprise all we are offered (SNP conference 3/6/68) is: 'The land and all natural resources belong to the people [which means the government] and will be held subject to the control of the proposed National Assembly.' This referred to all land.

Freedom from bureaucracy? Never. That at Glasgow would be no less away with the fairies (and our money!) than their counterparts in Westminster.

Freedom from England? Possibly, but do we believe this is what we really want? What we need, surely, is more freedom to decide our own affairs and this is exactly the opportunity which Mr Heath's much maligned Declaration of Perth is designed to create.

Scotland's involvement with SNP is an affair of the heart and, as such, will never be amenable to reason. It has dispelled the mists of political apathy, but unless the Conservative party learns to present its policy in a way which appeals to the heart, as well as the mind, Scotland will be saddled with SNP and it will be a case of Forward with Winnie or the Freedom of Fools, and it will be ourselves to blame as our standard of living descends. 'They' say that love is blind. 'They' seem to know!

It was a time of intense discussion about Scottish devolution and Britain's possible entry to the EEC. Despite France having a far greater proportion of agricultural votes I was strongly opposed, partly because of the way it would affect the Commonwealth, and partly because of worries if Edward Heath's obsession with Europe was in Scotland's long term interest. I wasn't even sure I wanted to remain a Conservative under the leadership of a man with such a sloppy handshake, but Taffy Landale, President of the Association, persuaded me to remain and eventually, at the end of 1969, to become chairman. Taffy was an outstanding man who had been Taipan in Hong-Kong. His first wife died unhappily in 1956, but he married Beatrice, his friend for many years. She made him happy and taught him how to be loved again as only the offspring of a Swedish nobleman, courtier at the Court of Tsar Nicholas II, and a Muscovite woman knew how. She never lost her accent. They asked us to dinner at Dalswinton. I remember that evening still, sitting between her and Kirsten, Grahame Gordon's wife, a Dane from Langeland, who told me Selma Lagerlöf's *Story of the Christmas Rose*, and afterwards sent me a copy of Khalil Gibran's *The Prophet*. The Cunningham-Grahams were there. Once Flag Officer, Scotland he was married to a great niece of Osgood Mackenzie. His hobby was polishing furniture, which he did with a clothes peg on his nose. William Clark-Maxwell took me to dinner in the Archer's Hall when he was speaking and described the Royal Company of Archers as looking like a lot of admirals rolled in spinach. I had been to *Dr Zhivago* at the cinema in Dumfries, had read Lesley Blanche's *Journey into the Mind's Eye* and was deeply moved by the relationship between Russia and where I sat. Very close to that table were those bearded priests processing around the church at Ennismore Gardens at my father's funeral, black hats and beards, swinging their censers as their deep voices echoed all the grief of Holy Mother Russia and her suffering people. As Taffy became iller and iller I telephoned two or three times a week to the flat at Cranmer Court to try to support Beatrice and when he died I did what one should never do. I tried to pick up the pieces and she went on a cruise to recover.

In the constituency it was General Election time. Molly Wilson had become agent. She smoked and had red hair – which speaks for itself – but was competent and organised her helpers skilfully. Looking back on Margaret Hay, ex Sheriff Deputy, who knew where to find precious stones in the Stewartry burns, and Mrs Duke, and a host of other workers, they were quite antique, although the young Conservatives like Rhonda Bodman, were energetic and thoughtful. Miss Hay's father taught her when things were bad – 'Drink your whisky and curse the Irish.' I canvassed the housing estates of Lochside and Lincluden, and learnt to stick up for myself, as well as collecting complaints to hand to the Council. On election day I visited every polling station in the constituency but by night was so exhausted it was necessary to lie on the floor with my feet on a chair before returning to Dumfries for the count. The Chairman's job lasted three years and coincided well with having to drive the children to school at the Convent, enabling me to visit the office at the Unionist Rooms in Loreburn Street most days. Unfortunately one winter was the year the Government mucked about with the clock which involved driving both ways in the dark along what Mervyn Crawford called the Lord's Prayer Road which twisted like a corkscrew between Dunscore and the flat lands, and past what the children called the 'smelly farm' at Nether Gribton. During that time Vice Chairmen of the Association were Arthur Jardine, undertaker, Margery Thomson, and Esme Grieve who was carted away in the train when seeing her mother off to Wales, and John Bell-Irving. Treasurer was Michael Johnson-Ferguson who taught his children to add by turning over a pack of cards faster and faster in time to a metronome. His Uncle Brian was Scout Commissioner, with me as one of his deputies without greater knowledge than having learnt to tie a reef knot at school in an air raid. I inspected boys at camp and asked them what to do if they sprained their ankles. They didn't know – nor did I – but they were told to find out, and the next time we met they showed me. Brian climbed ropes in his kilt which alarmed everybody on state occasions. There were Unionist meetings in Glasgow and Edinburgh. One dreadful night Molly was so cross we never exchanged a word for sixty miles each way. Every year there was a fete. One at Raehills was opened by Gerald Nabarro with his handlebar moustaches who had famously said: 'All publicity is good publicity,' although now he must be turning in his grave! That day Percy Hope-Johnstone, married to Peggy, our new President, showed me how to throw an egg onto the ground without breaking it. Six or seven years before I had learnt how tedious politicians could be at Moniaive when Jim Prior, sheltered by the only umbrella, spoke endlessly of the virtues of the Tory Party while his audience soaked. I have been one of the wet ones ever since but becoming drier!

I visited Beatrice – Lara is what I called her – on her return. Rachmaninov's Second. Piano Concerto was being played on a record by John Ogden in the Dalswinton drawing room and it was that introduction to listening to music which led me later to become chairman of the Dumfries Music Club. Early one August morning the following year I went to her flat at Cranmer Court and heard Elgar's Introduction and Allegro as I walked through the door. Whenever I hear it now it is still so poignant it makes me cry inside. She taught me so much of a life I did not know and in return I taught her about the countryside, and the birds and the flowers, and sometimes picked for her primroses and violets from the back of the roadside dykes. Once we went to Muncaster and walked through the arcades of rhododendrons to the Quarry in the Top Garden where Rh. megacalyx bloomed, and the johnstoneanums (named after the wife of the political agent in Manipur in 1882 – a useless piece of information!). In the middle was a New Zealand tree I called the Sinner's Cross. It and the megacalyx were killed by frosts in 1982, but I still dislike others visiting that special place.

She was twenty four years older than me, born in Moscow on a December Sunday in 1906. Talking to her daughter Karin, who has had a difficult life, we are not certain all she told us was strictly true. She said her father and her brothers were killed by the Bolsheviks in 1917 and she was taken to the woods by her mother who insisted she wore a blue ribbon in her hair although they had nothing to eat except what they found in the forest. Eventually they escaped on a salt train with only her father's greatcoat. She was educated in London and Geneva. Eventually she found a job at the League of Nations and married Karin's father, a nephew of Grieg. During the 1939 War she worked with the BBC Foreign Service while he was in China. After the war they parted. Karin went up to Oxford, then married first Reggie Bosanquet, the television presenter, by whom she had a sweet daughter, Abigail, and secondly, Estes Mann, an American from the Bible belt. Lara was a vile driver and in 1972 had a bad accident, terribly damaging an eye, but she later married Claude Crawford from Essendy which was a brief disaster. David Landale her stepson, treated her with great decency, allowing her to remain at Bankhead, a Dalswinton farmhouse, until she finally went to Cranmer Court where I visited her occasionally whenever I was in London. When she died she wanted her body left for medical research. After that was concluded there was a memorial service at Dalswinton, but nobody prepared me for what happened next. Leaving my office in Inverness one evening, travelling down the A9, Karin called. There was to be another service at St. Columba's, Pont Street in two days time and she and Abbie wanted me to do the talking. It was an almost impossible task, but I wrote this and speaking it in that wonderful church reduced myself to tears.

> My love, I have no fire tonight
> With you so far away
> No more I see my Clydesdale mare
> With all the stars her huffing breath
> Kindled each dawn from frosty air
> And sparks her silver shoes
> Struck from the stony track
> That led us long ago
> Across the morning on our way to plough.
> My love, I have no longer fire
> And when dark comes
> With nought but dreams
> Her stall will still be empty there;

No sound of munch contented
As she chews her evening feed;
No rustle of the shuffled straw
Around her feathered legs;
And I shall have to sit alone tonight
Setting my memories as snares
To try to catch the sound of geese
Sweeping in Vs across the moonlit sky
Beyond the distant firth that once was home,
But now my ears grow deaf,
My eyes no longer bright
With you so far across the years
And much too far away to light
The candle on the window-sill
To guide me home at darkening.
My love, I have no fire tonight.

This story sounds matter of fact, but whoever has collided with the romance of Russian culture, their music, and their quite different way of thinking will understand, whatever the truth, that I am scarred for life, for I loved Beatrice Bengsen, so help me God! And what she gave, however wrong, however brief, opened doors other people never find, and the music is still there despite my attempts to close my ears. All I can quote is from the Lara theme from *Zhivago*.

Some day we'll meet again,
Some day, whenever the spring breaks through,
You will come to me
Warm as the wind, soft as the kiss of snow.
Till then my sweet
Think often now and then,
God speed, my love, till you are mine again.

In March 1971 after several days studying rhododendrons with David Davidian at the Botanic Gardens in Edinburgh Phyllida and I flew to Hong Kong to visit the family of my brother who was attached to 7 Gurkhas. The following are extracts from my journal written for Lara.

Chapter 9

So lost upon the rim of time.

Patrick Gordon-Duff-Pennington
(1930-   ) *Patrick of the Hills*

Sek Kong
New Territories
2-8 March 1971

LEAVING HOME was unpleasant. Night train to London and aeroplane to Hong Kong. Frankfurt 1° frost; lovely flight over the Alps, some of the hills in cloud, others completely white and most dramatic. Cool wind at Rome where we stretched our legs. The Italian hills looked very rough – one had never before understood how the armies had been held up so long in the War. Over the Aegean as the sun went down and away through mountains of cottonwool clouds. Karachi in the middle of the night and dawn coming to meet us as we crossed the Burma coast. More hills, jungle, and many rivers, with a few villages, mostly quite small. Rangoon and the Irrawaddy – we saw the gold temple of Shwan Dagon glinting in the sun. Landed at Bangkok, temperature 82°. It was surprising how cultivated the countryside appeared. Over the Mekong and South Vietnam, a fearful parched looking countryside, but quite steep hills near the sea. We crossed the coast north of Quinhou and turned north past one or two carved coral atolls. Eventually to a Hong Kong bathed in thick cloud.

Landed at Kaitak, which has been made, as much of the colony, by tipping rock hacked from the hills into the sea. Astonished by the numbers of Chinese, the filth, the colourful signs in the streets, and the dreadful standard of driving – not improved on by sister-in-law Patricia or her language. Sek Kong is fifty minutes away in the New Territories over a steep road known as Route Twisk (the soldier who surveyed it). Banana trees, and terraces of water cress and vegetables gouged out of the hills. Some hills planted with trees during the past fifteen years, and everywhere purple bauhinias, mauve convolvulus, and purple and orange ipecacuanas. The hills are steep and the highest of all is Tai Mo Shan, the Godess of Mercy, above R and P's quarter. There are bougainvilleas and hibiscus in the gardens. The view is down the Sek Kong Valley to the duck marshes and Yuan Long where Ah Ching, the amah, lives. I never realised the New Territories, leased from China in 1898 for a hundred years, were so large. Little villages with poor shacks and vile sanitation. The air stinks and there are water buffaloes, and many ducks and hens, and copulating dogs and pigs, monasteries, and people. Pigs go to market stuffed in long wicker baskets alive, put in a lorry facing backwards in case they mess the cars behind – of which there are a great quantity! The few walled villages are breeding grounds for communism. Lovely butterflies, rusty backed shrikes, and kingfishers, and the ubiquitous bulbul. The sea is full of boats and above, the Amah's Rock. She was married to a fisherman and always climbed with their child to wave goodbye and welcome him home. One day he never came and she was turned to stone with the baby on her back to mark her fidelity. Between Sek Kong and Shatin there is a lovely fertile valley called Lam Suen with at the bottom the photogenic but filthy market town of Taipo where refugees live in unspeakable squalor on fleets of unspeakable boats. At the top of the valley the Kadoorie Farms rise from 300 to 1890 feet and the summit of Tai-Mo-Shan where hot air rises from the rocks. We visited it one afternoon and the terraces with the hakka women in black tunics and straw hats with black drapes, and the peach trees, pineapples, and asparagus, and camellias, and the Cocks' Summer Camp, where the cocks go to rest from the hens, were all very picturesque.

In places are prayer trees covered with papers on which people have written their wishes. The hills are covered with graves and the higher up the mountain the more important the people. After five years bones are scraped and polished, part of the reverence of the ancestors. The profession of bone polisher is very honoured. One day Patricia took us to Hong Kong Island to see the fabulous jade collection at the Tiger Balm Gardens belonging to Aw Boon Haw and Aw Boon Par. The rose quartz was the loveliest. At Repulse Bay a modern statue of Tin Hau, Queen of Heaven, the patron of life saving, was beautifully natural, but rather hideous.

The sigh of the wind in the casuarinas at night is a lovely sound.

Visits to Kowloon and a boat picnic to Lan Tau – a steep island with a monastery and three prisons, once the leper colony. I had a suit made for £20 in four days. We never took off our overcoats but it's lovely to see R. and P. again, and all the interest has made it worthwhile. Even a visit to the Chinese border was interesting, but where the colony goes in the future nobody knows. All is geared to commerce and profit. There are many rich people, but the discrepancy between them and the masses is shattering. Kowloon is vile, with the main drain running between two walls down the street. We think we have a pollution problem – it's nothing.

Brigade of Gurkhas Transit Camp
Barrackpore
Calcutta
9 March 1971

You can't imagine this place. Twenty four hours ago we were at the Kadoorie Farms in a cold Hong Kong afternoon, and now we are here in an old army cantonment, nothing like the Calcutta Aunt Mignon told me about. We flew into Dum Dum low over the delta which looked unprepossessing with most of the countryside water and a few islands of light. A charming Indian hostess met us, but was hopeless and put us on the wrong bus. She was so nice about it we couldn't be cross. There is a large new airport where the Customs were tiresomely formal, but eventually we got through – quicker than everybody else, only to find we weren't expected. Nobody to meet us, nobody at Movement Control in Calcutta, and no telephone working at the camp here. After an hour we resigned ourselves to a taxi (TFK 300), convinced we would be bilked and were told by the BOAC man the driver would be satisfied with 50 per cent more than the meter said. We embarked in a car belonging to an enormous Sikh, white turbaned, a long wisp of hair down the back of his neck. Another in front with a pink turban looked like grandfather and held firmly – with justification – to the dashboard. The moon was bright, enormous, and we kept it in the window in case we were going in a circle. The stench was everywhere. The road was dreadful and the driver dipped his lights by turning off everything. We careered faster and faster, shaving the hairs off dogs and cows in the middle of the road. So much for sacred cattle! Everywhere on the walls the Hammer and Sickle. Eventually the place became busier with gigantic erections like wedding cakes, and lights, and the beat of drums, and people.

We passed many army barracks, and many political meetings. The driver was unsure where we were going – so were we but he was intelligent and kept stopping to ask for 'British Regiment of Gurkhas'. We came to a gate with a hill man standing by it. Luckily Roderick speaks Gurkhali because the same night watchman had seen a hand trying to climb the railings shortly before. Now the man has no hand.

Nobody expected us but they were all polite. We sat inside the mess while an orderly was found. He offered us rum or beer and cigarettes for R. and eventually found us two quite comfortable rooms with a bathroom and fans. Outside frogs and cicadas made a tremendous din and the bougainvilleas were beautiful in the lights. Mosquitoes everywhere but we went round with a 'bomb' and had nets. A lizard scuttled up the wall.

I slept badly. Woke to a beautiful morning with tea at 6.30. Outside a drongo bird, like a blackbird with a long forked tail, and sparrows, and mynah birds, and something akin to wagtails, and an aeroplane revving up over the fence. We inspected Large White pigs, hens, and the vegetable patch with the Gurkha officer, and eventually had breakfast on the lawn under a tree. The place is like all army camps, but feels empty with only two British officers. Desmond Houston, a major from 10 GR, called – a bachelor with a cold and the MC. His only comment on picking up the paper was: 'No more than forty last night dead in the local riots!' The other is a civil major, Bob Burnett from the Pay Corps on a nine month unaccompanied tour. Eggs and bacon seemed out of place. It was horribly hot.

We discovered nobody expected us until 22 March, but people are efficient and we leave on the Delhi express tonight at 9.00 p.m. changing at Mokameh, Barauni, and Katihar hoping to arrive at 4.15 tomorrow afternoon. To the bank with RAPC man after he had changed into his uniform – nobody is allowed out in civilian clothes. Another amazing drive through crowds of people, and markets, and rickshaws and cattle, and there were even a kingfisher and some pigs in the street. People dying in the streets, lured from a bare living in the Bihar countryside by the thought of food and work and money in this cesspit. It has changed my views about who is badly off in the world. The bank didn't want to know us and Bank of Scotland travellers cheques were useless. The place was teeming. Indian army lorries drew out of their barracks filled with infantry, rifles at the ready. Tomorrow is election day in W. Bengal. The situation is unsettled with the communists trying to persuade the voters to boycott the polls. The politician's problem, difficult anywhere, is quite insoluble here. Population increases so fast there's no hope of catching up. Wages are low, prices high. Is it the climate, the history, the outside world – I just don't know, except that what we think is a crowd is nothing compared with this. Handouts to the poorest only make them breed more. Starvation so lacks humanity, but it is depressing when one thinks of armchair politicians at home who 'know' the remedy and haven't, in reality, the slightest notion of what all this is like.

Hile
13 March 1971

Left Barrackpore at 6.15 p.m. to catch the 9 o'clock train from Howrah, a journey of half an hour at home. A Gurkha sat in the back of the open Land Rover with his favourite kukri with instructions not to use it unless absolutely necessary, but to chop off anybody's fingers if they interfered. The crowds were ghastly, mostly political meetings and processions armed with staves, the only orderly ones organised by the Communists. The Indian government had drafted 200,000 extra troops into West Bengal for the elections. They stood at every street corner, in lorries, rifles at the ready. I have never before been in a place which felt so evil.

At the station one could hardly move on the platform. There were hundreds of beggars, mostly children, and the pathetic whine of 'Baksheesh' everywhere. Many are starving, many have trachoma. I have never seen people dying of starvation before and you can imagine the effect. It isn't a pretty sight and will be a weight on my conscience for the rest of time. Eventually the train appeared at the end of the platform. There was a frantic rush and before it reached the buffers the crowd piled in through doors, through windows and, for all one could tell, through the roof. We travelled in a first class air conditioned sleeper as far as Mokameh. The whole five hundred mile journey cost £7. Awoke at 7.30 as the sun rose over the Indian plains which were quite green. Except for the tiny size of the plots it might have been East Anglia with park-like trees everywhere, mostly mangoes. A few patches of water with people doing laundry, washing, then slapping it on a rock. Mokameh is an unpleasant railway junction. We ate sandwiches before embarking in another first class carriage, little more than a box with a bench and full of people. As we left the station a man, looking like a Pathan, eased himself over the threshold and squatted in the corner for three or four miles and as quietly melted away. The whole train seemed to be filled in the same way. Nobody had tickets so how do the railways manage? We crossed the Ganges to a bigger and smellier junction called Barauni. Nasty omelette in a restaurant upstairs, shared with Customs and Excise officials quizzing a large contractor about a load of cement. Everywhere people used the platform as a public lavatory. The next train was better. We shared a carriage with two Sikh officers in the Kumaon Rifles on their way to Assam. The Indians are still extremely sensitive about the Chinese. Their mountain warfare instructors are taking life seriously and training up to 18,000 ft. to try to avoid repeating the fiasco of the India-Chinese war, when Krishna Menon closed all the ammunition factories and troops were sent from Madras with no clothing except a pullover. Some were cut to pieces, twice as many died of exposure.

At each station there was a noise like a Thornhill sheep sale on a Saturday afternoon – people begging, selling tea, tomatoes, tangerines, and anything you might have wanted, including some rather fetching peacock feather fans. Up the trees on the stations the Biharis chopped branches for their goats below. The country changed hardly at all, although there were larger herds of water buffaloes and crowds of whitish draft oxen pulling carts of rice straw. Bihar is supposed to be even poorer than Calcutta, but one could not see it. Over every village red flags flew, but we have since heard Mrs Gandhi has won the election. They say the Green Revolution is beginning to bite and with more fertiliser and better seed India may start to tackle the starvation problem. Unfortunately I think there must be more to it than food – more a frame of mind generated by centuries of living in the way they live, and possibly the climate.

We reached Katihar at 4.15 in an afternoon dominated by flies. A Gurkha Land Rover met us to drive the hundred miles to Dharan. Tea in a wood in delicious shade with a light breeze. An elephant passed and a clown on rather a dashing horse. The roads were narrow and busy. Houses mostly made of split bamboo sections roofed with bamboo leaves. We crossed the border at Jogbani. Luckily the customs man was there which he often isn't! The egrets were flying home and the moon rose with a quality of timelessness. Not a hill in sight. The road filled with bullock convoys carting sal wood to the sawmill at Biritnagar. Eventually we met the jungle and the British-made road running for five or six miles through great stems of trees. Suddenly we saw the mountains rising very steeply to 5,000 ft. north of Dharan Bazaar which we reached at 8.15.

We had a bath. I had two as I never saw such filth. Horrid little lizards which, looking as if they had been skinned, eyed me with as much distaste as I viewed them. The rooms were comfortable and there was a good bearer who washed and pressed everything. Dinner at 9.30 with Adrian Gordon and a funny old stick called Richardson, over 60, who loves the place and spends eight months a year walking the hills on his welfare job. We spent a day in Dharan. R. organised the stores. I went round the Resettlement Farm where they hold one-month courses, a hundred and sixty men at a time, teaching them building and agriculture. The houses they built, substantial with two floors, cost under £50. The biggest agricultural problem is erosion. They are encouraging more people to terrace and irrigate their land and to use compost. The country we came through yesterday was badly farmed, but here, at 5500 ft., as far as one looks are terraces with rice and maize, and tangerine and lemon groves, and many peach trees which are now in bloom.

In Dharan it was the two day holiday for Holi, the festival of spring – which sounds unexciting after reading about the Feast of the Excited Insects in Hong-Kong! A party in the evening where R. and I did more than our fair share chatting up the sticky old trouts, before slipping away at 11.00, to be woken by the porters at 4.30, rather short of sleep.

Left at dawn by Land Rover and started walking at 5.15, Adrian Gordon climbing with us for the first hour and a half. Crowds on the roads astonishing, enormous loads in baskets fixed to their backs with shoulder straps and head bands around their foreheads. Steep climb to the old Limbu fort and we stopped halfway for a tangerine and tea, heavily laced with pepper. Descent the other side even steeper along a path bordered with buddleia. Stopped at the bottom of a sordid river bed for lunch at 10.00. One pays for firewood, but cooks wherever one likes. Awful flies. Squads of porters carrying kerosene and salt drifted by. One family had an old woman in a basket carried on the son's back. After lunch which took two hours we walked along a woody track beside the Tamur River, swift clear blue and very wide. We crossed the river by a new suspension bridge and paid a toll on the far side. Then an unspeakable walk through a grilling afternoon, up, and up, and up. Nourished by Uncle Edward's romances from Burma about never drinking on the march I refused water until so severely dehydrated it was useless. We reached a shop on a promontory at 3,000 ft., and staggered until 5.15 when we reached Dhankuta.

It is a beautiful village with terracing and substantial houses draped with dried marigolds about the doors. I felt miserable and was very sick down the loo, a substantial pit in the ground. We stayed with Don Paterson and his wife who were working for the British Medical Trust, carrying out a large scale TB inoculation programme financed principally by big industrial firms. Two student doctors from Guys who had wangled the trip were there, and an odd chap, about nineteen with draping hair, an agent for the drug firms, who spoke no Gurkhali but knew a surprising amount about the country. At night two weddings, with one bride carried along the street, her bridegroom on a grey horse, accompanied by a drummer and various other instruments. As they passed people let off fireworks.

I ate little and thought I was going to die which depressed Roderick, but two larch acetate pills and a night's sleep on the floor helped. We left at 7.00 to walk four hours to Hile. There had been no rain since last year's monsoon and the dust and heat were frightful. Up through pine trees and onto a track past the Nepalese army barracks. Two brass cannons and a smashing bugler. We watched them changing guard, much impressed by their smartness. Discipline is strict. A party of girls passed with red rhododendrons in their hair, rather smart but very cheeky. Yesterday we met somebody whose comment was, according to R., 'Christ! There's a white man!' We never saw another until returning to Dharan – nor a wheel. The parties on the road have new transistors, a blaring reminder of 'civilisation'. I still felt ropey so we stopped to sleep in the local shopkeeper's house. According to the porters he is stinking rich, but he tried to charge twice too much for an old white cock which must have blessed our meanness. We sleep tonight on his verandah, the rejected cock roosting on the rail beside us. Clear skies and a cool breeze here and we thought when we visited the village we could see the snows in the distance. There was a single vulture in the sky, vast and graceful, and the local Lester Piggott was training a pony for the races, arms and legs flying, sitting on a saddle with high pommels fore and aft. There is a Tibetan colony here and the place is a-flutter with grey and blue and white prayer flags. Tibetans one meets on the track have large flat faces. They wear moccasins trimmed with fur and strange carpet gaiters. Our porters are Dan Kumar Rai, a funny little man, a vile cook, newly married, but all eyes for the Paterson's cook. Lakshmi Limbu from near Taplejung. Limbuan is the only part of Nepal never conquered by the Gurkhas. Long ago they concluded a treaty exempting them from land tax, a situation greatly resented by the powers in Kathmandu. Head porter is Birker Bahadur (brave), bow-legged, nearly related to a monkey, a Gurung from Ayslakarche, some way to the west.

We spent an entertaining half hour in the shop and saw shelves stocked with luxuries such as Afghan Snow (for your complexion!) and Brooke Bond A1 Dust Tea which looks like the sweepings nobody else will touch. A sofa in the corner and a hen and chicks which kept dashing in and out. Going to the loo is a problem. They are more respectable than in India and there is little cover! Tomorrow we hope to leave before the moon goes down at 4.30 as it is much easier walking in the cool. Although it is interesting I feel strangely homesick in this foreign land.

> Two hours west of Amphura
> At the House of the Chetri
> 14 March 1971

A good day's march of about 25 miles. The map is difficult to measure as there are so many diversions because of erosion and the locals measure distances in time. Left Hile at 6.15 and covered 8 miles to Sinduwa by breakfast. A glorious walk along a turfy ridge at 7,500ft. We had our first view of the Himalayas and the air was like wine. Over our shoulders flew a flock of snow white geese, wings tipped with black. Later I wrote this:

I have tramped the tracks of high Nepal,
Seen Everest's far snows
Blue in the morning moon;
Slept by the fire
Under the stars on terraces
And counted skeins of snow geese passing by
Over towards Makalu.

I have heard
The deep notes of the horn players
At the mountain weddings
And watched the whirling of the quern
Spinning in the hands of the children
At the house of the Chetri.

I have admired
Some attitudes of this mountain people
Who measure distances in time
Not miles. They question, though
They do not answer one,
Nor do they often smile.

But through it all my heart
Is aching for Scotland
With its washing of grey waters
And its rocks;
Is waiting for
The calling of my children and
The softer speech and gentler eyes
Of my own people who
I love, and to whom I belong,
Even in this far place
So lost upon the rim of time.

Breakfast is a lengthy performance of $1^{1}/_{2}$-2 hours. We walk again until 5.00 when the meal is cooked. Tonight we were 'in bed' by 6.30. The food is loathsome – rice, stringy chickens butchered with a kukri, and other concoctions, heavily laced with vile spice, and so bulky they are cold by the time they are finished. Tonight we caught the chicken on arrival. It cost 7 rupees instead of the 20R the old man tried to charge at Hile where we purchased a quarter pig for 7R instead. We entered the first forest after breakfast and climbed to 8,000 ft. through 30 foot mahonias and arboreum rhododendrons. Tiny blue gentians on the path, brilliantly vivid, and in the damp places miniature begonias. As we admired the view we had a fright. There was a grunt behind us. Tiger, we thought, but it was luckily an enormous water buffalo browsing. There were redstarts and green parrots, and rather lovely green and yellow birds like warblers, but none could compare with the wildness and freedom of the beautiful geese.

It is hazy most of the day which is bitterly disappointing. We walked until 5.00 around vast slides of erosion. Nobody seemed to worry that as fast as they cleared or burnt the jungle the erosion became worse.

We took an instant dislike to our host. The Chetris are the moneylenders of Nepal, maintaining a tight hold on cash and land. Our loft is airy and clean. The porters sleep in the shed below. There is rice straw for bedding and an old quern for grinding the maize.

Tehrathum
15 March 1971

We slept badly and left at 5.15. The speed at which it gets light and dark is astonishing. The sun rose towards Kanchenjunga but the mist was too thick to see the mountains. We had intended to cross the 10,000 ft. Tinjure Dhanra but the porters refused to sleep in the jungle because of the bears. The erosion was still very bad, but we shaved and breakfasted beyond the Pillow of Amphura. There was a child with toothache and a dottled uncle. The school, which doesn't start until 10.00, came gawping for their geography lesson. We reached Tehrathum after descending through pleasant pine trees. The Government has tried to control indiscriminate felling and there has been some replanting, with erosion noticeably less and well formed terraces. It is a pretty place and fairly important with substantial houses and a paved street with Government offices. A smart 'expert' tries to persuade the locals to increase productivity by using sulphate of ammonia for which he is the agent, being the proud owner of School Leaving Certificate, Kathmandu. The rocks are young and crumbly, and this, coupled with erosion, burning, and sulphate of ammonia, is likely to damage Nepalese agriculture.

The people of Tehrathum are nasty. They give a civil 'Namaste!' but are sly and resemble some of the least prepossessing figures from children's editions of the New Testament. There is much corruption and the Chetris have a strong hand on the money. In the bank we saw an evil looking customer with a shotgun. The schoolmaster had a pain in his stomach but explained most people bought books for cheap wallpaper, their walls being covered with pictures of Mao, the King of Nepal, Ganesh, and Siva. Houses are clean and substantial, a few with glass windows, but the cooking is done on the floor.

Farms are beautifully terraced and irrigated up to 8000 ft. but people are poor and resistant to new ideas. I am disillusioned with the people and would like to go home. Tomorrow we turn north to Taplejung. TB is bad and I can't stand them walking up behind me, coughing and spitting. The man R. has come to see, who is being paid as pensions officer, is not here and is persona non grata. His assistant is supposedly doing his washing in the Tamur, one day's march away. My trousers need a belt!

Sikumba
At the house of the Sherpa of Gangtok
16 March 1971

Darkness at Tehratum disturbed by jackals. The village dogs sleep all day, but bark all night at their howling. I slept on a terrace, my knife under the pillow. A good morning's march after 5.00, past the hurdy-gurdy at Amphura, and eventually came to the first substantial river we had seen for some time. Bathe and breakfast in the river bed in my flaming scarlet pants under rocks on which white orchids grew. Backs of my legs badly sunburnt so discarded shorts for trousers. The postman passed at a jog, armed with traditional lance and bell, badge of the King's authority, prodding those in his way up the backside. The postal service is organised on a Panchyat (local district) basis, each council employing four or five men who exchange mail at the parish boundaries.

A terrible afternoon's slog to Sikumba, just below the jungle, reached at the darkening. Our host is a Tibetan, arrived in Nepal after a short stay at Gangtok in Sikkim. He has a marvellous face and reminds me of a drawing in Aunt M's room. The wife is a coy old devil with a gold bangle and keen on being photographed. The alert son wants to become a Gurkha, but the rest of the family are unprepossessing. The Sherpas live a Spartan existence above 8000 ft., often among the snows. The family had never heard of Scotland but were interested in improving their farming.

To sleep we shared the veranda with a family of swallows and a broody hen. Inside the house was a fantastic sight presided over by a figure we dubbed Pater Familias. Imagine a rabbit hole filled with smoke and this enormous ghoul in the firelight, earrings flashing, long oily ringlets falling below a filthy bandana, and a long skirt wrapped higgledy-piggledy around his middle. At intervals he leaps up in a dervish dance and then squats silent. Everybody coughs and spits, but the porters are enjoying the party and the girls. They have sung for a long time, slightly drunk on the *rakshi* (rice wine) for which they have paid too much. I like the swallows better than the Sherpas.

By the Banks of the
Tamur River
St Patrick's Day 1971

A terrible night, the family relieving themselves in relays, tripping over our legs, then jumping across the ledge of the veranda. The dog, which had fleas, tossed and turned on our feet while the broody hen kept clucking in the nesting box by my left ear. We left at 5.00, the jackals still howling, and climbed from 6,000 to 10,000 ft, through jungle, full of magnolia, viburnum fragrans and rhododendrons in bloom – *arboreum*, *lanigerum*, *falconeri* and *campanulatum*. We reached the top of the Pobbalgang Dhanra and sat on a rock watching Kanchenjunga in the sunrise. Under our rock I found one of the little hairy rhodendrons, *Rh. cetosam*. We descended a ghastly Jacob's Ladder even more abruptly than we had climbed and at the bottom had a gritty shave. Children drove the family goats to pasture up a path most people never used and, frightened by the strangers, fled into the trees. Gradually we moved into a place where R's very good Gurkhali cut no ice. We are in the heartland of the Limbus.

The tiny poor yielding cattle appear to have Jersey and Ayrshire blood, which the locals deny. Along the track are banyan and peepul trees shading walls built as family memorials where porters can rest their loads. Most have a plaque in Nagri script, with the sun and moon on either side of something resembling a toasting fork – a holy sign also imprinted on the ends of the priests' houses.

At the foot of the hill (2,000 ft.) we reached Dumahan by the junction of three rivers, with two suspension bridges which made R. queasy. Locals said their prayers before crossing but I relied on Rowena having said enough Hail Marys at school! We met a Tibetan horse smuggler with a pigtail come, according to him, through impossible snowdrifts on his way over the border to the monastery at Wallumchung. Having coaxed the pony, dun with black mane and tail, across the first suspension bridge he was trying to sell it to an Indian dealer but unfortunately it would face neither bridge again and our smuggler, a good mannered man, was having a long think.

The village was disgusting, so we spent the evening by the river eating potatoes and our one tin of pilchards, which was a change from endless unpolished rice.

Taplejung.
18 March 1971

I lay a long time watching the stars, thought about Topke Gola beyond the snowy peaks of the Mewa Khola and Kanchenjunga, but then much more of home and Scotland and the children. I am not really enjoying this journey but it gives a chance to reduce the mind to bare essentials and at the end will perhaps make me easier to live with. It is difficult balancing unselfishness with the need to take decisions.

I woke in the night, badly bitten by ants. Over the river a fisherman fiddled with his lines under the rocks in the light of a fire. The hills were ablaze with burning jungle and the erosion problems constantly increase. Left at 5, for a stiff three and a half hour climb to Taplejung. Kanchenjunga reappeared and to the left Khockling, 13,000 ft. with a monastery which people visit to gain fertility.

The porters believed it worked, but said the monks were robbers, and for me four daughters seemed enough! We met a smart little man, ex-Indian Army Gurkha who tried to persuade us to go to Wallumchung, 'very historical place'. Later the District Officer, Bandu Pant, told us politely he would have to put us in jail if we tried.

The Welfare Officer, Purna Bahadur Limbu, was quiet and conscientious. He had been through the war – Syria, Aden, Western Desert, Sicily and Italy – and is greatly respected. He gave us a wonderful education. In the afternoon we bought provisions and sat in the bazaar drinking tea, before visiting Bandu Pant, Commander-in-Chief and County Clerk, who wore sunglasses and a large black moustache and had been expelled as far away as possible when he became too powerful for the Kathmandu Establishment. A company of the Nepalese army (150 men) are based here, ten men manning each of the three border passes for a month at a time. All supplies are sent up, four days march in each direction. The school was large, 360 children, including some boarders. Teachers are very left wing and mostly Communists, particularly at Dingla and Tehrathum. A year ago a Chinaman appeared but was drummed out of town when he started to run down the King. We sat crosslegged on the floor eating tangerines with the skin of each pig peeled for us, probably for the only time in our lives.

Disease is rife. 85 per cent of the Nepalese population have TB and there is much smallpox among the Sherpas. We met no Peace Corps, but saw two Khumbas with American type boots and modern rucksacks; Khumbas were Tibetan brigands, but now use Nepalese bases, mostly in the far north near Mustang, to harass the Chinese.

The people of Taplejung are better looking and seem nicer than those met elsewhere. At evening we had soup and goat and whisky with our coffee. Purna came to celebrate and explained agriculture was difficult and that only education could cure the erosion. Land costs £40-£120 an acre in the hills, much of it mortgaged to the Chetris and the Bauns who are universally loathed for their business acumen. Interest rates are so high it is almost impossible to redeem mortgages. Cattle are local – water buffalo for milk and the smaller humped breed for draught work. Communications are difficult and map measurements give no impression of the time and distance people have to travel.

The Terraces at Changi
19 March 1971

A long lie. Rose at 6.00, invited to tea with Bandu Pant at 8.00, so left instructions for our porridge at 9.00 by which time we were still wading our way through curry, chupattis, eggs and tangerines, so it was an effort for our stomachs to return to the Welfare Office for proper breakfast. Our host talked in English and Nepali – which I understood better – of the difficulties of most of his family being in Kathmandu and the horrors of his post. The District Officer seems VIP and it is astonishing they are moved annually, probably as a central government manoeuvre to stop them going native. We left after breakfast, a very hot walk down the ridge to the Tamur, a horrid man tagging along behind, deserting his father who had been collecting his pension and was travelling in a basket on somebody else's back. At the bottom we fell in with our horse smuggler from Wallumchung. The climb from the river to the west was steep, hot, and deadly dull. By dark we had found nowhere to sleep as the priests, our intended victims, refused to have us! We settled on the terraces here, the jackals screaming wildly, and my stick is close at hand as the fire dies down.

A pathetic ancient passed wanting us to do something about a grandchild who had died. It is astonishing it happens so seldom as there are no chimneys and they light the fire in the middle of the living room floor. The reason given is the white ants because well smoked timbers are considered resistant to attack. There is a desperate shortage of doctors and medicine. The headquarters at Dharan has four army doctors handling 30,000 cases a year, but it is often a week's march to reach them. The British Government view the £90k. p.a. in the military estimates with a jaundiced eye, but it does provide aid to Nepal. The Nepalese civilian doctor from Dharan, a highly qualified surgeon from London where he was offered a job at £6k. p.a., is here paid £1 a day. Very homesick for Scotland.

At the top of the Milke Dhanra
20 March 1971

Rose at 4.30 to a beautiful morning and a walk through prosperous villages before it became too hot. Breakfast at 9.00 under a tree with dried-up fruits like pomegranates, which the goats and cattle were eating. We met our first beggar in the hills, a nasty Chetri farmer who complained his land was bad. Afterwards a long steep walk through the jungle to over 10,000 ft. Many magnolias and I found *Rh. shepherdii, arboreum, barbatum* and *thomsonii* above 8000 ft. There are clumps of pink primulas, tight rosettes of flowers in the rocks. At evening we came to a *bhatti*, a hut. The Nepalese have no idea about timber and people had chopped the beams for firewood. We had been introduced to a man in Taplejung who had a brush with a bear, but life became altogether too realistic as we settled down. There were ear-splitting yells of 'tiger' in the hills a mile away. It sounded as though the man was in the animal's mouth. The porters became agitated as more and more people took up the cry below. They said an ox had been taken. We stoked the fire higher. Afterwards thunder and great jabs of lightning across the hills made it very dramatic.

The cold became intense. The hut sloped outwards and my toes kept slipping into the frost. The porters kept the lamp burning all night and in the morning there was snow immediately above us.

The Terraces of Chittang
21 March 1971

We climbed early to the top of the pass. The sight unveiled a moment of glory. As we woke Kanchenjunga was immediately in front in the starlight. On top we saw Everest and Makalu, and all the rest of a magnificent panorama. Perhaps this was what we came for. 'Great things are done when men and mountains meet and not by standing idly in the street.' They were majestic, beautiful, but they do not speak or move like the hills of the Highlands. They are aloof and have no fairies. I can't make up my mind if it is merely something in me which hears these voices in our own hills, or the light, or the wind, but I know for certain I have seen nothing more beautiful than Laggan in all her moods. What I came for, to see these high hills, has left me more homesick than ever.

As we descended, after an hour, the vultures gave a convincing demonstration of air power. Nobody likes them but they can certainly fly. We saw a *mirgar* (deer) and a brilliant red and blue bird like a flycatcher. We passed tombs and temples, with grey prayer flags, usually a sign of Tibetans or Bhotias, before breakfasting at Captain Lalbahadur Gurung's house at Nundhaki. We felt exhausted after our night high up and proceeded slowly to Chittang. Some nasty Bauns refused us shelter, so we slept soundly on the terraces, undisturbed by dogs or jackals.

From the House of the Chetri at Pipla
22 March 1971

Left at 5.00 for Chainpur, a smart place astride the trade routes. The DO's house was spacious, with a courtyard and garden, and glass windows. Most houses have curly tiles on the roof, although Government offices have tin. Every other shop was full of brass workers making pots, and we watched a photographer taking pictures of a very self-conscious youth. We bought twelve sweets in a bag (made of the Maxims of Mao Tse Tung), and a packet of disgusting biscuits (3/6 and the price of a dozen eggs). Food is still horrid, but the two of us and three porters are living for 16/- a day. We breakfasted on terraces outside Chainpur, where the local school came for the usual geography lesson and for a good stare. At 2.15 it thundered and poured with rain, and we eventually found shelter in this slender bamboo house. The cattle looked better bred and better fed than others we had seen. Two daughters sit on a speckless floor grinding an enormous basket of maize with a hand quern. Each has one hand on the handle and the other on their hip, and as they work they grin at one another. The picture is full of movement and circles, like a Russell Flint. The little host has had malaria and looks miserable. A bossy competent medical assistant has entered, taken a blood sample and a smear, given the old boy his pills, and recorded the performance with a nail on the wall. He looks sixteen but made a neat job. We shared a veranda with a dog and some pigeons. Life has been unfair to this family, who are kind and hardworking but Birker says we need not worry as they are very rich. As I fell asleep I thought of the moonpath over Findhorn Bay to Morven, something I haven't done for a long time.

The House of the Tamangs
23 March 1971

We left at 5.15 and saw Everest in the moonlight but had to wait two hours to cross the Arun. A monkey with brown breeks pelted the boys with pomegranates as they sat under the tree by the ferry. Dan Kumar went to look for the ferryman returning half an hour later to announce: 'He's coming – probably!' There had been a dispute as to which village was on duty, but eventually he came and we crossed, squatting on our haunches in a hollowed out tree trunk, propelled precariously by bamboo poles. The river is broad here and rises far into Tibet. There were cormorants, a few birds like plovers, and a beautiful white capped redstart. We disembarked and walked half a mile across the dried up bed of another river before climbing desperately steeply through woods. The soil became red and the country seemed to have changed with fewer people and less farming. At breakfast, marred by red ants, we still saw Everest and the Arun River, a yellow-grey milky colour, not beautiful. There were green parakeets and afterwards we watched eighteen vultures trying to claim a dead goat from a dog which was still in possession half an hour later.

People came down the tracks with flowers threaded in chains around their necks, returning from a local festival. We met a girl, dressed like a cutlet with soup plates in her ears. At a distance of five yards walked her brother who announced proudly he was driving her over the hill to be betrothed. Climbing all day from 1500 ft to the Pass at 6,000 ft. we became very tired and the porters nappy, but they made a hopeless guess where we should go for the night. Eventually we came to this spotless and beautiful house on the top of a ridge. Outside the prayer flags flutter, a loud beating noise in the breeze, sending their messages to heaven. My bites itch. Thank goodness we have the histamine cream. In the night two horrid Chetris came and lay on the veranda beside us, but after thirty minutes of mutual irritation they left. We are becoming rather odd. It feels wrong if we go to bed later than half past six.

Bhojpur
24 March 1971

We left the Tamangs at 5.15 and are staying with Tilak Bahadur at the Welfare Office, where the white ants have vandalised his timbers. We had a good wash and breakfasted by the river before climbing to Bhojpur. We watched cranes eating frogs on well irrigated terraces. The village is dirty, with a big school, barracks and hospital. As we passed the court the yard was crammed with suitors. There are two photographers and a football field. Prices are high because there are so many government offices. Officials are very nasty – too toffee-nosed to talk to anybody and conscious of their education. We watched people preparing to plant maize. Rice is planted May-June for harvesting five months later. Tilak's farm which his wife and four children work while he does the welfare jobs is four hours away. They have no surplus, but enough to eat. We entertained him to supper. R's tongue is pink from eating sweets which worries him. Tonight there are good views to the Temke Dhanra and tomorrow we turn for home.

Munga
Lady Day 1971

Left Bhojpur at 5.15, a long easy walk along the ridge to where the Pikua and the Pilua join, before breakfast in a sordid encampment of flimsy huts. The place was alive with flies and in the middle a blaring wireless, something missing for over a week. Goats and pigs and cattle everywhere. People shared their food with them and the mangy dogs not because they wanted to, but because of being outnumbered. Afterwards we entered the river bed, a rickle of rocks, fearsomely hot where the sun struck the gorges. A constant stream of people making for tomorrow's market in Bhojpur. Few signs of agriculture, although there were one or two patches of rice planted optimistically in the river bed. Every half mile we waded across water, two feet deep in the shallows, but the impression was of desert and where there were neither boulders nor water there were great stretches of burning sand. In late afternoon we reached the junction with the Arun. Crossed the Arun ferry at Munga Ghat where there was a disagreeable scene with the porters about the price of tomatoes which, after the drought, were only the size of a thumbnail. Dan Kumar swore his were best, but I think it was because the girl selling them was the prettiest. Luckily he refused to cook supper and we had the most satisfactory meal we had eaten for some time cooked by Birker. He reminds me of Puck – short grisly grey hair, a ghastly red, white and black hat, bow legs. He dashes into company, exactly resembling a monkey – to whom, without doubt, he is closely related – and collapses on his haunches in the corner usually quite without comment. Having listened to the conversation for some minutes he almost knocks one down with a torrent of words accompanied by a broad grin.

Night by the river was clear and still. I lay a long time watching the stars and saw two satellites crossing. Tomorrow we return to Dharan. I have lost three inches around my middle and the new trousers are having trouble staying in place.

Dharan
26 March, 1971

We shaved in hot water, leaving Munga at 6.00 to walk down to the Arun ferry along a level wooded path. I lay on my back in the sun reading *Other Men's Flowers* while breakfast cooked. I do admire Wavell, both for his mind and as a soldier. It became hot and unpleasant. At the new suspension bridge we bought eight bananas for 1R (10 old pence) and drained the water bottle which always tastes disgusting with the tablets we have to use. We need more and more salt as we near the plains. At one o'clock we reached the junction of the Sun Kosi and the Arun, and a little later, what must be the most curious shipping office in the world. An old crone, nearer 100 than 90, sits on a bench in the inner sanctum of a bamboo hut issuing grubby scraps of paper covered with hieroglyphics. We part with 3Rs each (2/6) which entitles us to a 'seat' on the 4 o'clock boat to Chattra, a journey of an hour and a half. As we waited, across the river a man scooped endlessly at the water with a large hand net. At 5.30 a loud shout rose from the bank and a sail appeared round the bend, only to put in to the side while someone hauled it down, wrapped it round the mast, and laid the whole outfit in the bottom of the boat. It arrived twenty minutes later. Thirty people poured in – and so did the water. It had been made for twenty, and known to take seventy. We sat for five minutes. The helmsman's wife appeared and read him a frightful lecture. He disembarked, a Daddy Long Legs of a man, dressed in bloomers, with a coif of hair he kept pulling. He said not a word, but eventually they trooped into the distance towards the shipping office. We sat, some got out, everybody chattering at the top of their voices. At 6.30 Daddy Long Legs reappeared with a frightfully smart man in white trousers who proceeded to check off the tickets against the money. To everybody's surprise they balanced!

Finally we left, two men rowing like billy-oh, and the helmsman standing in the bow with a tiller. We careered towards the rapids but Daddy Long Legs was skilful. Monkeys in trees on the bank and a large Buddhist temple. It grew dark and the waters became quieter. Suddenly we catapulted into the plain where the river is almost a mile wide. We reached a bamboo landing raft near nowhere and were decanted to walk a dark mile to Chattra. Suddenly we came to sand dunes, and arc lights, rusty bull-dozers, and lorries. It resembled the desolation of war. Finally we reached a 'road' and found a lorry, already full, which offered to take us to Dharan. We wedged ourselves in. There was a goat under my legs and two men on the roof of the cab. We stopped, and kept stopping, offering lifts to more and more people. We reached Dharan in an hour and a half, smothered in dust, but relieved to find a bath and an enormous meal. I am glad to have been on this trek to learn to understand a little the vast distances and enormous problems of the country. It has been interesting, but there is no wish to return – even to watch the flight of the snow geese in front of Everest and Makalu.

Having completed business in Dharan we travelled on what was at the time the only tarmac road in Nepal, through the flat wooded lands of the Terai to Siliguri, arriving the day war broke out between East Bengal and India. The station was crowded with troops and chaotic officials, but we eventually caught the train for Darjeeling which had to reverse to surmount the steep bends. We returned for a night to Dharan, then flew from Biritnagar to Kathmandu, staying in the Hotel Shanker, an old palace with marble pillars where waiters moved through dining rooms flicking egg shells onto the floor with their napkins. We wore army boots and everybody thought we were Russians. It was rather grand so we moved to a guest house spending two days sightseeing around endless temples before flying to Pokhara in Western Nepal, below Annapurna. We wanted to visit the Marsyandi Valley, home of many rare rhododendrons, but it was a restricted zone as the Khumbas were fighting the Chinese on the border. We met their mule trains returning for ammunition, sick animals being dumped on the nearest farmer to be retrieved only if they recovered. Trouble at the airfield when a crowd of irritated would-be travellers lay in front of the plane, but after returning to Kathmandu I flew alone, via an unpleasant night in Bangkok, to Hong Kong where my sister-in-law, ex-army matron, dosed me for hookworm as a prophylactic measure! It had been an extraordinary experience, but home was a relief. The sequel was showing slides to the WRI (Women's Rural Institute) of Amisfield who were horrified to find a mouse nesting in the projector!

Chapter 10

When a man gives out much, he absorbs much;
And it is good to live for the gods a bit; that is why some folk
Made pilgrimage to the Western Isles of Scotland.

Jessie Matthey, *Life of Tobias Matthey*

THAT SPRING was beautiful and I wondered why I had crossed the world to seek my soul. Scotland was home and I went with Iona, now aged ten, to the cattle sales in the Western Isles, moving from stance to stance and up through the Uists and Benbecula from Castlebay in Barra. We bought no cattle, but each day the sky was blue, reflected in a sapphire sea, with gannets plunging into the waves for fish. The first night the calves escaped from the pens, jumping into the harbour where a sailing ship was anchored, before running home to their crofts. On top of Heaval we sat on a rock beside an eagle, and I learnt to love the Islands, a mysterious continent, made stranger when Glasgow Airport had to consult the tide tables before giving the time of the Barra plane. We landed on the beach, the air full of the cry of birds, and along the road or across the heather, old wives enticed single cows and calves, walking in front with a wisp of hay while husbands followed behind. It was the start of another perspective in my life from whose wonder I have never escaped. We went on the little ferry from Eoligarry, where Compton Mackenzie lived while he wrote *Whisky Galore*, past Eriskay of the Love Lilt, with a lowland dealer lying on the bottom of the boat convinced he would be sick. Several years later I returned to Lochmaddy to help Ray Brill and Alastair Alexander with the grading of the calves for the cooperative, staying with Mrs Ferguson, No 2, Locheport. It was not to be the last of my visits to the Uists.

On the farms it was a time of huge change with intensification of animal and grassland production. Heavy stocking rates entailed the erection of more buildings, better handling facilities and increased fertiliser use. We kept a regular check on pH status using magnesium limestone and basic slag, but eventually deserted artificial compounds for slow release Humber fish manure which greatly benefited our permanent ryegrass/clover swards which had suffered when, led by Peter Maclaren, who had a stutter and a lovely wife, we had a brief flirtation with the nitrogen bag. It ended when I wrote a ditty about the 'acres and acres of blue drunken grass' for the *Journal of the S.W. Scotland Grassland Society*, concluding:

> And a cow that survives
> In the end on our books
> Needs an iron constitution
> As well as good looks!'

For two years we mucked out Robin Thompson's broiler house which gave me asthma and grew bigger and better docks in the Kirkland fields. We made silage awhile, but cutting it with a reaper and carting it with a buckrake through the narrow entrance of the barn, before rolling it endlessly to control the temperature, took all day for many weeks. Using a thermometer deluded us into thinking we were scientific, but the smell of my boots at the back door all winter scarcely justified the effort.

A grass recording scheme was administered by Idris Hunt and John Frame from the West of Scotland Agricultural College at Auchincruive, which also used our financial figures for their annual surveys. A new dipper and bughts at Killyleoch, and portable cattle and sheep weighing machines enabled us to carry out regular dosing programmes and to sell stock at the weights the market demanded. We treated young cattle for husk in spring and administered what Bill Stewart called a Bastille Day dose on 14 July. He was an excellent single handed vet whose career had commenced with racehorses in New Zealand. Having found his customers crooked he withdrew and set up in Dunscore where he led a stressful life, attending one difficult calving at Kirkland in his dinner jacket. Eventually Rory Cessford, whose wife had an English setter with an enormous litter of profitable puppies, replaced him. Their expertise saved money and time, and instead of haggling endlessly with medicine men on the Whitesands in Dumfries on market day – a Byzantine process resulting in some salesman undercutting the firm which produced the medicine – we bought everything from the vets or Jack Bryden at Woolgrowers.

The beautiful Irish cows were slaughtered when, attempting to speed up an increase in stock, we bought ten in-calf, as well as ten bulling heifers from Pointzpass 229. They were infected with brucellosis. Subsequently we bought 46 milky Northern Dairy Shorthorns at a farm sale near Eynsham in Oxfordshire which each reared eight calves a year, mostly purchased through a reputable dealer. Unfortunately one load from Sturminster Newton was mixed with a load from Chelford, and the Wiltshire and Cheshire bugs were as incompatible as many people's computer systems. The result was a fountain of skitter, requiring calves to be dosed with salt and water every four hours, night and day, and forty six cows to be hand-milked. That temperamental summer is an exhausting memory. It concluded with a hundred young cattle nobody wanted, but over the years dealers who bought our cattle in Castle Douglas – George Barbour of Auchengibbert and Jack Mounsey from Cockermouth – paid fair prices. Although the foot and mouth outbreak of 2001 brought dealers a bad name, the service they provide has been vital to the northern livestock industry ever since the days of the Falkirk Trysts.

On entry to Killyleoch and Farmersfield, eventually occupied by Bobby Carson, a connection of James Taylor who he assisted, the whole farm was covered with Stinking Willy, the result of continuous grazing with only cattle. Dykes, wrecked by cows scraping their mangy necks, were incapable of containing sheep, but with top wires and electric nets they were gradually improved. We turned to ewes which bit the rosettes out of the ragwort in spring. No matter the demands of public life I was always present at lambing time, leaving home at five, and learning over the years which field corners individual ewes chose to lamb. It became a sixth sense. We had good motherly Greyface ewes, purchased as gimmers at Castle Douglas and mated with Suffolk tups. Once a fox drove twenty five lambs onto ice which collapsed and drowned them, and occasionally, having helped a ewe to lamb, and gone elsewhere while she prepared for a second, it was heartbreaking to return to find the first one taken. They say foxes only take carrion, but it isn't true. In 1976, a year of terrible drought with fields burnt brown, we started a flock of 150 Clun ewes, entering the Meat and Livestock Commission (on one of whose committees I eventually sat) Recording Scheme, which proved a useful discipline, although weighing lambs at birth with rain pouring down one's nose and entering them in the book before tagging and castrating them was a fair imitation of hell. For the Cheviot Sheep Society Centenary Dinner I wrote these indifferent lines aimed at Michael Scott of Troloss, a renowned Blackface breeder.

The Ghost of Glenochar

Oh! The ghost of Glenochar
Was born long ago
When the fields of Dalpeddar
Were covered with snow.

They whitened his face,
A right ugly beast,
And took him to Lockerbie
Dressed to deceive.

He got never a bid,
Unlucky they were
So they took him back home
To eat at New Year.

But the bold boy deceived them,
Slipped over the dyke,
When the dog was asleep
He got onto his bike.
He served every ewe
On Dalpeddar that night,
Then took away eastwards
Before the first light.

He made for Leadhills
Where he lived in a wood
Of ugly dark sitkas
Below the old road.

Tom Scott was amazed
When he went to his lambing
To find the bold boy
Had nicked well with the ewes.

So he wandered around
Like a soul in despair
Till the day that he found him
Come out of thin air.

At the sheep sales that year
Old Thomson was rich
With the progeny got
By that randy young tip.

Eight years he performed
And all was forgiven
After most of his peers
Had been taken to Heaven.

They decided one day
That enough was enough,
But one final fling
They would give to their tup.

As they sped past Troloss
Through a slit in the trailer
He spied what he'd dreamed of,
The bonniest ewe.

Brockled her face,
Her horns were well set –
She was far the best ewe
Michael Scott ever bred.

As autumn returned
They intended to loose him
With the best forty sheep
That a shepherd could pick.

But one night in October
With the moon over Daer
He decided to flit
And his thoughts ran afar.

So he jumped in the burn
And swam down to Glengeith,
Where out from the waters
He clambered at length.

As he came to the road
He suddenly thought
Of the love of his life
That he'd spied from the trailer.

A fruit they'd forbid him,
If ever they knew,
The harm she might do him,
That bonniest ewe.

But nothing could hold
The bold boy from his fun,
So he slid down the road
On his ugly white bum.

For the Lanarkshire Council,
Aye strapped for spare cash
Had not gritted the road
Which was covered with ice.

When the moon settled down
Beyond Queensberry's top
And the first streaks of dawn
Had slid up from the East
The laird of Troloss
Strode off down the road
On his morning patrol
Of his pedigree sheep.

Imagine his horror
When came into view
A hole in the dyke
Where he'd left his prize ewe.

While she stood with a glow
On her admirable head
By her well polished feet
A Cheviot lay dead.

There's a rowan tree there
In the park at Troloss
And that's where the ewe
Confronted her boss,
With a quite illegitimate
Bonny tup lamb.

Michael Scott left it too late
To mark the wee brute
So what did he do
But bring him right out
To sell in September
At Lanark tup sales

Fifty two thousand pounds
Was the price that he made
The priciest 'Blackface'
Clarke ever sold.

So drink to the Cheviots
And drink to their herds,
And drink to the Ghost
That still stalks at Glenochar
For none can surpass
That libidinous tup
Who I'm sure is still laughing
At the back of the bught.

In Annan I once bought a score of Teeswater Cross ewes and a dog from David Brown at Borgue, along with a very wild cross ewe with two spikes for horns. We called her Carnegie. Each lambing she disappeared for three weeks returning with beautiful twins. Difficult to control she careered around the bughts with my stick around her neck until suddenly stopping to catapult me over her head, grazing my face on the concrete. We bought another six old ewes from Sam Vallance of Poundland who didn't want the laird, who was my laird's brother, to have them, when he retired. Originally from Borrobol in Sutherland, one Cheviot was six years old, with one tooth and a lame leg. For five more years she produced triplets and reared beautiful lambs and when putting her in the lorry I was so upset, we had to take her out again. She had twins for two more years. Her breeder, Lady (Beans) Wigan, competed at the sales with two other redoubtable Sutherland widows, Mrs Tyser of Gordonbush and Lady Paynter of Suisgill. She once fell in the Helmsdale with the ghillie on top of her and catching a chill was confined to bed. When the fish started running she sent for ice to keep in her mouth until the doctor came to pronounce her temperature low enough to return to the river. We speaned the lambs promptly, selling many of them for slaughter straight off their mothers. Eric Houston of FMC usually helped us draw them and when an acquaintance died his comment was: 'Patrick, you have to remember we're all in the drawing pen now!'

In 1969 we took over the Home Farm at Muncaster. John Whitelaw, originating in Wigtownshire, was grieve. I visited every week or two, 108 miles each way, paid the bills, and began to revive my interest in the gardens. John was hard, inconsiderate of his two helpers, and mean to land and beast. He was on a profit sharing basis but in retrospect his desire to show profit meant the farm was starved of essential resources. Fences were in a mess and the buildings inadequate and neglected. Nonetheless Muncaster stock sold well in the markets, and John was honest. He was like Billy Goat Gruff with his long suffering wife Maisie, and constantly complained about daughter Carol who won all the local beauty competitions, having to be primped up month after month like a champion heifer for the Royal Show, coming back engaged to a different fellow each time, including our ex-student, Alastair Mackintosh, who was boarding as a single shepherd with the Whitelaws. Carol was briefly estate secretary, but left sharpish when father-in-law found her sitting on the recently-widowed curator's knee in the office. Philip Denham-Cookes, the next curator, with his wife Iris, did much to keep things going in the house which had opened to the public in 1968. Philip had been in the RAF, and farmed briefly near Dumfries, before becoming agent at Bliffield. He had a fiery temperament, looked like the Sandy Whiskered Gentleman, and formed an unlikely alliance with Charley Carlisle. His mother was Ursula Bloom, who competed with Barbara Cartland and was reputed to have written more books than anyone alive or dead. At the end the poor soul trundled around London supermarkets putting tins of asparagus, which she loathed, into her trolley, while her minder followed returning them to the shelf.

The farm was stocked with 900 Mule ewes producing Suffolk cross lambs, and 80 Bluegrey cows, purchased as heifers and served by Charolais bulls – too many for land which poached badly in winter, with little shelter and inadequate buildings. Lambing percentages were high, but so was the death rate. We did however install a proper dipper and modern handling facilities.

The garden was well stocked with wild-sourced plants and six gardeners, the head being David Robertson, son-in-law of Lee his predecessor, and knowledgeable. David Davidian, the rhododendron guru from Edinburgh, visited occasionally. He grumbled about the new curator at the Royal Botanic Gardens who had removed some of the shelter from his precious plants and eventually felt so strongly he was reputed to have farmed out delicate stock to friends with window-boxes around the New Town, knowing they would care for them. He despised hybrids, and when asked the pedigree of a particularly beautiful flower his inevitable comment was: 'Naughty little bees, Patrick!' The badly neglected greenhouses cost a fortune to heat, but a new mist-spray propagation unit was erected, with a modern greenhouse in what had been the kitchen garden and was now the standing ground. Contract and design work had been undertaken outside to the detriment of the gardens. There was a complete lack of costing, and an indiscriminate propagation programme, conducted by Bob Godsell, who churned out masses of cuttings which were neither sold, repotted, nor planted out. He had a brilliant eccentric brain, and it must have been heartbreaking, but he shrugged his shoulders and continued teaching illiterate people to read while the garden became increasingly overgrown. I wish now I had taken more time to learn what David Robertson and Bob could have taught me. Neither my parents-in-law, nor any of the agents, nor I, provided the lead which the knowledge of those two men demanded, and which would have saved the garden from becoming the wilderness it was when Phyllida and I came to live at Muncaster in 1982. Management was paralysed by the thought of losing ever more money, an occasional agent, an often absent owner, and a rudderless business.

Grandfather's unthinned woodland nurseries had been increasingly drawn by a dense canopy of enormous beeches, planted in 1783 by the first Lord Muncaster, and many had matured into spindly plants vulnerable to the wind. Blown timber was extracted by cowboy contractors who didn't care tuppence about damaging the plants. Unmarketable logs lay where they were left to spread honey fungus. Later Arthur Wilson, and his son Murray, were skilful at felling and extraction doing minimum harm. The malignant neglect of the garden was uncompensated by contracting income or the sales of plants, hanging baskets, and wreaths at which Marion Robertson excelled.

With the vigour of a new broom I attended a weekend course with eleven others at a hotel near Northampton to discuss Nursery Costings. We were asked to enlighten the colleagues on each other's businesses. One stated immodestly, in a heavy Dutch accent: 'I run my greenhouses on a such-and-such system. I grow 3 million euphorbia, 3 million chrysanthemum a year. My turnover is £1.3m. and my profit £750k.' The other had a turnover of £750 and a profit of £400k. I felt idiotic saying Muncaster's turnover was £30k., and the loss £6k., and my mother-in-law kept three donkeys to eat the grass. It did, however, teach me a lot.

Briefly, in the 1960s, Judy Biggar came monthly from Farm Business Records to do the Kirkland accounts. She was skilful without being pushy and taught me how to organise paperwork. When she married Finlay McGowan her place was taken by a young man whose name I luckily forget. He caused chaos and one whole year's accounts had to be rewritten before the accountant could understand them. Later we employed Fiona Waugh as secretary. She came from Effgill near Langholm and had passed top out of Kirkley Hall, but was continually ill. In the end she unsuccessfully married Brin Arneil who had written a thesis on blackbirds. Her mother, a sculptress, kept Pharaoh hounds and judged at Crufts, but was removed from the panel when one of her dogs bit the judge at a show. Thereafter I wrote my own cheques, kept my own records, and although the need to know is a family failing – after one Muncaster meeting my son-in-law recorded in the minutes: 'Iona's father said she could do with half an inch off the end of her nose' – it does keep a constant finger on the pulse of the business. The combination of Uncle Edward's and Judy Biggar's tuition has enabled me to be honest with myself about figures and has simplified life far beyond the costly confusion of City lawyers and accountants, who are delightful but expensive company.

Over many years I became familiar with lawyers, accountants, stockbrokers and auctioneers. The family solicitor in London was John Gilbart-Smith of Fladgates in Pall Mall, an urbane Old Harrovian who played squash at lunchtime, was kind, changed my name by deed poll satisfactorily, but took ages to transact business. When Uncle Edward died in June 1973 my mother transferred to Christopher Parish at Macfarlanes. Following her up the London streets that summer was an experience. She strode into the Trustee Department of the National Westminster Bank. 'Close my account – you're useless!', and she fired the accountants before going to lunch at the Ritz where she took a swig at her whisky flask in the ladies' loo, before entering the restaurant where she drank water. It was a difficult time for her, not made easier when her eldest grand-daughter, in constant revolt, absconded twice in a week from Constance Spry's Cordon Bleu School at Winkfield and was taken by her and Phyllida to see an unpractical psychiatrist who said she needn't go home with her family. As they boarded the train at Waterloo to return to Rotherwick Prunella took off up the platform, pursued by her recently bereaved grandmother who pulled her hair saying: 'Now listen, my girl!' whereupon the onlookers surrounded them and summoned the police. A young constable told her she was seventeen and a free agent, but luckily a Dixon of Dock Green character appeared asking where she intended to go, relating the tale of his own daughter who thought she could live independently in London on her wages from Peter Jones. Prunella lived in a state of high rebellion and with her sisters warrants a separate book.

The Pennington lawyers were Thicknesse and Hull, later William Sturges and Co. who had made a considerable living from the family's tangled affairs. Their office at 16 Great College Street, resembled a scene from Dickens – dark panels, spiders, and the smell of expensive leather. The senior partner was Roden James. His successor Rae Shephard who had been at Hartley's in the 1930s, a Guards officer in the War, was unqualified, and totally useless. A bon viveur, he took the family to lunches at Boodles, the expense being added to his bills. Once Veronica told us Bobby was in financial straits. I visited James to enquire if we should help. Unfortunately it was Friday afternoon. A passer-by murmured: 'Didn't you know it was poet's day in London' (Push Off Early Tomorrow's Saturday). Next time I made an appointment and in response to my enquiry if father-in-law was badly off James stood at the top of six steps, legs astride, thumbs in braces, pronouncing: 'My dear boy, poverty is comparative!' Once Rae Shephard asked us to meet him on the fourth green of Sunningdale Golf Club in a snowstorm to discuss 'important business'. It resembled a spy story, he dressed in British warm, and an Old Etonian tie, with a brown pork-pie hat pulled over his eyes, while we shivered, snow creeping up through soles of city shoes.

Rae's place was taken by David Morris who over time has done much to simplify the complications of the family business. It took him many years to sort out Grandfather's and Bobby's affairs with the Capital Taxes Office and when I visited them in Shepherd's Bush before their move to Nottingham I could sympathise with the grinding boredom of the work and marvelled at Mr Still's good nature. While waiting I read ten current commitments to service in all of which they were in breach! Some of the family have been heard to curse David, but to me he was always kind, occasionally visiting Muncaster, and once having me to stay with him and his wife Maggie who entertained a family of foxes at the end of their garden in Putney. Eventually the Muncaster business was transferred to Brian Stevens, and later to Andrew Lane, of Withers, with Cartmel Shepherd dealing with local matters.

In 1971, Bruce and Edna Watson, my brother's parents-in-law, asked us to take in Rona Dent, a daughter whose husband was trying to prove she was too mad to look after their two children. She wasn't, having learnt to drive at the expense of our car and our gatepost! Bruce, an ascetic Glaswegian, ex-tea planter in Assam, had married Edna whose first husband drank, drowning himself in a well in India. They lived in a house in Wiltshire with kingfishers sitting on a branch outside the windows. From there Roderick and Patricia were married in 1965 just before my father's death, and there at my niece Nicola's christening I met Angie Thorne (Penrhyn-Jones), an actress with a lovely personality endlessly famous for her part with Penelope Keith in *To the Manor Born*. John Dent's grandfather, Dog Dent, was the MP who introduced the Bill for Dog Licences. On marriage John took Rona to America where he taught at Phillips Academy, putting her out to work. She hurt her back, had an operation which went wrong, and returned to London for another. While she was in hospital he ran off with an Australian actress in the next door bed who had taken an overdose and when Rona came out they barred the doors against her before taking the children to America. She did secretarial work for us, and when she had settled down we let her the old farmhouse in the village before trying to help recover her two very young sons. It went badly. She was on legal aid with a lawyer in Brighton. Eventually we went to speak for her in the Law Courts in London and my heart rose when the judge arrived with knickerbockers under his gown. The enemy lawyer turned to Phyllida:

'The only accommodation this woman has to offer these children is a farmhouse, at the end of a row of cottages, in a little village in Scotland, and over the door, my Lord, is written the date 1786. Now, Mrs Gordon Duff Pennington, are those the sort of conditions young children should be brought up in?'

Sir George Baker: 'Mr W., I must intervene. Plainly you know little of conditions in Scotland. I was born there, brought up there, and educated there, and have to point out that houses, particularly farmhouses, particularly of that age, have usually been well built, well maintained, and well modernised. In addition to which, Mr W., I have to inform you that your chambers in the Inner Temple are a great deal older.'

John Dent was told to pay up for the children's maintenance – which he didn't. Six months later we returned to court under a different judge, where I read the 'Ballad of the Belstane Fox' under the desk.

Judge: 'Why didn't you pay up, Mr Dent?'

JD: 'I didn't think Sir George meant it!'

Chapter 11

The prime use of the land is for the employment of the people.
Douglas Calder, *Chief Planning Officer, Inverness*

IN SCOTLAND Ardverikie legal business was conducted by Howard Butters of Dundas and Wilson, tall, slim, and precise, but never knowing which way to look when the family verbally gutted each other at AGMs. My perch was the office log basket between mother-in-law and Aunt Joyce to deprive them of ammunition. Howard's son John took over, wise, swift, and decisive. Although of unhealthy complexion, he was fit, sometimes camping overnight in the hills on his way to meetings. When asked: 'I suppose we'll soon hear you're one of those idiots wanting to sail the Atlantic single-handed?' 'Actually,' he said, 'I did last year!' At fifty he decided there was more to life than law, so bicycled around the world, returning to marry Sarah Cockburn, daughter of a Scottish judge. He lived in Moray Place, doing public work, entrusting his clients to Robert Turcan. Also there was Aunt – who wasn't – Elspeth Hobkirk, past Governor of the women's prison in Greenock, whose ex-customers sometimes tapped her shoulder in the street enquiring: 'How ya doin', hen?' Deputy head of the ATS in the War after youth at Cleddon in South Wales, she had spent time in Riga, of which she painted lovely colourful pictures. She sheltered and encouraged me as I spent increasing hours on NFUS business at 17 Grosvenor Crescent, Edinburgh where Dumfriesshire sent me in 1972 as a Council representative. Thither I went, driven sometimes, petrified, by Aird Smith of Drumhumphry who was colour blind and ignored traffic lights. I served on the Livestock Committee under Sylvester Campbell and John Cameron, both later Union President, and was Vice-Convenor for four years under George Anderson of Kair, Fordoun. From 1976 I sat on the GP Committee, sometimes sharing spectacles with the Pigs Convenor, Fiona Dalrymple, and for six years was Convenor of the Hill Farming sub-Committee, the largest committee in the Union, whose secretary was Richard Henton. A notice on his door proclaimed. 'You are entering Cattle Country. Eat beef, you bastard.' In 1972 Harry Munro was Director, an ex-airman who disapproved of me. The President was Jim Stobo of Fishwick, with unfulfilled political ambitions. Later, when chairman of the Scottish Quality Lamb Association sitting opposite me at a Border Area dinner where Alec Douglas-Home was speaking he was enraged to find 'NZ Lamb' stamped across the skin of his meat. At Council Meetings the Press liked me. I wasn't reticent and my name was very long at a time when journalists were paid by the word. Years later Auslan Cramb was kind enough to write a headline under my awful picture: 'Outrageous, outspoken, and outstanding.' Committee days left indelible impressions. After lunch provided by Mrs Carrick, the caretaker's wife, Henry Christie, Milk Convenor, always did his teeth in the gents. Seamus, later Duke of Montrose, when others introduced themselves by christian name said 'Lord Graham'. I thought 'Corr!' but amended my views when offered a hand, black with tractor oil. Later, visiting Winnie Cooper at the Ord, Rhynie in a snowstorm there was nowhere to sit except the floor. Robbie, her late father, had been a well known Blackface breeder, and when his widow seemed rather patronising I said: 'You know, I too keep sheep.' 'Aye,' she replied, 'I kent ye was a wurkin' loon – I lookit at your haaands!' – which were covered with violet foot spray.

In 1974 Mr Heath took Britain into the Common Market, removing all support for beef, forecasting a secure future for unlimited production. The market collapsed. Irish cattle poured into the ports until there was no space to kill our own cattle in Scottish slaughterhouses. On 10 November the Livestock Committee lobbied Parliament. Returning to a London roost at evening the Underground stuck at Sloane Square where, to my mother's horror, I stood on the platform addressing the crowd on problems facing the Scottish beef industry. The following night was spent on the picket lines at Merkland Dock in Glasgow. I am glad I was there, because when people thump the table at meetings demanding militant action I know they weren't. Not many were. It was a boring night around a brazier wearing father's greatcoat from 1917 with holes from the phosphorous bomb at Inverness Tattoo. The police came, helpful, and one black cat and four black rats. Towards dawn a disapproving Sylvie Campbell and his bag men appeared. Eventually the Government reacted when the Welsh rolled a rock onto a railway line and something was done to rationalise the situation. It was the start of Green Pound aggravation which, as currencies stood, acted as subsidy on imports and tax on exports. It negated our tick for Europe which we had wrongly assumed meant free trade in a large market with uniform prices across the Community.

Several years later I demonstrated again, leading a march with John Cameron and Henry Christie to the French Consulate whose countrymen were dumping our lambs in the sea. The odious and unimproved Jacques Chirac was their agricultural minister at the time, a chauvinist to the tips of his toes. Three of us entered and the Consul, shaking, but with unblinking eyes, stated firmly: 'Gentlemen, I must inform you it is the duty of any government, whatever the law, to protect the interests of its citizens.' I wished that man might have been Prime Minister of Britain!

My primary duty was to the Dumfriesshire and Stewartry farmers who sent me to Edinburgh, and it was necessary to know as many as possible – and their worries. At the 1974 election Heath lost. Wilf Shaw and I were accused of stupidity after we wrote (I wrote and he sent!) to the local MPs, Hector Monro and John Brewis, that we might advise our members against voting for them in view of their Government's mishandling of the beef situation. Harold Wilson won the election and in 1976 I succeeded Jim Brown, an able farmer from Birthwood, Biggar, as Hill Farming Convenor. Scott Johnston, by then Director, called me and said the poison chalice was mine, but it was the start of twenty five wonderful years stumping about the Scottish countryside, learning to speak out, but also to find reasons why a reluctant Treasury needed to support the hills. It was a social matter, but the sensible structure of the industry with the hills producing healthy store stock to be finished or used for further breeding on low ground farms added greatly to the validity of the case. I wrote to Scottish rural MPs in longhand and frequently spent weekends telephoning Government Ministers – a habit detested by their civil servants and the Union. For the next quarter century the Central Lobby of the House of Commons became my middle class version of 'underneath the arches' when cold and wet. It infuriated me that most NFU publicity was for big grain and milk producers while those in the Less Favoured Areas (LFA) were ignored except for occasional press releases which appeared in agricultural columns of the national press and the *Scottish Farmer* and were read only by farmers and their wives. I located the Consumer writer of the *Glasgow Herald*, Heather Rose, asked her to lunch, and presented her with a bunch of red roses which proved a good investment. She gave hill farmers a whole page in the Consumer section of the paper. Victoria Hainworth wrote a sympathetic article in the *Radio Times* in which I was reported as questioning the right of a spider to be given precedence over the livelihood of a small Lanarkshire farmer who desperately needed to drain a bog. An angry environmentalist telephoned the following day. I also made friends with Joan Mackintosh, chairman of the Scottish Consumer Council, asking her to speak to an Area meeting in Dumfries, a night never to be forgotten when the dog stole the pâté off the table at Kirkland before supper. Later I sat with Laura Grimond and Father Colin MacInnes from South Uist on Joan's Committee, producing a report on Consumers in the Rural Areas. She remained a too occasional friend, and became Legal Ombudsman in Scotland before retiring to Auchterarder. NFU management was dubious about my connections and determined to keep agriculture in a separate box – a disastrous policy for its members, who comprised less than 2 per cent of the electorate and were beginning to be in desperate need of allies.

In 1976 the European Sheepmeat Regulation was agreed, bringing essential money into the LFAs, but the headage payments and later the Sheep Annual Premium Scheme have wrecked the structure of Scottish agriculture and given rise to the current environmental crisis with the divorce of farming business from the land. My first meeting at DAFS before the Hill Farming Review provoked Boyd Gordon's comment: 'If you do not moderate your tone you are not welcome to return!', but he became a trusted friend. His successors and their superiors have since been unfailingly kind and courteous in our dealings, always making allowances for their eccentric customer, despite having their own worries with a domineering Whitehall. Those who remain clearest in memory are Ronnie Cramond; Sir Muir Russell, later Permanent Secretary to the Scottish Executive; Kenneth Mackenzie; Tony (Shirtsleeves) Cameron; Charlie Mackay, educated at a side school at Tongue whither he went in bare feet; Donald Collie, who played hockey; Richard Grant, responsible for the Red Deer Commission, and his successor Isabelle Low to whom, on her appointment, I sent a postcard with a stag to remind her of my interests and her responsibilities but spoilt the effect by spelling both her names wrong. Although subsidy was essential to keep men and dogs – and families – in remote areas it demanded a more progressive attitude from hill farmers themselves, a view reinforced by meeting Robin Armstrong, in charge of the Hill Farming Research Organisation (HFRO) farm at Sourhope and listening to John Arbuthnott delivering a lecture at their headquarters at the Bush. I began calling on Ian Cunningham, HFRO Director every two or three weeks after accompanying him to Tyne Tees television at Newcastle. It was my first time on the box and I was nervous, made worse by the staff striking in the middle of the programme, during which the make-up lady cut my hair. Having been nice about the Shetlanders whose sheep had been driven into the sea by a blizzard, it was overwhelming at the end when a man from Lerwick swung himself from the beams and grasped my hand. Ian Cunningham and his wife Nancy have been friends ever since. His successor at HFRO, John Eadie, had insufficient credit for his work because he hated writing up his research. They pioneered the two pasture system, a simple grazing regime requiring minimum funding, but failure of too many advisers to promote its benefits set back hill farming's contribution to the Scottish economy by many years. Successive Treasury officials from the time of Mrs Thatcher have never understood development and research are intimately connected. Their increasing unwillingness to fund one without supporting the other has been against the national interest.

Hill Farming Reviews in Whitehall were heavy occasions. The English, Sidney Fawcett and Oliver Allison, nice as they were, were unprepared to fire bullets for fear of upsetting traditional arrangements with MAFF. At my first meeting I was nervous until remembering an entertaining and totally unsuitable story about the father of the Minister sitting opposite – a relaxing thought. After another, boarding the train at Euston, two Indian children approached with a man asking me to see he was all right. At Rugby he started to wave. I thought he was new out of Bombay – which he wasn't. Deaf and dumb he pointed at his paper. Sign Language learnt at St. Peter's allowed us to communicate. He disliked Idi Amin, having been his passport clerk in Uganda, had three wives in London, Leicester and New York, with thirteen children, and was a ship's chandler in Hamilton, Scotland. I explained on my fingers difficulties hill farmers faced with HMG, and was astonished, alighting at Dumfries, to be tapped on the shoulder by a geography teacher from the Campion School at Hornchurch who thought his pupils would be interested in my conversation with the Indian. He took my address and two years later called me to arms. Boarding a train at Hook was my first encounter with an anonymous Valerie Profumo, the start of a distant but lasting friendship with her and her husband, two fine people whose memory is still unfairly raked over by the gutter press. We parted at Waterloo, she to the dentist and I on a lonely terrifying journey to Hornchurch for a worthwhile encounter with students who had never seen Scotland, let alone a hill farm.

Six years I was Hill Farming Convenor and for two of them Honorary President of the Union which made me many friends, and before each Hill Farming Review six weeks were spent traversing Scotland collecting information from auctioneers, banks, College offices, as well as farmers and their wives. At Kinlochlaggan the Inn had closed and the Post Office. The Highland and Island Cinema no longer came. Rural communities throughout the hills were withering, fuelling my indignation – and my eloquence. When it snowed I usually made for Tomintoul or Hugh MacInnes, Farmton of Glenkindie at the foot of Strathdon, and held stormbound meetings at Lumphanan Crossroads. Once my photograph appeared in the *Press and Journal* up to my waist in snow at Auchorachan in Glenlivet, a message diluted by a report on the opposite page of the Maconochies receiving £4k. for a bull in Perth. Another night, slithering on ice and drifting snow down the Avon to Dufftown, I could reach no further than Lal MacDonald, Dalbuiack, Carrbridge who everybody assured me would never give me shelter, but he and his daughter took me in. Once a fiddler, after supper he said: 'Mairy, the laddie likes music. Put on "Lament for Mary Queen of Scots on her way to the Scaffold",' an appropriate tune, in time to which he waved his pipe. Recently widowed, he installed me in the former marital bed, awakening me at 3.30 a.m. to drive to Edinburgh. We stood in the steading discussing the stars before I set off through the frozen night. Such kindness I met in so many places, and was glad after twenty four years of friendship to be at the funeral of that knowledgeable and capable man.

There were speaking engagements throughout Scotland – and Orkney and Shetland, who dislike being lumped with the rest. When called up in 1939 the Shetlanders wrote Bergen as their nearest railway station which the southern English couldn't understand. Days were spent, before evening meetings, visiting farms with the Area Secretaries to see problems on the ground. To Shetland and back by air cost as much as Edinburgh to New York return and was sometimes frustrated by winds and once by a pilot who overslept. Florence Grains, the Iron Fist in the Velvet Glove, was Secretary there. Jonathan Wills, candidate for Parliament, once lighthouse keeper at Muckle Flugga, ran Radio Shetland. I stayed with John and Wendy Scott at Gardie on Bressay where helping John to carry feed blocks to the top of the Noop of Noss, dive-bombed by bonxies, with the sea all round, and a hundred and fifty islands was magic. Once we travelled to Unst. We visited the Budges at Bigton, and Willie Mainland, and the Irvings at Bixter. Emerging thence one night into a snowy wasteland we found the incongruous sight of a Norman Frenchman who had cut off his finger in the fish factory at Walls and was on his way for treatment at Scalloway, where the wicked Earl Patrick had built his castle using white of egg as mortar. To Shetland, too, drifted Andrew Harmsworth, our ex-student, once my brother's brother-officer in the Queen's Own Highlanders. He married Sarah, a general's daughter from Dorset, and when his father Michael, who drank a bottle of whisky each evening and dined at midnight, was asked to stay for the wedding he replied: 'I never stay with strangers.' Andrew became religious and was living testimony to 'the Lord will provide' when they lived one whole winter in a beach hut on Shetland with two infant children without a cross word while they waited for a house.

Orkney was different, full of Norse relics, a fertile place of skilled cattlemen like Scott Harcus, plagued by its distance from its main market in Aberdeen. One summer we went with Neil and Barbara Findlay, and four children, on a boat hired from Jamie Bruce and skippered by Jimmy Flett, ex-captain of the North Isles Ferry, famous for amazing feats of seamanship in impossible gales. An excellent tutor on the pedigree and performance of the island people he described how, in a fog, seeking the channel between Eday and the Calf of Eday, he whistled to find if the seabirds had green legs or red to identify his position, then shouted. When the echoes from both sides coincided he knew he was on course. One night we entered the harbour at Whitehall past Papa Stronsay and the grave of an eight foot Dane on the Romaynes' farm. Every second house was empty since the herring fleet left and the young ones gone. We landed on Eday, and at Rousay went at breakfast time to Reo Ritchie, a drunken character who lent us his unlicensed Land Rover. I wrote in a letter:

> Last night I was in Rousay,
> Dancing with the children at the Flower Show dance.
> Reo Ritchie took us to Trumland,
> Gave us gin.
> I poured it in the flowers when he wasn't looking,
> A tumblerful completely neat.
> In the morning we had fresh fish
> And I walked among the fuchsia hedges on the hill.
> The flowers in the gin were dead.

It rained incessantly, with machines bogged in the silage fields and anxiety about winter keep. We visited St. Magnus' Cathedral and often in the distance watched the church on Egilsay where Magnus was murdered by Half Dan Longlegs. I shall never forget sailing from Scrabster past the rose-red cliffs of Hoy, first sight of land for so many mariners returning from Atlantic convoys, and then the entrance to Stromness harbour where we had only dropped anchor ten minutes when a small boy appeared enquiring who was on board. Unfortunately it was George Burger, the Area Secretary's nephew, and was the signal to visit his farmers, despite having promised Phyllida I would have nothing to do with agriculture for two weeks. Howie Firth ran Radio Orkney and as elsewhere I was expected to issue a war-cry.

Although Eddie MacDonald was Secretary of both Caithness and Sutherland, speaking at their meetings on consecutive nights was difficult. Maurice Pottinger and the men of Caithness expected me to listen carefully to interminable complaints, while the Sutherland men wanted to know my thoughts. At Golspie were Robin McCall, his brother Alan, Willie Murray, and Mike Burnett, shortly to become President of the Union before departing temporarily for missionary work in southern Africa. Margaret Thomson, daughter of Lord Migdale, grand-daughter of Carnegies of Skibo, became a particular ally. A firm but gentle touch made her a talented and successful stockwoman. Having read of Ospisdale in the *Scottish Farmer* it seemed sensible to seek her assessment of the current situation. Hilda, her helper, told me she was out, but if I telephoned at night she would be home. Still out, she was up in the steading feeding her hedgehogs. Ever since I've known her as the Hedgehog Wife of Ospisdale. Although we seldom meet she has remained a warm-hearted and wise counsellor. Typically she befriended Harry, a young heron found smothered in soot on her bedroom chair after it descended the chimney in a storm, and with him she seems to have an understanding.

Having spoken at Dingwall one night a crofter from above Strathpeffer, Kenny Mackenzie, bent on trouble, well oiled with a twirly stick, rose to his feet. 'We have heard an awful lot of eloquence from the speaker, but what the hell happens?' I removed my jacket, rolled up my sleeves, and we fought. To my astonishment, at home arrived a letter saying he was well pleased with the service – and we remained in touch until his death. Also in Ross-shire was Air Commodore Duncan MacDonald Somerville, Loch Droma. After all my efforts it was maddening to read his letter in the *Scottish Farmer* saying nobody did anything for hill farmers. I put Bess in the back of the car at Kirkland, never slackening pace until Loch Droma. The Council had improved the road between Garve and Silver Bridge and his lambs were sticking in heaps of tar left by the Highway Department. He addressed his MP, Hamish Gray, later Lord Gray of Contin, but unable to provoke an answer eventually wrote saying as he obviously knew little of hill farming would he please come and put the slates on the roof – a calculated insult as Hamish Gray's family were slaters.

Around Fort William Jock Hunter, Legal and Commercial convenor, held sway. Lochiel's factor, married to Joan, a saint, he became John Cameron's Vice President, which wasn't a success. Although knowledgeable and always kind to me, his judgement and loyalty were capricious. In Strathglass Iain Thomson, author of *Isolation Shepherd*, the Union's Highland and Island convenor lived at Breakachy up Strathglass. He thought I poached his preserves but his kindness remains unforgotten when he and Betty took me in after a pitched battle in Aberdeen with Russell Fairgrieve, MP for West Aberdeenshire, who lectured the Danish Christian Democrats on the compassion of the Tory Party. It was too much and I suggested he needed to buff up his ideas of compassion when he couldn't bother to visit his constituents in the aftermath of a blizzard. He demanded my dismissal from the Union and complained to Hector Monro about his awful constituent, only to be told if he had attended his business the incident would never have occurred. I was so furious I never slackened pace until reaching Breakachy and since then I have questioned whether any political party can command unquestioned allegiance or a monopoly of correct policies. What remains certain is that an over centralised state may be desirable for the convenience of the rulers, but can never be in the long term interest of its citizens.

In 1976 there were worries about winter keep in Morvern beyond the Corran Ferry which could only carry half a lorry load of hay at a time. The long route around Locheil was little better, the clearance under Drumsally Bridge having been measured by Captain Tony Bailey RN, known as Fox, with his umbrella. One Arctic night I stayed with him and Kali at Inversanda, leaving at dawn to watch his hounds at work. From a ditch, near the turning to the White Glen, jumped John Livingstone of Carnoch, a collie at his heels, a shotgun slung from his shoulder. 'I did not believe in the Captain's dogs,' says he, 'until one day, standing on the top of the hill along comes a fox and goes to ground at my feet. A piece of binder twine and the poke off my piece was all that I had, so I twiddles it round my stick and lights it with a match, pushing it into the hole. It singes the red brute's tail, so out she comes and they kills her at my feet. Now I pays my subscription.' Followed by: 'My father was a man of Kintyre and he would tell me how they killed the last fox in Kintyre before the Forestry Commission brought them back.' Foxes and trees competed for hill farmers' dislike, but the price paid for poor land for forestry at that time saved many a Highlander from bankruptcy, as well as providing work in the establishment stages, although insufficient care was taken about who would be responsible for the fences or where the trees were planted. A pulp mill was built at Corpach, but its processes were outdated before it started, crippling initial employment hopes. A huge investment in housing drained the population from hill areas in their search for higher pay and new homes and nobody would pick up an axe on a Monday morning without an injection of cash into their back pocket.

Chapter 12

*This is certainly a fine country to grow old in. I could
not spare a look to the young people, so much was I
engrossed in contemplating their grandmothers.*

Ann Grant (1755-1838) *Letters from the Mountains*

AMIDST THIS increasingly chaotic life the claustrophobia of an untidy home
made me run away. Peter and Frances Shand Kydd sheltered me at
Ardencaple on Seil, and the Borradailes in Somerset. The doctors gave me valium
– a course not to be recommended for any seven year itch! Several times I went
to Tiree, gazing across to the Dutchman's Cap and the Treshnish Isles, visiting
Gunna at the time of the seal calves, looking for green stones on beaches, starting
to learn the romance of the Island seas – the excitement of the ferry at Oban,
sailing past Kerrera and up the Sound of Mull to Tobermory, before turning by
Bloody Bay to Coll and then to Scarinish. I met Neil MacFadyean, the ninety-
something father of John in Kerrera, delighted to have beaten Donald Pos Ban,
thirty years his junior, in a race. Once I worked an hour or two with Neil
Maclean and thought how good it would be to be a crofter in the Western Isles,
but staying for a meeting with Pat Ford, the vet in North Uist, with the gale and
the sea outside, I realised my constitution was too frail to withstand Atlantic gales
when feeding cattle. Pat competed for customers with the Wee Free Minister
who persuaded one of his followers to tie up a cow's tail with red ribbon to cure
abortion. Rev. Morrison's son, a journalist of unspeakable prejudice, later became
the Tourist Minister in the Scottish Parliament. When testing cattle on Vatersay
Pat had to survive for a day at a time on unlimited whisky and an oatcake, and
not much else. The widow who took me to the Islands remarried but has, with
her husband, over the years remained my constant friend – as have so many
others who have cared for me on my wanderings.

I returned to Phyllida and the family to whom I had been disloyal and
unkind, and now, everyday life without her there after forty eight years is
unthinkable. Her steadfastness, her love of family and her inheritance, of her
church, her ability to smile at someone she dislikes and shrug her shoulders
when things go wrong; her complete sincerity and will to work, are an
uncommon combination. Although I have strayed through the years, I have
always tried to give back as much friendship and affection as possible to those
who have been good to me and have been loyal to organisations for which I
worked and people I have served and loved. The news today that Phyllida needs
a heart bypass brings me face to face with myself and my shortcomings.

Once I contemplated an official job with livestock in the Highlands and Islands but Ronnie Cramond persuaded me, that after life in a large pool, dealing with Ministers and Civil Servants, working in a small one would kill me with frustration. Now, after thirty years wandering around Britain, learning to speak my mind on rural matters, the experience has confronted me with the fact that I am totally unsuited to detention for twelve months a year in a remote castle on the West Cumbrian coast, cut off from my vast acquaintance and the intellectual challenge of life in Westminster or Edinburgh. By nature a tinker, I love people, not possessions, and find enormous pleasure in helping them by making connections between my large circle of contacts. I feel imprisoned in a house, free on the road, all of which makes the writing of this book an uncomfortable experience of psycho-analysis – and me extremely difficult to live with, which perhaps goes back to the time of the falling-in-the-burn at Trinafour. At the end one is driven to the terrifying conclusion that not only do people change but in reality it is impossible for anyone to find in one single person the varied intellectual challenge and emotional response they need, and so my restless road went twirling on, desperately needing to be told I was loved. Later frustrated by detention in Muncaster these lines were written:

The Missing Word

Nobody knows.
Not once, in all of the years we were wed
Did you actually tell me you loved me
Though all of the rest of the world
Has always assumed that you did;
Not once, by the touch of a hand,
Nor the glance of any eye,
Nor a word's caress
Did you tell me;
So I grew to believe
I was there as a habit,
Less valued
Than all the four children we had, or our dogs;
Less valid
Than all of the care of the house
And the chattels
Your grandfather gathered to fill it,
And the beautiful garden he made.
I wanted so much to be loved for 'me'
For myself alone,
For the warmth and the kindness I owned long ago
When we both were young,
And not for the use I might be
Propping a monstrous irrelevance
Others had left to decay –

Wrangling with lawyers and agents, trustees,
Who knew even less than I knew –
Who made money for them,
And used the estate as a game.
All this I could do, and have done,
But the hours of cajoling the figures,
Of talking to trippers, and keeping the peace,
And enduring alone,
Have taken their toll at last.
All this I have done as a service for you,
Could have done it a long time yet
If only, you'd told me sometimes
That you loved me for me, and not for the things I could do.
I know it's my fault,
But now it's a little too late,
Soon I must go
Out of your life to a place
Where I can't feel hurt
And I can't hurt you,
Where I'm me
And not just part of a house
That can never be home.
I suppose
That somewhere deep down I must love you still,
But it's cold and I'm crying inside
At the thought of the loss of the years
And the life that we shared.
'I love you,' that's all that I needed so much to be told –
Only a word.

At one hill farming meeting the Nature Conservancy's proposal to reintroduce the white tailed eagle to Mull was on the agenda. As it had already done so there was little to add, but it was alarming to read in Bannerman's *British Birds* that it sometimes lifts lambs to a great height before dropping them to see if it can catch them before hitting the ground. It seemed unlikely that Bert Leitch at Laggan Ulva would welcome the experiment. I admire his daughter Kirsty who once came with a war party from Aberdeen University to Ardverikie to see the mechanics of a Highland estate and seemed astonished I knew her father. Another student, Andrew Crompton, sent me these touching words that sum up better than any of mine, my feelings for the land and the people of the Highlands.

I met a funny man one day
On Ardverikie Estate.
He drove me up and down his land,
With Mr Chalmer, an old mate.

We saw sheep and deer and suckler cows
And sitkas by the score –
And even a white elephant –
A house beside the shore.

He kept us well amused that day
With poems and stories too,
And advice to trust your own ideas
And only those you knew.
He said to trust the Colleges,
The HIDB as well,
But his views towards economists
Were all too clear to tell.

You see he has no time at all
For the money grabbing man
Who is only out to farm
For every penny that he can.
Instead he tries so very hard
To keep the jobs around.
He thinks this more important
Than the monetary pound.
And it gladdened me to see a man
With such ideas as these
At a time when every farmer
Feels the monetary squeeze.

So I wish him luck, good fortune,
With the lands within his care,
And should I return in future years
I trust he'll still be there.

But alas if he has gone
I will watch the swans depart
And remember the funny man I met
Who farmed straight from his heart.

I spoke at meetings in Mull and Islay, and Arran, and Bute, and all through Scotland. Mostly it was NFU, but sometimes the Blackface Sheepbreeders, (BFSB) on whose Council I served for a while, and sometimes the Young Farmers (YFC) who were kind – even respectful – in those distant days. They made me feel useful. At Aberdeen the BFSB Chairman, Pat Glass, upset me. Having driven 250 miles through snow it wasn't endearing to have to listen to a tedious oration about his visit to New Zealand, a long assessment of life as it was by Sylvester Campbell, and then to be told it was time to go home. The nicest people were often boring! At the mention of each of the places I went a mental photograph of all the people's faces still flashes through my memory and time spent on their farms or in their homes was more useful in identifying problems than any meeting or committee where the personal slant put on them in kitchens by wives and families was diminished. There are two apt sayings: 'Meetings breed meetings as rabbits breed rabbits only quicker,' and 'A committee is a place where otherwise sensible people take extraordinary decisions which they know in their hearts to be wrong.' Even better is from *Glimpses*, thoughts on life by Brendan Kennelly, Irish poet and Professor of Modern Literature at Trinity College Dublin.

> In heaven's name, is there anything boring as a meeting
> Where decent men and women sit
> For hours that feel like days
> Grinding the minds and arses off each other
> Yapping shit!

In Mull a strange alliance of Raymond Nelson, Glengorm, ex-Rifle Brigade, married to Janet, a lovely American; Robert Wilson, the vet; and John Angus MacDonald, a socialist crofter with a certain turn of phrase, who lived with his sister Chrissie at Lochdon; together with Donald MacGillivray, Glenforsa, and Hugh Macphail was beginning to move the community away from its nickname of the Officers' Mess gained when so many service men settled there after 1945. Attempting sensibly to retain as much local production as possible to cater for the quadrupling of the population in summer Glengorm grew tomatoes and a slaughterhouse was established. It was costly to send animals to market in Oban and much too expensive to bring them home from a bad sale. This the dealers understood and island stock was often undersold. Authorities in London and Brussels also understood, but it was hard trying to din into their heads that mainland areas such as Kintyre or Sutherland faced the same logistical problems as the Islands, often doubling costs. The vet sent oysters to Edinburgh from a fish farm in which he was involved, the empty van returning with cigarettes which he distributed to cash machines on his rounds. One snowy day John Angus was pulling out his hair. His tractor wouldn't start for which he blamed that 'bloody Tatcher woman'! Meetings were in the Western Isles Hotel at Craignure where the chairman was George MacRae, a skater, who had worked in the Falklands, and had three passports. Returning to Mull years later with Rural Forum it was impressive to see a community which had done so much to help itself.

On the Islay ferry the McGill and Smith traveller begged me not to miscall the clouds of geese which ravished the island, creating constant need for reseeding and making the Islay farmers his best customers. It raised once more all sorts of conservation issues and it was mildly shocking to be told by a girl from the RSPB in answer to a question about what would happen when there were too many geese to be accommodated on their own reserve that they would just buy more land. George Graham who ran the Co-operative was the Area Secretary and an ideal guide. Later I served with him on the committee of

SAOS, the body embracing the Scottish agricultural co-operatives whose Director was Edward Rainey Brown, later to succeed Scott Johnston as Chief Executive of NFUS at a most difficult time. Whisky was offered from dawn to dusk wherever we called which may have been good for the distilleries, but rapidly taught me to say 'no'! Over the years I returned several times to meetings and to the Islay Agricultural Society dinner where the loyalty of the farmers to their vet who had 'problems' was impressive.

In Mid-Argyll Archie MacIntyre from Minard was Secretary and for a meeting at Lochgilphead Phyllida and I stayed on a windy night with Robin and Susie Malcolm, listening to the sea outside, remembering the pibroch, 'Sound of the Waves on the Walls of Duntrune Castle'. Robin recalled how Seton Gordon once appeared demanding to play it on the ramparts, departing afterwards without a word of thanks. I had attended a protest meeting by the Five Men of Argyll about the disastrous beef prices at the Excelsior Hotel at Glasgow Airport and felt an identity with them – Robin Malcolm; Robert Paterson, Goatfield; John Warmerdam; Baxter Nesbitt; and Rankin of Killochonoch. Scotland has seven or eight separate identities, and Argyll a charm all its own. Peter Shand Kydd was on midget submarines in the war and claimed to have been the only officer to signal his admiral saying 'Sheep crossing the deck' as he passed through the Crinan Canal. At Dunan in Cowal a nasty interlude helping Archie Fletcher calve a red and white cow (MRI) up to its hocks in mud before going to the Cowal meeting and another night to the Blackface Sheepbreeders at Strachur. Archie Macleod was in charge of the College Office at Oban. The favoured son of every crofter's wife in the Islands, he ran the Advisory Service with practical common sense and a deep knowledge of his customers' needs.

Campaigning was conducted in the stormiest seasons. One October night I found Chou Hayes (MVH) who is everybody's friend. She had farmed with her husband in the Scilly Isles. In 1947 his aeroplane crashed off Rum and she was left hanging onto the tail with the spaniel while he swam for help. Widowed in the 1950s she had returned with David and Helen to Scotland and ran the farm at Barbreck, assisted by the Ritchies, stocking it with Beulah ewes and Murray Grey cattle. After a year she moved to Craigdhu, a place she has lovingly crammed with connoisseur's plants, and even a tree which kept her supplied with lemons for gin and tonic until the greenhouse was demolished in a storm. One dried up lemon remains in the bottom drawer of my desk. For twenty five years she has been my friend and adviser. Occasionally I stayed there when there were always flowers beside the bed, and sometimes Gretta from Donegal was there who lived nearby and helped. Hours spent by that fireside have always meant happiness with no axe to grind, and good advice, and news as we discussed the state of the nation and the lunacies of the faraway world. I telephone her weekly and her children thoughtfully let me know if she is ill as they know I might worry. Following one visit I wrote these words.

For MVH

Came to the House of the Black Rock
Again last night
At evening time –
Campanulas and geraniums
In the kitchen window, and outside
The sun on the evening heather.
Beside us, in the garden,
Full of the spirit
Of my friend who made it,
Eucryphias stood
Wide-open-eyed above the house,
And the *Pyrus salicifolia*
Weeping uncontrolled
For the old Argyll that time has destroyed.
We walked to the top of the hill
With the dog,
Hearts full of lament for the changing land
And the greed of men.
We took our salt and sat by the fire
Full of the memories
Of that first rainswept night
When I came to the House of the Black Rock.
Today I go, out of a long ago,
Back to my private wars,
Full of an untold sadness at leaving the place
But at peace, looking forward
To our next meeting.

And now, after finishing my book, she went and died having given me, two days before, three seedlings of the myrtle smothered in bloom in the yard which she had asked Helen Taggart to pot up for me.

Further east winter was always worse and I slithered from Edinburgh through deep snow to one branch meeting at Luib, arriving early enough to be filled in by the woman who ran the hotel, on the pedigree and performance of every man and sheep between Tyndrum and Aberfeldy. For the evening she remained in her chair with a parrot on her shoulder to ensure I had learnt my *Who's Who*. That night was spent at Lochdochart with Willie John Christie with whom I had conducted a bad tempered argument in the Press about Galloway cattle. Antony Rosen was another with whom there was a later scrap about the virtues of agribusiness, but in the end both became friends. At Crieff a platform was shared with a drunk but entertaining Nicholas Fairbairn MP. That night the hotel loos were frozen and the back of the roadside dyke seemed preferable on my way home. At the junction where the Cultybraggan road enters near Braco, although there was a blizzard, I could wait no longer. The wind and the snow blew everything in my face – a mistake!

I learnt the value of visiting farmers and their families in their kitchens, and hearing their worries on their own ground, often most vividly expressed by wives. That knowledge eventually became the foundation of my work with the Scottish Landowners' Federation (SLF) and the Deer Commission for Scotland (DCS). Sadly this approach is considered irrelevant by the bureaucracies of modern Britain, fearful of becoming involved. At that time, in the 1970s, I shoved coins into draughty phone boxes to communicate with Edinburgh, but even then there were indications that livestock farming's future lay with science, financial management, and organised marketing of stock and no longer with the brushing and combing of our cattle in the byre after tea, with the old intuitive skills of stockmanship and the time to treat our animals as individuals. For someone who never attended agricultural college this was an amazing admission. We had a student, Anne Marie Tracey, doing agriculture at Edinburgh University who shocked me saying it was possible to get her degree without ever having been on a farm. Subconsciously my work drew towards the academic and educational establishments both in agriculture and forestry which until then had never been mentioned in the same breath. One night I spoke at Wye College against Professor John Bowman who said hill farming was a waste of national resources and the hills should be covered with trees. I told him he was no more a scientist than I was, and that he had only thought of an idea and was determined to make the facts fit. The debate ended with the students and their professor in my corner and poor John Bowman alone. He was quite nice and of course I felt bad! Conservation bodies were largely ignored by Government. Farmers still considered their job was to produce food which somebody else would sell. This attitude was fostered by a subsidy system without which we were at the mercy of our foreign competitors. The 1970s were a time to seek allies elsewhere – Noel Robertson, Bill Mutch and Murray Black from Edinburgh and Ken Thomson from Aberdeen were particularly helpful. I spoke twice at AGMs of the SSPCA, and eventually the formation of the Farm Animal Welfare Council shed light on some unacceptable conditions in which we kept livestock but, as fast as standards were imposed by EC Regulations and Directives, Britain was confronted by other states unwilling to enforce similar conditions on their own producers, which gave them an unfair cost advantage in the British market. Although understanding the philosophy of Britain in Europe, after thirty years I still cannot understand the arithmetic of British membership.

Ann and Murray Black and their three clever daughters became particular friends. Anne was the daughter of an Irish farmer and auctioneer who sent her to school in Dublin. Thinking she was becoming too fresh, he brought her home to cool down by driving the pigs to market along roads without banks. Murray taught ESCA students and ran the College farms and the Bush Estate where such pillars of enlightenment as Ian Cunningham, Brennan Soane, and Bill Heal at the Institute of Terrestrial Ecology (ITE) operated. Iona did her

HND at ESCA, was late for her graduation and learnt to parachute with the University TA, landing on her first and final jump in a tree above the frozen River Earn. Her first job on leaving school was rearing deer calves in the garage at Adverikie, brought to her by Ian Mackay (RDC) one of the Pait boys from Loch Monar, later taking them to the HIDB farm at Rahoy in Morvern. She soon left as nobody worked.

Relations between NFU and HIDB were cool. John Bryden, their land officer, produced a hare-brained idea for a Committee of Public Safety in each community to oversee the way farmers managed their farms. There was a sniff of the French Revolution about the suggestion. Thank goodness the scheme was frustrated, but John Bryden is Professor of Geography at Aberdeen University and many of his stupid theories have been resurrected in current legislation for Land Reform before the Scottish Parliament. In 1990, as convenor of the SLF, I wrote:

The Scottish Socialist State
(Standing the World on its Head)

We are the majority –
Therefore we must be right!
We believe that the injustices of the past
Can only be rectified
By destroying the descendants
Of those who, we are told,
Destroyed the lives of our predecessors
By condemning them to a life of slavery
In industry.
Because we are the majority
We must be right –
Therefore we will erect a society
Based on theories
That have been proved at fault
In countless other states.

We are not interested in other nations' failures –
We must repeat those failures for ourselves.
We are not concerned for economic truth
Or mathematic certainty.
We will prove that wealth
Need not be made –
It only needs to be shared.

Our enemies say
The inevitable consequence will be
The poverty of the state – and *all* the people,
But they must be wrong because
We are the majority
Who therefore must be right!

We see the private ownership of land
As the ultimate injustice,
And furthermore
We can peddle the product of our prejudice
To a vast public wishing to believe
Our simple politics.

We do not believe
Those landowners who say
They have worked for most of their lives
With those who they employ.
We do not believe the farmers
With a hundred cows, a thousand sheep
Who say they have lambed their own ewes,
Calved their own cows –
Those who have worked for them
Have had more out of the land
Than they themselves.

In fact
We do not understand
The realities of life in the countryside.
We don't believe we have to
But we must continue to pretend we do!
We must only come to it unchanged,
And *rule* it.
We are the modern Ostrogoths
Who will destroy all those we envy
Even if we destroy
Those who may follow in our wake.

We believe in *power*,
And we who come from urban places
Whose ambience has been destroyed
By a multitude of socialist defecations
Will now begin to destroy
And dominate
The Scottish countryside.

There are bad landlords and bad tenants, but having visited Russia and Hungary, and listened to tales of older people, state management of food production by those understanding neither the soil nor the feel of the land under their feet, is a fatal remedy for a nation's ills.

Agricultural education was important. I later sat on a Committee at Aberdeen University discussing its future along with Maitland Mackie, briefly Vice President of SNFU, where his correct ideas were at that time too advanced for a rather conservative membership. A most competent farmer and businessman, with the aid of Brian Pack, he built a highly successful dairy processing business, later becoming Chairman of the Scottish Agricultural Colleges (SAC), a difficult post to which his extraordinary talents were eminently suited. Another keen on education of agricultural students was Neil McCall-Smith of Connachan near Crieff, a noted producer, who achieved massive increases in sheep productivity although the laird accused him of wrecking his grouse moor. He took Michael Scott, Troloss as a student on the strength of his leaping in the burn to recover his hat in a gale. Rowena was at Connachan for a year where she learnt new extremities of language from his daughter Mary before attending Elmwood Agricultural College at Cupar. She started in too posh digs in Bowling Green Road sharing with three girls and two boys who disliked the landlady inspecting their rooms, infuriating the poor woman by locking the doors and climbing out of windows on sheets. The final straw came when the boys hung a red light outside to test the system, after which they were invited to move. I visited Neil and Debbie often. Mary married Roddy Macpherson, who was, for a brief unhappy spell, head of FMC in Scotland. They built an ugly house at Bracketriggs above the Foulford Inn, have two daughters, Ibby and Rose, and another farm at Lauder where Mary hunts in winter and swears at her husband. Roddy spoke in Dumfries one night when Phyllida was away and there was nothing to eat in the Kirkland fridge except orange jelly.

At Connachan Rowena lambed the heft at the back of the hill by the Round Corrie, reached by pulling oneself across the river in a basket on a wire which hadn't been mended. I wasn't pleased, having heard of Neil's care of students, to find our youngest daughter up to her waist in the middle of the Almond, her dog in her arms and snow and ice flooding past. Nevertheless she learnt a lot and Ibby was a bridesmaid at her wedding in 1987. Neil was never the same after Debbie died, but he came to the small meetings of forward thinkers we began to hold annually at Ardverikie to discuss the revitalising of the Highland economy. We kept no minutes, but their contribution enabled us to improve the working of Ardverikie which at that time, thanks to Geordie Chalmer, began to be seen as a progressive influence in the Highlands. Geordie had been evicted from his farm in Kenya where he had married Anne Crowther, daughter of an Indian Army General and an Irish wife. He joined the firm of Bingham Hughes and Macpherson (later Finlayson Hughes) in Inverness who took over management of the estate from Bill Lang, Glen's assistant and successor, who was nice, but weak. By 1963 it was obvious that he was not the man for the job. Neil McPherson and Ken Hughes supplied Mike Steward to be succeeded almost immediately by Geordie in 1965. When Neil Usher surrendered the tenancy of Aberarder Farm, Lang had replaced the 500 Blackface wethers on Moy with 1,000 ewes from Lanark, totally unsuited to the poor grazing on Creag Meagidh where their heavy fleeces balled up in snow. Willie McWhirter, head shepherd, moved to Carrot Farm at Eaglesham, his place taken by Davie Macleod and when he retired the two young shepherds had little zest for the hill and early morning gatherings. 85 per cent lambing in Neil Usher's time slid to 45 per cent with high ewe mortality. By the early 1970s it was decided to cut the stock to 800 with one shepherd, a dog trial man. The sheep grew leaner, the dogs fleeter, the herd fatter, and lambing descended to 30 per cent – insufficient for replacement stock. Lambs and cast ewes averaged £3 and at the November term the shepherd left for Northumberland. We gathered the ewes, drawing the worst half to sell in Inverness where they made only £3 at a time when they should have been strong and ready to tup. The remaining 400 were placed behind a fence on 1,000 acres at Inverpattack, herded by Gordon Duncan the stalker, and the Chalmers with their charming but useless dogs.

The following spring lambing remained 30 per cent, but mindful of Lord Rothschild's dictum about selling early we marketed all lambs at the end of August to allow ewes to go to the tup in a rising condition in November. We bought four old Swaledale tups from Donnie Munro, Pitmain, Blackfaces from Kingledores in the Upper Tweed Valley, and North Country Cheviots from George Murray in Sutherland. The results were spectacular with lambing over 100 per cent and rising later to 135 per cent, ewes with twins being taken off the hill onto the in-bye land. Prices rose to average in one season almost £30. In the mid 70s we felt strong enough, with the aid of an Interest Relief Grant from HIDB, to double the stock, erect fences at Tullochrome to allow the resting of Inverpattack grazings, and plant two shelter belts. One thing was certain – with the scarcity of hill dogs and hill shepherds, together with unacceptable black loss, we never again wanted to run sheep on large areas with open marches. The system allowed better utilisation of pasture, 85 per cent of whose growth was within six weeks. Winter grazing capacity was the limiting factor even if alleviated by supplementary feeding.

At the same time we limed and slagged the greens at Ardverikie for the deer. The stags were fed nuts in winter since Grandaddy died in 1958 to draw the better stags away from the marches where they wandered off after the rut, never to return. The present condition of the stags is a tribute to the dedication of the stalkers since then.

In a modern sheiling system cows and calves for summering were driven on foot across the hills by the Junors from their farm at Foyers on Loch Ness side. The operation ran well for several seasons to mutual benefit but had to end when the bull, after finishing work, became bored and wandered away to Rannoch in search of fresh female company.

The intellectual elite inclined to denigrate deer forests and their owners, but a letter from Granddaddy in 1911 to the Secretary for Scotland stated his agricultural operations at Braeroy had consistently lost money and the only sensible remedy was to lease it as a deer forest. Braeroy was sold in the 1950s to George Mackie (Lord Mackie of Benshie) and Crichton Stuart who tried reclamation with pigs. The next owners, the Tapps, Kent farmers, ran an operation with their breeding cows wintered on an arable farm in the east returning to the hill for summering, but there was a dispute over money which underlined the fact that one farmer needed financial control over the whole operation. The Porters in Angus, astute businessmen, still demonstrate the potential of transfers between Scryne and their farm at Cashlie far up Glenlyon, but high transport costs for a short season were a problem even in 1976. The Government predictably sheltered behind European Regulations regarding the illegality of subsidising costs whether on the mainland or on the Islands, which, also badly affected, much needed applications of lime. Much hill grass remained wasted owing to selective grazing by sheep and deer whose narrow muzzles picked out the finer, more valuable species leaving dense mats of unpalatable nardus and molinia to harbour ticks and cause deterioration of the sward. Too many stocks contained animals with bad mouths and bad legs unfit for covering their ground, while the fittest had probably never had a lamb or even seen a tup. All eild ewes were ruthlessly culled as soon as possible after lambing when still valuable, a process simplified when scanning was introduced. Lord Pearson of Rannoch, twenty five years later, is still pressing the use of hill cattle where their broad mouths and their droppings, with their heavy feet in places where bracken constantly encroaches, must have a potential for improving the productivity of upland grazings. The problem remains. The Government wants the benefit of grazing animals but does not want the cost of underwriting hill farmers' livelihoods.

Most dairy and arable farmers in the Union thought me batty, believing money 'wasted' on the hills would be better spent on them, and content to prolong a system of glutted autumn markets totally within their control. The cause of cattle worsened with the BSE crisis, the crucifixion of the export trade, and the introduction of the OTMS (Over Thirty Months Scheme) although the production of quality beef was boosted as dairy bull calves became unsaleable. There were fields of well bred beef cattle again for the first time in a generation, instead of the mongrels produced in decades of 'Beef from the Dairy Herd'.

Ardverikie and its connection with the Laggan Community occupied much time and thought for twenty years from the 1970s. Iain Richardson, retired doctor, was a moving force with Geordie Chalmer in achieving television reception, the setting up of Laggan Stores as a community shop after Davie Miller retired, and a new Laggan Hall. He had eccentric drive. He and his sons poached, as if by legal right, and his long suffering wife, who had a tumour on the brain, dealt with the upbringing of six unconventional children. He gave up medicine because of her illness and moved to the old manse when it was sold. After telling me she would approach other landowners Jean Macpherson gulled me into putting up half the price, which at that time we could ill afford. In the end she never asked Bobby or Gerry Feilden, and never produced money herself. She had a school in London about which she wrote an interesting book, was considered by some to be raving mad and was married to Tommy. He ran in the marathon in the 1948 Olympics. Tommy was a brave soldier. In Jugo-Slavia, in 1945, where he had been working with the guerrillas, he single handedly took the surrender of a German general and twenty three thousand men. Even at 82 he retains phenomenal energy and at their invitation we attended the Clan Macpherson gathering in 2002 presided over by the Chieftain, Sir William Macpherson, a famous judge, who had been at Trinity with me in 1948. When Tommy was knighted in one New Year's Honours list Jean was scandalously reputed to have returned the grocer's bill addressed a week before to Mrs Macpherson, Balavil with the comment that they ought to know she was Lady Macpherson. Despite this libellous dig I'm quite fond of them both.

Rowena lambed once at Dalchully for Godfrey Owen, a Shropshire farmer, married to Margaret who knew all about irises, started operating at 5 a.m. each day, never appeared to sleep or eat, and regularly drove north at that time. Jeremy Porter, ex Guards officer, married to Scilla, was the previous owner. Lying in bed one night they were woken by poachers turning in the yard. Jeremy, in his pyjamas, leapt with his rifle into his Land Rover, pursuing them to the road end where they miscalculated the turn. He held them at rifle point in a spotlight until the passing of the mail bus which delivered them to the police. Being released on bail they were finally fined by the Sheriff, but boasted they had poached every night between which more than paid their penalty.

Godfrey Owen became ill and shortly before his death Dalchully was sold to Alex Herbage who led the community by the nose. Thirty two stone with a small German wife, doors had to be widened and computers installed in all the rooms. He employed armed guards which astonished Laggan who guessed he was an arms dealer. He also owned Sutton Scotney in Hampshire where he kept what was supposedly the finest collection of modern art in the country. On expulsion from France headlines proclaimed 'Return of the Prodigal Tonne'. He instituted the Laggan Games and had his own Sutton Scotney Games to which he would transport any inhabitants who wanted to attend. He employed local tradesmen on grand projects, complaining that the HIDB refused him grants which, according to Rowena, he put about locally were refused on my advice. That was untrue, but the Board kept a dossier alleging he had been jailed for fraud. I took the precaution of denying the story and he said wouldn't dream of thinking it had anything to do with me. He bought an AA stot to be brought out for Smithfield where Winston Nicholson won the supreme championship for him although having to pay to get himself and the beast to London. Eventually it was discovered everything was courtesy of the National Westminster Bank which foreclosed, leaving many small local businesses with unpaid accounts. Dalchully was sold to Jane Ramsden and Hugh Morrison who came from their deer farm at Luss where Hugh managed the estate sporting. They worked incredibly hard and it is sad that in 2002 they decided to move to France because of the idiotic solutions the Scottish Parliament seems intent on imposing on the Scottish Countryside – in the name of democracy.

Between August and mid-October we always spent time stalking at Ardverikie. My parents-in-law invited the same people, all good company, but some of them finding increasing difficulty climbing hills. Billy Fox-Pitt nearly had a heart attack walking up grouse on Aberader. Rosamund Birkbeck collapsed in my arms when helping herself to soup at dinner, and Vera Smith-Bingham infuriated me saying on a misty day, 'Cyril hasn't gone stalking today – I can't think what you do in Scotland if you don't go stalking.' Cyril was a vile shot with a stupid short barrelled rifle. Once, firing at the target and missing three times, his wife grabbed the rifle to show him what to do, hitting the stag in the teeth, much to John Duncan's delight. Sometimes there were paying guests – usually Danes or Dutch. A chemist came with his keeper but returned, having been sent to the easiest beat, exclaiming, 'I came to shoot zee stags, not to go mountaineering.' A Spaniard, intensely proud after killing a stag, produced his whisky flask saying he understood it was traditional to have a dram. Gordon Duncan pointed to the nearby spring as a source of good water, into which the customer promptly emptied the contents of his flask. Three years a party of Danes came for whom I stalked on the Binneins, an exhausting business as they sometimes shot three stags a day. The stalkers had the ponies and the snowtrack on the other beats and I had to drag stags long distances through rocks and over the deer fence, before a final pull to the Lochside Drive through the tussocks in the wood. Often it was eight o'clock before finishing and I lost a stone in a week. John Anderson, a delightful little man who shot well at the target, was unable to keep his rifle steady because of his excitement when aiming at real deer. After he left there was a bottle of pills in his bedroom labelled: '*Godt fur nervose skytter*' which meant 'good for nervous shooters' and not what I had thought! Once chairman of a mayonnaise factory he sold it to RHM, remaining on the Board. One day he said: 'Gentlemen, I have an intuition this is the day we should buy bottles.' The stupid chairman announced: 'Mr Anderson, modern British management doesn't recognise there is such a word as intuition in the dictionary.' 'In which case,' said John Anderson, ' a very good day to you, sir!' and he never returned. If you have studied my life so far you will realise how much we agreed.

Those autumn days among deer, guided by John and Gordon Duncan, Ewen Mackintosh, Murdie Maclean and Dougie Langlands, and the numerous ghillies and ponymen who assisted them were golden times for which it is impossible to give adequate thanks to the memory of my father and mother-in-law – even if she kept meat until it had maggots and the grouse until they were almost flying out of the larder window. She hated house-keeping. At one dinner chocolate sauce was served for the venison instead of gravy which the foreign guests assumed was a delightful Scottish habit. There was a massive throughput of cooks and butlers, one seen dancing the Highland fling on the lawn with the housemaid, both of them drunk as lords.

Tom Maclauchan ruled the big house. Born on a croft far out on the hill from Brig o' Brown, he was gassed in the 1914 War and taken prisoner, thereafter drinking his way to 1939 with his colleagues in the TA. At Dunkirk, with six fellow Seaforths, having organised the evacuation of their colleagues, when it was their time to leave, he suddenly remembered a case of whisky under the pier. As the Germans hadn't arrived there seemed time for a party before leaving. In their merriment they stared straight along the rifle barrels of the surrounding Germans and Tom was imprisoned once more. After 1945 he never touched alcohol again, looked after the house as if it was his own, and, without malice, cursed to their face anyone, including my mother-in-law, who he thought wrong. He entertained a large flock of feral greylag geese, descended from a mother and six goslings brought in the back of Bobby's car from Muncaster. They squatted in the yard, sailed in the back bay, and multiplied. It became an increasingly messy performance crawling through their shit when stalking. On his death, the key to Bobby's business room had vanished but was eventually found in the lining of Tom's cap. The place was never the same without him. The spelling of his surname for his funeral was a problem. His sister produced eight different versions. They buried him at Nethybridge with the sun glinting on the snow opposite the place I had poached the partridge in 1945.

Accompanied by the Kellys we often stayed at Gallovie for the hinds, playing bridge at night, and for some years sharing Christmas with the Chalmers either there or at Kirkland. At other times we Christmassed at Ardverikie, once having a teenage party for the children with a hundred and eight guests sleeping all over the house in beds or on the floor. Geordie and I laid a trail for parents and children one Boxing Day, unfortunately failing to give ourselves enough start to take account of Tommy McPherson's athletic CV. At the end the remains of the sawdust had to be thrown in the face of him and his daughter Ishbel at the garden gate. There was sunshine and snow and once, on top of Meall Each na Sgubach with Ewen Mackintosh, we saw the brockenspectre, our shadows walking on the clouds. It brought back a night before the battalion went to Austria when Neil Macpherson and John MacDonell, who had been at Trinity with me and later became a financial adviser to the archbishop of Canterbury, set about climbing Ben Alder in the dark – a silly thing to do which frightened John out of his wits.

The Inn burnt down and was badly rebuilt. At one stage it was successfully tenanted by the Smalls, but after Veronica insisted that if others could make money out of hotels so could she, it was taken in hand until its decommissioning left the estate with a loss of £60k, partly because she insisted on counting the cigarettes and linen to ensure staff were honest. Bobby had told his wife she was useless at business, and she appeared anxious to prove him right. The Chalmers moved from Gallovie to the Inn, now called Camas Cillein, remaining there until buying Strathmashie Lodge for their retirement.

There they began to make a lovely garden and do up the house with the aid of their son-in-law, John Lister, who unfortunately rode off into the sunset on his bicycle. Because of family troubles they had to sell, moving to a house they built themselves in the hills above Moniack where they are making another garden and live among many friends from Geordie's youth.

Wanderings with SNFU continued and frequent exposure to the media was considerably to the advantage of everybody and everything I represented. Even people in prison heard my voice, and across the world. On the Underground between South Kensington and Victoria a woman with a little black velvet hat leant over asking: 'Are you Patrick?' 'Ye-es.' She nudged her neighbour. 'That's Patrick!' On enquiring how she knew she said she had seen me on TV in Brisbane, Australia. I reckoned I'd made it, but what I had said she hadn't time to tell. One man suggested growing tomatoes on Ben Nevis. Regrettably the only way to reach a large audience is through the media who are not always reliable about transmitting messages but I have been lucky with journalists who have crossed my path. The ones I would trust with my life are Gillian Harris and Patience Wheatcroft from *The Times*, Arthur Anderson and Isabel Fraser from BBC Scotland, Fordyce Maxwell from the *Scotsman*, and Eric Robson. I hope mentioning them won't cost them their future. Patience and her husband appeared under strange circumstances with a letter to *The Times*, of which she is Business Editor.

> Sir, I fail to understand why Patience Wheatcroft is so opposed to Church Schools when she seemed quite content to send her two sons to a school which has just spent £8m on a new chapel, has two clergymen on the staff, and compulsory services on Sunday.
>
> Yours faithfully,
>
> Tony Salter (Mr Patience Wheatcroft)

It made me smile so much Enquiries gave me their number, and we've been friends ever since.

In Arran I stayed with Margie and Donald Currie and with Donald McNiven. Being driven over the String Road by him on a frosty night after a meeting was frightening. Evelyn Sillars was the local councillor. Charles Fforde, son of Lady Jean at Brodick Castle, both a little to the right of Genghis Khan, said many correct things, but at unsuitable moments, which severely damaged the cause of private ownership. I don't know whether he married her, but his fiancée was supposed to have hit him over the head with a rolling pin. Years later, having spoken to the primary teachers of Cumbria at Grasmere, I slipped on the icy steps of the Prince of Wales Hotel and hit my head, after everyone had gone home. Being due in Arran the following night I staggered to the morning boat at Ardrossan and it was the only time I have ever seen the sun rise in the west.

Throughout the south and south-west of Scotland, in the Lothians, Perthshire, Fife and Kinross, Angus and Aberdeenshire I sang my heart out, staying often in bitterly cold farmhouses, always given tea and a welcome and throughout that time it was strange. Those to the north of the Forth and Clyde always wrote to say thank you and until my last year those to the south never did – with the exception of Wigtownshire. I supposed it was something to do with the Covenanters. When I became County Chairman of Cumbria NFU in 1986, with few exceptions, nobody offered me tea, or supper, or a bed and nobody knew who John Cameron was when I suggested him as a speaker for the annual dinner despite his having done so much for the British sheep industry. Moving to Cumbria in 1982 was like going to a foreign country and a severe culture shock.

Between farming, Ardverikie and the NFU there was little time for diversion. One whole year we stopped the newspaper and didn't feel lost, listening to the news on the wireless – what everybody born after my grandmother seems to call the radio. We tried to educate ourselves artistically. My ancestor had bought a small watercolour, 'Promenade du Boulevard du Temple' by Swebach des Fontaines, most of whose output was destroyed in the French Revolution. This we sold at Christie's in 1964 and with the proceeds purchased a Bronze Goose by Phyllis Bone who had sculpted the animals at the bottom of the Scottish War Memorial; two pictures by our friend Cyril Wilson, a dowser; a MacTaggart; and others by Anda Paterson and Mardi Barrie whose picture 'Mountain Sky' completely captivated me when I saw it in Aitken Dott's. It reminded me of all the spiritual qualities of the mist in the Ardverikie Corries. We attended concerts at the Edinburgh Festival. Viveca Andersberg made her debut with Elizabeth Söderström in Dvořák's Requiem and later became a friend when, as Baroness Åkerhielm, she came to Muncaster with her husband Kim who was head of the Swedish Landowners. Once we stayed at their home at Dylta, near Örebro which was filled with her singing as she moved around the house. She drove like the wind with a telephone in one hand and the steering wheel in the other. Kim showed us his forests and his crayfish traps. His mother Leah, half Danish half Swede, told us how she smuggled things to her family in Copenhagen during the War. Old and wonderful she met us at the airport with her stick having hitched a lift, leaving the Estonian au pair at the edge of a cornfield with her car which had run out of petrol. In Edinburgh we attended the Fiery Angel when the lights failed, and were at the Usher Hall in 1968 when Menuhin played the Beethoven Violin Concerto as the Russian tanks were rolling into Prague. Afterwards I wrote:

> Before he began he stood on the platform
> And addressed the audience:
> 'On this dark dark day
> I wish to dedicate my performance tonight,
> As did Beethoven his life

> To the great and indomitable
> Spirit of man.'
> The audience were all in tears
> And as the notes floated from his instrument
> They seemed to speak to everyone
> 'There must be a God,' they said.

Many years later Phyllida and I went to Prague with the National Art Collection Fund, staying in the Maximilian Hotel with a party led by Lucy Abel Smith, in bright blue patent leather shoes which prevented us from losing her in the crowds on the Charles Bridge, and Harriet Fennell from Ireland. It was moving to see the statue of John Hus and to go to the Castle where the Defenestration of Prague took place, starting the Thirty Years War in 1618. What Eton history hadn't taught me was that the two deputies ejected from the window down the steep cliff below landed in a midden and walked away unscathed. We were shown the Brevnev Monastery church by a young girl, Marcela Koupilova, who tried to convince me I wasn't going to hell. In two letters afterwards she wrote very movingly of her grandfather's farm, and her husband and baby. We visited Lucy's friend, Geraldine Mucha, whose family was originally from Orkney. She had endured the communist years with her Czech husband with whom she had returned to Prague in 1945 and was trying to revive the memory of her father-in-law, best known for his poster of Sarah Bernhardt, produced for a printer in a fix in two days one Christmas time. I sent her two poems to set to music.

Scottish NFU AGMs were tiresome set pieces with little chance to prevent Ministers who came from giving predictable answers. At Peebles I took on Hugh Brown, a delightfully modest man. At Renfrew Shirley Williams addressed us, having milked cows in her youth, and she was later encountered on a sunny summer afternoon in Robert and Janet Balfour's garden at Brucefield. Robert was Chancellor of Stirling University for ten years and I sat at his feet on a Heritage Committee at Robert Gordon University run by Jan Magnus Fladmark, a Norwegian with a farm in Gubrensdal. Through those times Henry Plumb, a Midland farmer afterwards President of the European Parliament, headed the English NFU. Now a life peer he is still a voice of sanity amidst Britain's agricultural chaos. At one SNFU Council Douglas Alexander, chairman of the Publicity Committee, in an act of suicidal courage, took on the Press and got away with it. Then there were countless Area dinners. Once sitting next to Henry Crawford, representative of the TGWU, he shocked me with a tale of having his hat shot off his head by an irate farmer as he walked away. The permanent staff were unfailingly courteous and conscientious and when it was time to move to Muncaster I missed them and everything they did to help me – in particular Richard Henton and John Coutts. In retrospect my contribution to Scottish agriculture seems tiny in comparison with what it gave to me. Jim Gourlay's comment: 'Just remember the average farmer is an absolute shit,' wasn't true.

The media loved a row. Gradually one's technique improved, finding the ability to produce brief off-the-cuff comments which officials so dislike. The first encounter was in a darkened room in the BBC studios in Queen Street with a tiny red light on some infernal machine and a reminder to turn it off when one left. The dividend came when one was trusted with people to show around farms. The first was Jean Archer, in charge of Meat and Meat Products at MAFF, encountered in a slaughterhouse near Northampton whither they had sent me to see the grading standards under the new European Sheepmeat Regime. She wore spongebag trousers, which she continued to wear at receptions in the Berlaymont Palace at Brussels, a habit unappreciated by her superiors used to the silk dresses and dark suits of her colleagues. As she had never been to Scotland and was in charge of all-important hill subsidy negotiations in Whitehall it seemed a good idea to invite her for a week's introduction to our problems. It seemed such a simple request, but it had to go through Ministers, the Scottish Office and both NFUs to see if anybody objected. It was spring and as our tour progressed the weather was marvellous with little evidence of disadvantage, until we came to Glenlivet where a violent snowstorm snapped the unthinned Forestry Commision plantations in an area where the Department in Aberdeen were reluctant to admit there was anything but fertile soil. It opened the lady's eyes, which considerably helped our pleas for recognition of the hill farmer's plight. To Kirkland in 1978 Alasdair Hutton, our MEP, brought David Curry, ex-*Financial Times* European Correspondent, both on the Agriculture committee in Brussels. David and his French wife Anne stayed, sharing a bottle of the best claret, and from then until now they and their family have been among my closest friends. David, later MP for Skipton and Ripon, was the son of Abba, charming ex-headmaster from Leeds who fell off a telegraph pole in the Army. Anne Roullet David met at Oxford, the daughter of a La Rochelle shipbuilder killed by the Nazis. A sculptress whose work is in considerable demand she has created a beautiful garden at Newlands End. A twin daughter, Isobel Bilgen, adopted by me as honorary god-daughter, is building her name as an up-and-coming garden designer. Married to Tarquin there was on their engagement a problem with Jasper, her jealous Alsatian. David is brighter than most MPs and became Minister of State at MAFF under John Gummer, with whom he moved to DOE. As shadow Agricultural Secretary in William Hague's team he resigned, unable to subscribe to the Tory Party's anti-European stance. As chairman of the Rural Affairs Select Committee he seems happier, has more time at home and a diverse job to which his knowledge eminently suits him. I wrote for David and Anne two ditties when he was Minister of State at MAFF with a wife exasperated by the ravages of roe deer in deepest Essex.

A Sad Tale – Not To Be Told In Brussels

It's no use loving the Minister's wife
Who's trying to immortalise Woy's* swelled head
As he asks for his gin with a tear of sherry –
Affected sod that he is!
And it's no use loving the Minister's daughters
When the roe deer have eaten the Minister's veg
That he'd drawn in immaculate drills last week.
So the balance of payments is wrong again
And his wife must buy foreign instead.
And the dear little deer are nought but a pest
As they stroll through the rows
In the neat weeded beds
Zapping the Minister's leeks.

Oh! It's 'Minister this' and 'Minister that'
In the portals of Whitehall Place,
But it's no use his secretary stating her case
When the roe deer have pasted the Ministers leeks
And wasted his weekend work once more.
And it's no use loving the Minister's wife
And the Minister's daughters as well,
When the roe deer have eaten the Minister's leeks
That he'd grown with such practical skill.

So 5.6 billion plus two rows of leeks
Is the up to date deficit now,
And worse, much worse, is still to relate
For his daughter's duck was squatting below
The apple tree Newton once had observed
In his studies of gravity long ago,
But the brain of the bird
Was not nimble enough
And was smashed by an apple
That dropped from above.
So 'Minister this' and 'Minister that'
Will not do on next Monday morning
For the suicide bird and the awful deer
Have jiggered the Minister's budget again!
And his wife and his daughters will have to make do
With the stew of their duck which hadn't a clue.

---

*'Woy': Roy Jenkins, Home Secretary in Wilson's Government, President of the European Commission, and Chancellor of Oxford University.

Chapter 13

...it's grand, and you cannot expect to be baith grand and comfortable.

J.M. Barrie (1860-1937)

1981 lambing was memorable for one day of awful snow with massive drifts at the top of Killyleoch, but 1982 was worse when Bobby, aged 78, telephoned, saying Muncaster had belonged to the Penningtons since 1200 and had lost him £50k p.a. for the past five years. Would we take over? Phyllida's highly developed sense of responsibility to her family's past made her say 'yes'. I wanted to say 'no', but was persuaded to agree when the accountant said we would be out in two years. Too old at fifty two we moved in September. My office, described as a place of understated quality, was in the top yard and was supported by a primitive gas stove which made me feel ill. My mother-in-law's peacocks squawked into my left ear from the roof opposite, the sawmill deafened my right, and above there was the shit of forty generation of hens which nobody had cleaned out, yet that was the one place I felt secure. The outer office was occupied by Sheila Macleod – pretty and fiercely loyal to Philip Denham-Cookes' memory – and her ugly Doberman, Heidi, neither of them approving of me. She did aerobics, was as thin as a rake, and answered 'Ravenglass 614' with a deep inhalation of breath. Underneath she was a really nice person, married to Uisdean from Sutherland, but withdrew when Iona took over and their minds didn't meet, which wasn't surprising as our daughter went on an Assertiveness Training Course and returned different. Office equipment was supported by a redundant ansaphone which, failing to understand, I called Gretchen Stevens of At Home Country Holidays who sent us Americans to stay, as the most likely instructor. The following morning at 6 a.m. in the office, the time I started work, there were six minutes of messages. On calling the first a voice informed me that the people concerned had left eight years before. It was not an auspicious foray into modern technology. Fortified by Uncle Edward's teaching about double entry book keeping I kept all accounts in longhand, added in my head, and quickly learnt a feel for the mechanics of the business. We needed to build the cash reserves in the summer, sending them away to the money men in Glasgow to recall them to avoid an overdraft before the next season. Unfortunately my cash flow was derailed when I went down to the house one day to discover Phyllida had bought 122,000 postcards from a photographer whom I disliked. As annual visitor numbers were only 31,000 it was unhelpful!

The forty estate houses had been rewired seventy years before. McWilliam's perpetual legal niggling about his landlord's liabilities had bled my father-in-law white. Rents were tiny. Charlie Carlisle still did the estate work although his war wounds caused him pain. It seemed sensible to sell Rougholme (McWilliam's Farm), the Grove (the original estate office), and Pennington House which, although their capital value was low, at least removed some liabilities. Bobby said he wished the proceeds to go to Phyllida's sisters. I exploded and said if he wanted Phyllida to succeed he mustn't do it. Even so he gave them all the cash in the New Muncaster Trust which had been set up to maintain the estate with money from the 1970 sale, which made life very difficult, but we did our best to ensure Lucinda, whose financial situation was more precarious than Annabel's, received 60 per cent. Phyllida took over on 31 March 1983. Bobby died on 13 January 1986 within the three years needed to ameliorate the tax we had to pay, but each daughter received a third of his life insurance which was a considerable help.

We became the first members of the family to live full time in the house since 1850 and our grandchildren are the first children to be brought up there since the 1830s. It was freezing. We sat either side of the Library fire of an evening in our sleeping bags. The house was reputed to have the first heating in Northern Britain since the Romans left sixteen hundred years before. It only operated in four rooms and was not used as it consumed $2^1/2$ gallons of oil an hour. The grids through which it was supposed to blow sucked in cold air. Later an American travel agent, named by me Elizabeth the Sick, threw up down one in the hall after crossing Hardknott Pass. Tax was to pay on the contents of the house and the trustees insisted we trace everything in the inventory at Grandaddy's death in 1958, a difficult task as it had been concocted by Curtis and Henson in 1962 in faded type with such entries as 'a chair'. Organised by James Miller, experts from Sothebys, dressed in overcoats, revalued the chattels in 1983 at prices astronomically higher than twenty one years before. During our searches we were assisted by an excellent young man, Robert Walker from Kendal, whose father was head of Provincial Insurance, recommended by Mary Burkitt, deeply knowledgeable Curator of Abbott Hall. Nights on end were spent matching the silver, searching for items parents-in-law had moved to Versions and Ardverikie, until eventually we were sorted out room by room and an inventory taken. Apart from the irritating expense it produced a valuable record, even if its value was somewhat reduced by Phyllida constantly moving furniture around the house. The valuation team taught us much about antiques which has added to the pleasure we can give the public who at that time we engaged eyeball to eyeball across the ropes on any subject from Mrs Thatcher to the price of pigs. The house was full of ribald laughter which I miss with the modern technology wands. Even visitors from the most disadvantaged parts of Liverpool encouraged us by saying: 'We don't want you nationalised. We don't want you National Trust. We want you here as a family with whom we can talk.'

The payment of Capital Transfer Tax was an unpleasant reality of life. A valuable putto had been given to Phyllida by her grandfather on our marriage and she decided to sell it, having a replica made by Caroline Clay. It helped considerably, but the following year, as I was explaining the awfulness of our situation to Waberthwaite Primary School the headmistress pointed to it: 'Oliver, what do you think of that?' to which the bold boy replied: 'It's rude, Miss.' Never having appreciated it, this was exactly my sentiment and it astonishes me how people surround themselves with ugly objects because of their financial value, treating them solely as investments. We applied for heritage exemption on large Pennington portraits and very pricey items for which we would have difficulty in finding cash to pay tax without ravishing the whole collection. We decided to pay tax on smaller pictures and furniture which could fit in our children's houses if the accountant's forecast proved correct. It was the correct decision at the time, but the transfer of non-exempt items to the next generation was to return as an awkward problem with Nigel Lawson's 1988 budget. Throughout our discussions with the Capital Taxes Office the support and tenacity of David Morris was outstanding. Sotheby's spoke dismissively about the books, but placed a large total value on them and gave us a most sketchy inventory on the 6,500 volumes. 'Shelf £100', 'others £50', except for those few books they sniffed as a possible sale. We applied for exemption which was initially refused despite explaining to the CTO that the beautiful octagonal room with its forty foot ceiling would be no library without its books. Eventually they relented on condition a list was produced of each title, its author, its publisher, and the date of publication. After four freezing weekends at the top of the library steps the job was done. Sorting out the valuation when our generation is taken to its fathers should prove simpler.

Iris and Philip Denham Cookes, the curator who ran the tourist side of the business, retired to Newtown where they made a beautiful garden. The caretaker, Ernie Bendell and his wife lived in the North Tower; Grace cooked and lived in the Cook's flat with husband Harry Simmonds who helped Jim Huddleston, the builder, and fell off a ladder; David Robertson was head gardener with five assistants, including Bob Godsell, a master propagator. There was a keeper for my mother-in-law's birds and animals which consisted of:

> 8 bears
> wallabies
> a kinkajou
> a monkey
> 3 donkeys
> a fox
> pens of exotic pheasants
> rheas
> chipmunks
> flamingoes
> sarus cranes
> a pair of black swans
> 28 peafowl

and 7 sexed pairs of parrots which had lived together for fourteen years without reproducing, as well as a quantity of ducks and geese whose droppings in the ponds backed up the drains and poisoned the plants. The bears, reduced to three by then, were sent to Birmingham when Veronica died in 1987 and were shortly afterwards expelled to Glasgow having beaten up the other bears at Dudley Zoo. The skull of Rupert, the father bear, with his crooked mouth sits on our dining room cupboard. The wallabies and twenty four peahens wandered into the woods, and the four peacocks were dismissed smartly after doing a thousand pounds of damage in the Garden Centre on a single night. A mink killed the pheasants and one black swan, whereon the other died of a broken heart. The rheas laid enormous clutches of eggs in careless places. One Saturday afternoon the police enquired if we had lost an ostrich, because one had been reported going like the clappers five miles away on the road between Waberthwaite and Bootle. By the time I reached the front door two young footballers were sitting in their car with an indignant bird on their knee which they had arrested returning from a match at Millom. One sarus crane preferred me to her husband. Whenever she saw me coming she ran up and down the chainlink fence with which my mother-in-law had vandalised the beautiful garden. We performed a ritual dance, jumping with legs astride – once for the American TV, and US visitors sometimes tapped me on the shoulder enquiring if they hadn't seen us before. The parrots we sent to Chester Zoo to re-investigate their sexual credentials. The answer was thirteen boys, one girl, and the female cockatoo was so astonished that on her return she laid an egg. We tried to rationalise the situation and were given a blue and gold macaw with few feathers. The following day, sitting on the dyke – not what Americans might translate – two old women were heard to say: 'What an awful bird!' as it declaimed in faultless English: 'F—— off you, F—— off.' The situation was remedied when Tony Warburton, founder of the Barn Owl Breeding and Release Scheme asked if he could come to Muncaster on being made redundant as the warden for the MOD nature reserve. The chain link fences have gone and the World Owl Trust is thriving as an independent charity, but is very much a part of Muncaster's life. Everyone loves owls and the first Millennium stamps – nineteen million of them – had Third Millennium Muncaster and a Snowy owl on them. I don't like animals in cages and wrote:

I know
How animals in cages feel,
For not so long ago I walked the mountain tops
And felt my legs swing free across the summer grass,
But now I'm here at Muncaster,
Imprisoned in a gilded cage by circumstance.
I've lost my freedom, lost my hope,
And never more may know the sun upon my moving limbs,

In the garden at Muncaster.

> The music of the wind among the rocks;
> So now I understand how lions feel
> In cages.

A sentiment owed to Virginia McKenna. With little cash and no spare time, by the end of March we prayed for spring, but when the house opened four days a week in mid-April we never saw the other side of the valley for six weeks. Because of our pathetic budget, on the advice of Ross Muir, a friend from Edinburgh, and with the help of Paul MacGoolagan from Square Advertising at Gargrave, publicity was directed only at visitors to the Lake District whence the bulk of our visitors came. I rewrote the brochure less formally which outraged Veronica who said, 'People like you shouldn't speak to people like that with such familiarity' – advice I continue to ignore. When returning to Muncaster she threw herself wholeheartedly into the game, always pretending she wasn't who she was and invariably ornamental. At Brackley the water supply was suspect. They drank Malvern water, Bobby sometimes filling half empty bottles from the tap before leaving them in the cellar without telling his wife who became so ill she almost died.

It seemed important to stop Phyllida's ancestral home being viewed as an isolated centre of privilege in less privileged surroundings where the population existed among inescapable memories of the Depression in the 1930s from which it had never recovered. We urgently needed to reconnect Muncaster with life outside to which my parents-in-law, because of commitments elsewhere, had been unable to devote sufficient time. Bill Deedes, returning in the late 80s to the scenes of his youth as a cub reporter, gave me dinner at the Hunday Manor Hotel with Chris Tighe, his *Daily Telegraph* correspondent in the north of England, telling how little he found changed in Cleator Moor. Unemployment high, mining dead, iron and steel dying, and farming in severe difficulties. Communications remain difficult and to entice new enterprises to the west in preference to a site beside the M6 enormous bribes would be needed. The nuclear industry at Sellafield and the Marchon chemical works were the only significant employees. BNFL was particularly bad at paying small business suppliers without unacceptable delay. That first summer was the year of the Sellafield leaks. Traditions of secrecy from MOD days persisted leading to rumours and half truths. Chris Merlin owned the Ravenglass shop which she wished to sell, but considered offers for it, and her house, unsatisfactory. Some years before she had sent her Hoover dust to US for analysis and now, recalling it, she wished to sue BNFL for devaluing her investment. This was manna from Heaven for the Press and unhelpful for our tourist business. Cumbria Tourist Board (CTB) was paralytic, changing their Director as often as their members changed socks. One refused to live in Cumbria, claiming it was too dangerous. At Commercial members' meetings the Central Lakes hotels were petrified their business would be damaged by association and I was astonished when they later gave me an award as Cumbria Personality of the Year. The result was deafening silence from the very people whose job it was to help. The Lake District Special Planning Board (LDSPB) was also unhelpful. Of its 30 members – 16 County Councillors, 4 District Councillors, and 10 Ministerial appointments – almost all lived outside the National Park, having little notion of the needs of the natives. Willie Rawling, Steele Addison, Trevor Farrer, and John Allen, who I replaced as an appointed member from 1987-93, struggled to represent our interests. We were not helped by the Board's insistence that the Western Lake District should be devoted to the 'quiet enjoyment of the people'. Planners still fail to understand landscapes the nation professes to love cannot be maintained without economic activity.

When news of the leaks broke the enraged population of Ravenglass super-glued Mrs Merlin's shop door on Monday morning. Sally Hardcastle, tough BBC journalist, landed on the beach declaring it must be evacuated to show how dangerous it was, but the housewives of Ravenglass surrounded her helicopter forcing its withdrawal to a nearby field where she interviewed me. The Press had a feeding frenzy. One local doctor produced an equation proving the further from Sellafield the greater the agitation until it reached its zenith among the population of Southern England who lived a stone's throw from the French nuclear installations. Jake Kelly, BNFL Press Officer, had an impossible task. Distinguished scientists with hands shaking like leaves without media training were put up to oppose the brilliant public performances from

Greenpeace and Friends of the Earth. I wrote some lines 'To Greenpeace and the Gentlemen [an out-of-date description] of the Press from the People of West Cumberland'

> Tonight I know I speak
> For many of the people of West Cumberland.
> We do not feel the threat
> You tell us lies within our lives
> Along the coast from Sellafield.
> We only wish you'd go –
> Back to the roaring south,
> To cigarettes and petrol fumes
> Which kill you much much quicker
> Than all the things you try to make us fear
> From nuclear power.
> Time was
> You did a useful job and pointed out
> Matters that needed rectified,
> But now it seems you will let no one win
> Unless they can agree with you.
> The people of West Cumberland
> Say 'Go!'
> Please leave us be.

Shortly normality returned with the appointment of Christopher Harding as BNFL chairman. He collected egg cups and understood the industry's need for PR. At great expense a visitor centre was opened to the public free of charge to draw people to the west coast and explain the basic facts of the operation. This became particularly important following the Chernobyl disaster in 1986. In the minds of local people, particularly those who had lost children with leukaemia, there remained the insoluble conflict between jobs and the health of their families, although many conveniently forgot there had been cancer clusters at Seascale as long ago as 1911.

In those far off days of 1983 Muncaster's need for publicity was soon apparent. Joan Freshwater introduced me to Radio Cumbria. She interviewed me about my favourite music and didn't mind being asked if she had pigtails as a girl. I contributed often, calling each week with news to interest them. Thus, on becoming Chairman of Cumbria NFU in 1986, my name was already known. Muncaster needed to diversify its income streams quickly without spending capital we didn't have. Our assets were a house severely needing maintenance; 320 acres of derelict woodland; three rented farms, one in-hand; estate houses mostly rather dilapidated; a no-hope caravan site set up so that it was impossible to generate income and employ a manager. An indifferent café was unprofitably franchised. The house and garden-opening business, geared to insufficient day visitors producing insufficient income. My father-in-law, considering we knew

PTGDP with Sir Christopher Harding (Chairman of BNFL), the man who collected the egg cups and set up the Visitor Centre at Sellafield.

nothing about publicity, insisted we employed a man from Tunbridge Wells, to help. Married to a bank manager in Orpington, he wrote on green writing paper, and sent large bills. We said thank you more politely than we felt, but remembered him when a grand-daughter bought two Buff Orpingtons at a farm sale.

Anne Matterson enquired about reopening the garden centre for no better reason than to get back at her ex-husband with whom she had run a successful business at Walkmill, Gosforth, six miles away. Funded by me and assisted by Betty Smith, daughter of Ada Cowan, ex-postmistress, and Heather Phizackerley, it became a tidy, pleasant, and totally unprofitable place, later let to Alan Clark while he was Garden Curator. Apart from digging up valuable seedlings in our garden and selling them on his own behalf he rapidly restored it to its former chaotic state. Alan was brilliant at propagation, a rhododendron bore sometimes encountered at night in the bushes with a miner's lamp on his head, and a disaster at human relations.

Phyllida answered an advertisement from At Home Country Holidays in Sussex run by Gretchen Stevens and her friend Angela Rhodes-James, married to Robert, MP and historian. They sent overnight visitors for which they never allowed us to charge enough saying those who paid top prices were invariably nasty. Over five years we entertained many, one season having a throughput of 250 in ones and twos. They were supposed to arrive at 5.30 p.m., as the house shut, their last hosts having telephoned to avoid repeating the previous night's menu. They often arrived at 7.30 p.m. 'Gee, Pat,' – an abbreviation I hate – 'we got to have a bath!' Sometimes it was 'shower' which caused problems – something we didn't have until a woman, whose supposedly sexy tan looked as if she was advertising holidays in the sun, persuaded us to invest. They appeared at 9 p.m. when dinner was spoilt, saying they must see the whole house and the whole garden and leave after breakfast. Sometimes I drove them a hundred miles a day around the Lake District and more than earned my £100. They wanted to dine off silver, only kept warm by pouring water through a small hinged aperture into the hot plate below, usually inserting one quarter into the heater and three quarters over ourselves. We were sometimes helping Mrs Simmonds and Mrs Bendell wash up at 1 a.m.

Most guests were perfectly nice, a few horrid. The first were the Wedgewood Society, brought by Hensleigh Wedgewood and his wife, memorable because a large Missouri lawyer fell through his bed above our room with a loud thump. The prospectus said only one party at a time, but there were odd glitches. One couple confused the date and walked in unexpected. Phyllida never blinked. Another couple arrived after midnight having confused Newcastle and Carlisle. Returning to New Jersey after the War, in 1947 he was unhappy with the way the Bank transacted his business and bought the bank on Monday morning. I envisaged walking into the Natwest Bank at Seascale, plunking a cheque on the counter and saying, 'You're working for me now.' Bob Stone, a wildlife and circus vet came from Michigan with Hatty telling stories of treating a giraffe with pinkeye and of a rhinoceros needing a health certificate which he rapidly supplied when, after investigating it through a peephole, the animal's tusk ripped up the metal panel, beside him like a tin-opener. A circus asked him to anaesthetise a lion with a thorn in its paw. The animal lived in a pit with a cage over it. Bob put on a belt with various aerosols before descending. The assembled company craned over the cage. 'Shht.' He squirted the lion's nose and without taking his eye off the animal repeated the operation with a different aerosol. Out of the corner of his eye he noticed the spectators slumped over the top while he and the lion were left gazing eyeball to eyeball across the pit. The President of Rotary International, Ted Capelan, came, setting a tape recorder under the dinner table without asking. When his head collapsed on his plate we worried it was a heart attack, but he was just checking his infernal machine. He propositioned Gretchen in a motorway café on their way south. Indians came to lunch and we gave them pork. A self-possessed girl of twelve was quite unfazed when a swallow swung through the door depositing its good luck token on the table in front of her. Perfectly poised, she mopped it with her napkin and carried on eating.

The couple from hell were the Ice Maiden, and her husband who had made $1 million out of people's bunions. His mother said they had risen too quickly and declared she disliked mice, which caused a local resident to make an indiscreet appearance. They left with their bedroom key and she made a play for their driver Jim Gavin, our Irish friend who organised the mowing machine races at Wisborough Green in Sussex. At home in California the Webbers employed an inside gardener and an outside one, and had a stairway lined with tanks full of creatures of the deep. They owed Gretchen money which I undertook to recover, but returning from the office for breakfast, my mind beautifully organised, the bloody woman was washing her hair and never appeared. Dorothy Frazier, headmistress of a school at Pocatello, Idaho came three times, once as an unpaid housemaid, but fell out on encountering Margaret Crawford, kissing cousin and scandalous friend from Australia, a spunky lady with a heart of gold, who disliked dogs and children. She arranged an annual tour of her so called relations from Gloucestershire to the Black Isle if she thought them smart enough and was amazing. In her late eighties she broke a leg in Outer Mongolia, and had to be hoisted onto the aeroplane of Madeleine Albright, the American Secretary of State, who just happened to be passing. She admitted to snobbery, had good taste with which she developed her property at Emu Swamp, supervised by Crocodile Dundee, and despaired of the chaos in which she considered we lived. She comes no more and we miss the old bat. I always forgot to buy soda for her whisky.

There were other gentler friends. Sue Gordon, who entertained Rowena in America, split herself laughing when trying to point out where she lived in Colorado on the only available atlas in the Library. She was rather alarmed to see it marked 'Sioux Indians'. We now have a large up-to-date *Times Atlas of the World*, but can't read the names without a magnifying glass. Then there was Mary Packard, secretary of San Francisco Opera, who everybody loved. For her I wrote:

Real cool

Mary Poppins
Flew in from San Francisco today,
Tall, elegant, beautifully dressed,
And in no time at all
She has restored this maddening place
To serenity.

I like Mary Poppins
Who is everybody's friend
And who comes back
Like a gentle wind
Each spring.

As soon as she's gone
We will return to our awful normality
But for today
She makes everybody feel
A little less mad

And a little less annoyed
At being alive.

Mary Poppins
Is real cool!
That's what I think.

An ultimate awfulness was a party of six Canadians. On disembarking they announced they thought they had the rightful claim to Muncaster and were putting a lawyer onto it. At dinner the leader examined a silver fork. 'Gee, Ethel, this is a Pennington fork', following up with identical comments about the spoon. Phyllida was away and Gretchen, acting hostess, was also cooking. On going to fetch the next course I found her dancing up and down on the kitchen table in a black petticoat and a state of fury. The guest's enthusiasm rapidly evaporated when told our annual costs.

Besides Gretchen another mastermind was at work, her friend, Catherine Althaus at the BTA who loved Bill Addison, but they were sadly unable to wed until he retired, not long before his death. He had introduced a rule that no BTA employees could be married to each other. We met on a blind date at the ticket barrier at Manchester Piccadilly. She sent journalists, paying more realistic rates than At Home, and providing us with Press coverage throughout the world. Over one woman's shoulder I watched her unbelieving scribble on being shown around by Phyllida: 'And do you know she does her own ironing?' Chung Lee wrote in lovely Chinese script. Nikki Yarkoff lay on the lawn to take her photographs, and Makoto Kobuta featured me as centre spread in Japanese *Playboy* in Uncle Edward's old overcoat with the dogs. The rest of the magazine featured nothing but naked ladies and was unfortunately sent to Bobby. Noticing it on his desk, Gretchen thought he might be shocked and hid it. On coming down to dinner his first comment was 'What's happened to my Japanese magazine?!' As a committed Scot, the headline 'England Freak' upset me. Makota Kobuta who had come to investigate ghosts asserted that in Japan they had no feet. Uschi Königer came from Munich. She christened me 'Awful' and liked the clink as I counted cash. Her husband had died young and I liked her very much. Accompanying her was Bob Koenig, ex-Czech jockey with houses in Denmark and Surrey who did work for Catherine. Ena Kendall featured me in the *Observer* article 'Room with a View'. Jerry Payne, friend of John Wayne, a lovely Irish writer riddled with cancer, later entertained Iona in his Los Angeles home, allowing her to drive his Rolls. Peter Hayes wrote for a glossy German magazine, pretending to be our butler and driving me to a TV interview in the Lammermuirs with David Dick, RSPB enforcer, about the poisoning of raptors.

Border TV, where I first met Fiona Armstrong who opened the new garden centre for us, and Radio Cumbria were very supportive, although one reporter, Jonathan Garrs, later rusticated to the Isle of Man, infuriated me, gatecrashing a party with Janet Langhart, a beautiful quadroon, married to the inventor of The

Pill, who was interviewing the family for Boston TV. J.L. 'Sir William, which is your favourite room?' She had a lovely voice. After listening to this famous woman Jonathon requested an interview on a 'most important subject' the following day in my office. J.G. 'Mr Gordon-Duff-Pennington, which is your favourite room?' The maddening man was through the door quicker than lightning, and of course I felt guilty for hurting his feelings. To Janet I gave a uniquely scented bloom of *Rh. brachysiphon*, a plant whose name is still transcribed in my mind as Janet Langhart. Ms Grace Ng of British Airways brought Johnny Yip, a famous Chinese pop star and writer, of whom we had never heard, with Mr Cheung his boyfriend; L. Greenstreet Kan – racing correspondent of the *Hong Kong Times*, who said he never bet, but probably did; and two others. At dinner Mr Cheung sat beside Gretchen, contributing nothing, silently slumping lower and lower on his chair, until suddenly his face lit up. Gretchen thought she was stroking the dog but it proved to be Cheung's knee. Worse still was Vera Beljakova, correspondent of the *Johannesburg Sunday Times*, aged 38, daughter of White Russian lecturers at Nottingham University. She appeared having had an injection of mountain lamb glands in Switzerland to rejuvenate her. She was dressed in her 'boob toob' and was expecting her French lover from America. We took her to Ravenglass Fair in May, equipping her with a more suitable wardrobe for £1.50 after which she insisted on attending the fortune teller, Madame Eileen. Eileen Moore, unbriefed, told her a tall dark stranger was coming across the sea to claim her and she should remain beside the fire – our fire – until he came. Much to Bobby's fury she translated this literally. We were not pleased when she called the BTA complaining of her disgraceful treatment and that we had even bored holes in the bottom of the silver tin beside her bed to make the biscuits go soggy! She demanded an extension to her free stay, but was put on the BTA blacklist having failed to realise Catherine was a friend of the natives. Eileen (73) still supervises the cleaning of the house and tells the tea leaves with uncanny accuracy.

Catherine has remained a good friend. With Bill gone she still had her cats who ruled her with a rod of iron. On going to stay with her in Parsons Green I wrote as a bread and butter letter:

Nedd and Ben

We live with some conceit
In 1, Irene Road,
Our coats are very sleek
And we know we are superior
To cats in other streets.

Our names are Nedd and Ben
Although the visitors are apt to call
Us n'cats, or chats, or beasts
We have a servant quite unlike
The cats along the street.

She feeds us coq au vin,
We dine at half past six,
For us no smelly mouse
Like other cats in Parson's Green.

We're too well bred to work
Like cats in common roads
Who do not have a maid to serve,
Who pee upon the Persian rugs,
And slaughter little birds.

Because we do not pay
Our cleaner very much
A part time job we make her take
In order that she can afford
To have a little break.

We do not pay her stamp,
Pretend she's self employed,
And on the whole we're happy that
She knows her place as servant
To these two conceited cats.

Others came in constant streams. A cousin, Priscilla, asked to stay. At the appointed time Phyllida was appalled to see it was the one with a husband and four children from Drummuir and not the expected spinster. Relics of our forgotten past appeared, usually late, not realising the twisted road. Nancy Ingham, Bernard's wife, brought one party sent by BNFL on 'spouse control' to keep them quiet while their other halves were locked in learned discussion at Sellafield. During John Guinness' chairmanship we were sometimes entertained at Sella Park, BNFL's very upmarket guesthouse, meeting many interesting people. Once I sat next to Marjorie Wallace, investigative journalist, whose determination through her own battle with ill health achieved so much for schizophrenics with her foundation of SANE in 1986. Marchon also entertained us one night, and the following day the head man's wife, Missy from Texas, came with Diana Paul, married to Robin, the English head man, who was interested in stars and lived at Eden Close in Kensington. She wrote poetry under the pseudonym Imogen Brown and sent me 'Meals-on-Wheels' to which I replied:

Imogen Brown

Oh! fascinating female, you
Who suddenly appeared to me
Among my awful daily mail,
Along with bills and tax demands
To brighten up my dingy day
With tales of fish and Mr Brown,
And meals on wheels in Kensington

Next time you come
Be sure to bring
A bit more sun and Robin Brown,
But if the rain does not relent
A rod and line will likely land
A fish upon your window sill
That's big enough for Brown and you,
And Mrs Jones who'll be content,
And even grumpy Mrs Pratt,
And all the wives round Eden Close
Will call you then the heroine
Of Meals-on-Wheels in Kensington,

Dear Mrs Brown I fancy you
Because you brighten up my day.
I hope you'll live to ninety nine
And be my friend from now till then,
So I can add my voice as well
To all the ancients in the street,
Who sing your praise each time you call
Fair Imogen of Kensington
Disguised as plain Diana Paul!

Terry Spencer came with his wife Lesley to write an article for *Time Life*. His previous piece was about a murderer and he left us to visit Yasser Arafat. We found them poised with their camera at midnight above the bowl of the loo beautifully decorated with blue roses. Olaf Salmonsen who worked for the Red Cross, and his wife Signe Moland, a distinguished lawyer who fought hard for the disadvantaged, were favourite guests more than once. They entertained us in Oslo on the way to a forestry conference at Elvirum, and again when they met us at Stavanger en route for the North Cape on the coastal steamer. 1940 seemed very close where the German Stukas had dive bombed places we had stuck pins in maps. We visited Trondheim Cathedral, a dark and moving place where the Norwegian kings were crowned, and the Arctic Cathedral at Tromsö whose east window was painted white to prevent the congregation looking out when they were meant to be concentrating on higher matters. We sailed up the Trollfjord where it was almost possible to touch the cliffs on either side, an amazing experience spoilt by the phoney atmosphere they tried to create by playing a tape of Peer Gynt. The reindeer at the North Cape were mangy, and it was a relief to fly back from Kirkenes to be met at Bergen by the Salmonsens who drove us back to Oslo up Sognefjord at cherry time and through Gubrensdal, visiting an old hotel at Rudesheim, with its turf roof which Signe had owned. The year before I had taken two Norwegian journalists, Gard Espeland and Berit Metlid, around south-west Scotland. They invited me to dinner at Gard's home. Afterwards we walked in the moonlight across the Akerselva Bridge and saw the old factory where long ago the girls made clothes watched from the opposite bank by Rudolf Nilsson and Oscar Brathen who immortalised them in their poems. Gard's ancestors were Sinclairs who came from Caithness in the seventeenth century as mercenaries to fight with Gustavus Adolphus. Most were massacred in Gubransdal, lured into the valley by the vision of a beautiful woman on the hilltops. The Salmonsens once arrived at Ardverikie with a suitcase full of clothes and left with clothes in a plastic bag and the case full of chanterelles.

For two springs lambing time was a terrible miss, but leaving the office would have worsened the business chaos. John Whitelaw had shared the farm profits since 1969 which was a mistake as he starved the farm of resources, but I insisted on an extensive refencing programme. Shortly after its completion it was maddening to find twenty tups strolling down the front drive and the bull and his harem sunning themselves in a clearing in the Top Garden. There was no money to undertake conservation work in the house but we scraped together £1,000 for Clare Wilkin to clean and reline Tom Fool's picture at the top of the stairs. Two years later she brought her fiancée, a modern art dealer, to lunch. On entering the Library the youngest daughter was heard to say: 'I can't understand modern art. Some idiot in the paper last week paid £500k, for a plain white canvas with a dot in the middle.' 'Oh dear,' said the man, 'It was me!'

Echoes from the Scottish NFU remained. In 1978 Alasdair Hutton MEP had asked me to meet a European Committee at Patna, Dalmellington as an outstanding example of urban dereliction in rural surroundings, before taking them to visit Frank Hunter Blair who bred Dun Galloways at Marbrack, and to listen to the problems of Carsphairn. In the evening Alasdair telephoned to ask how it went. He commented it was fine friends I had when told the man who really understood was Signor – whose name I perfectly remember – supposedly the head of the Mafia in Sicily. Back home he was wanted for two murders. He had crinkly black hair, a sweet smile, and a ravishing secretary in dark glasses.

At Muncaster despite my best intentions I started attending boring NFU branch meetings at the Brown Cow at Waberthwaite or the Pennington Arms at Ravenglass. Peter Dowling was branch secretary and Michael Postlethwaite, a man of few words, the chairman. Peter read the whole meeting, including the minutes word for word, but did so much beyond the call of duty for his local farmers, helping to fill in their subsidy forms, that his early death was an enormous blow to an agricultural community bypassed by time. One evening of mischance they elected me to represent them at County meetings which happened fifty six miles away at Newton Rigg near Penrith. It was a chance to meet many of the Cumbrian farming community. I was often driven by the County chairman, Bobby Salkeld, of Low Leys, Lamplugh, who had an encyclopaedic knowledge of farms and farmers whose road ends we passed. Reaching his home wasn't always easy and entailed crossing Cold Fell which the Sellafield workers used as their rat run. One morning, stopped in a lay-by to let them past, the car was written off, splitting my chest up the middle. Someone

David Turner and PTGDP counting the cash in the kitchen at Muncaster in the 1980s.

produced two ambulances, but that night, to Phyllida's fury, I staggered six miles to address the Bootle Horticultural Society in my pyjamas. People were kind but lacked the passion of the Scots, although when Michael Jopling, the neighbouring MP, stood next to the stocks in the Square at Broughton-in-Furness, it was impressive witnessing Kate Mawson, from a dairy farm at Seascale in full flow. Michael was a Yorkshire farmer, a decent person, who having been Margaret Thatcher's Chief Whip, became Minister of Agriculture, a post he held with some discomfort at the time of the Chernobyl explosion. I was appallingly rude to him at the NFU AGM in London in 1986 and ended with: 'I can say I love you in Welsh, but don't think I will today.' It was unjustified as he was working hard to push the CAP in a more sensible direction. I wrote to apologise but had back the rudest letter ever written – so rude, in fact, it was going to be framed and put in the downstairs loo. He is now Lord Jopling, too far away and too late to be a friend, but I have never forgotten the Russian toast he told to a meeting at Sedbergh: ' I drink to your death – and I shall be there when they bury you in a coffin made from an oak tree whose acorn I shall plant tomorrow.' Michael and Gail, wherever you are, please forgive that awful moment of ill manners in Kensington Town Hall.

By sod's law in 1986 they made me County Chairman. The Secretary was Roger Ward, with a mind like a gimlet, later moved to London. We developed an excellent working relationship even if he sometimes felt slightly precarious having to include me in his responsibilities! A new HQ was completed at

Penrith, opened by Willie Whitelaw to whom I donated a ditty written for a radical paper at Cambridge whose sub-editor, Gretchen Stevens' daughter, was sacked.

Thoughts of an old Oxford Blue on the Establishment

I only went to Oxford
And that was just because
My mother had high hopes for me,
A fairly hopeless cause.

I've been a party chairman
I've propped the NFU,
I've partly owned a castle
And farmed a field or two

But deep inside I'd much prefer
To find a different place
That understands irreverence
From which I can't escape.

It clings to me tenaciously,
That wish to dig a pin
In any set establishment
That thinks it's sure to win.

I do not like the Tories,
Dislike the Labour left,
The SDP and Liberals
Of policies bereft,

So because I'm always guaranteed
To say what can't be said
I think perhaps I'd better stick
To being an anarchist instead.

In Invernesshire someone asked me to stand for Parliament as a Conservative, but Russell Johnston, the Liberal MP, had paid so much attention to the plight of the hill people it would have been churlish to stand against him. In West Cumberland Jack Cunningham has represented Copeland with considerable political nous for many years, although he often seems unpopular with his constituency party, so my political agnosticsm remains intact at a time when it is considered unfashionable to vote for a person rather than a party – which makes me remain the perfect floating voter!

In the 1980s British Agriculture was, as usual, in some sort of terminal chaos. Milk quotas were introduced on 1 January 1984, geared to a holding's production in 1983 giving dairy farmers a substantial capital asset, transferable either by lease or sale and not tied to the land. There was injustice. In 1991 a newspaper told a tale from South Wales so unjust something needed to be done.

The paper refused to give the man's name, but they told his lawyers. I asked if he wanted me to have a go, after which Raymond Caswell from Berthlwyd, Llangynin, near St Clears telephoned and said: 'Oh! Well!' He had arthritis, and his wife Eirlys, who lived on cider vinegar. Milking cows must have been agony. In 1983 he had bought a farm near Laugharne on overdraft for a son, and purchased Friesian heifers to calve in 1984. As a result the farm's production in 1983 was nil. He went to the tribunal, and better went. Still they refused to award him quota. After six years he took MAFF to the Court of Appeal where he won, but they took him to the House of Lords who upheld the Ministry. By this time interest rates were high and he was in desperate plight. Luckily David Curry was Minister of State. His officials advised that if he gave in the floodgates would open to other appeals, but the papers were still on his desk and he promised to respond in a month. After four weeks two letters were sent to the lawyers, one saying he couldn't help, the other giving Raymond 450,000 litres of quota which was all that he had asked for in the first place – which revealed a brave and just Minister, more intelligent than most of his colleagues.

Another time in the Central Lobby I met Edward Kolawole, Environmental Health Officer from Camden Town. Coming from Nigeria in 1978, in 1990 he married a wife from Kenya and they had a son. Six years later, to have their next baby, she returned with their child to her parents in Nairobi. The Home Office refused re-entry and the poor man was distraught. Again with the help of David Swift, our neighbour of *Drop the Dead Donkey* fame, and Charter 88, the Minister relented. When I telephoned to see how the battle was going a voice the other end said: 'It's wonderful – you can talk to her. She's sitting beside the fire.' Do you remember Yeats' 'An Irish Airman foresees his Death'?

> Nor law nor duty bade me fight,
> Nor public men, nor cheering crowds,
> A lonely impulse of delight
> Drove to this tumult in the clouds.

And each time it is worth it, however small the victory.

Leaving Kirkland was sad, particularly for the children. Anthea had married Tim Osborn-Jones the previous summer and it was she who felt most keenly the sale of the only home she had ever known, but it was essential if limited resources were not to be spread too thinly. Muncaster had fallen into a bad state largely because Phyllida's parents had been unable to live there throughout the year and it was vital to concentrate our energy in one place if we were to succeed in re-connecting the house with the people of West Cumbria. For me too it was a wrench bidding farewell to twenty three years of happy memories. I still think of Jimmy Glencorse, Strathmilligan doing all his work with a horse and riding his bicycle. Worse still was leaving friends from the Scottish NFU, particularly Richard Henton. Jim Sharp, from Lauder in the Borders, became hill farming convener and we travelled a little together to introduce him to one or two people and problems in the Highlands. Too many discard their experience without passing its benefit to their successors who, at the turn of the century, increasingly appear to think it irrelevant to modern society. Meantime we watch the young ones make the same mistakes we made.

On a winter night Richard and Patricia Henton drove me north in a car for two as we watched an aurora's curtains of fire across the A9 from Dunkeld to Laggan. For everybody the ensuing months were a time of grinding adjustment. We started weekly meetings of all staff together to explain what was happening, in an attempt to avoid the spreading of rumours and to reassure them that maintaining their jobs was a priority. At the top of the drive Arthur Wilson cleared a jungly mess and we planted a temporary windbreak of six foot Leylandii against the west wind. Unbelievably they were stolen, the same night. We thought people would be scandalised when we felled dangerous trees, but as Arthur's saw screamed two old women were heard to say: 'Isn't it wonderful, something's happening at last!' We left the in-laws' rooms unchanged to welcome them whenever they came and Phyllida's sisters resented the changes far more than their parents. One asked, 'Why do you have to change everything? It was quite all right in Daddy's time!' but it wasn't. The figures spoke for themselves.

Another trauma was adjusting to the mindset of the London NFU, but many Parliamentary contacts remained on all sides of the House of Commons – which was as well because in 1986, my year as County Chairman, at the end of April, disaster descended on West Cumbria with the fall-out from the Chernobyl nuclear reactor. I rapidly learnt the distance from Windermere to Chernobyl and was probably the only person in the County to know. They monitored my radioactivity in a concrete container at Sellafield – an unexpected relaxation – and Jake Kelly, BNFL's Press man, arranged for all newspaper cuttings to be sent to Muncaster. They soon made a pile level with the office ceiling! Initially Government had no intention of compensating farmers unable to move or sell stock, but by September plans were in place to monitor sheep, allowing lambs with readings below 1,000 becquerelles to be sent to market. Gathering the fells was unproductive work and after intense lobbying it was a relief when the scheme was introduced. By the time store sales were in full swing fell farmers were in such a ferment that MAFF called a meeting at Broughton-in-Furness attended by three hundred people. Staying at Muncaster an American TV team were allowed to attend, but not film – which caused us to hold a further indignation meeting at home the following day. In the front row at the Eccleriggs Hotel sat Lou Howson, a Scot from Windsor Farm in Wasdale. An ardent supporter and adviser to the Labour Party, he was an indifferent farmer with a good heart and quite verbose. When somebody suggested the MP for Penrith and the Borders as a possible helper to our cause he commented; 'Och! Yon Davie Maclean, he's nocht but yin o' Mrs Thatcher's knicker washers!' Throughout that summer John Bradbury and his staff were immensely supportive. He was an outstanding man who felt frustrated because he wasn't in the Civil Service fast stream and couldn't rise as far as his abilities should have taken him. For six months the Press were maddening, telephoning daily. Half an hour was spent on each call only to be persecuted by a different reporter from the same newspaper the following day. I wrote to Mr Gorbachev inviting him and his wife to stay to see the effects of an accident in a place miles away, with a long history of difficult times, sympathising with the population who had been dispossessed around Chernobyl. There was no answer, but the request made *Pravda* and apart from the Communist Party of here and there the New York Fire Brigade and Cumbria NFU were reputed to have been the only independent organisations to have written letters of sympathy.

It was ironic that the fallout set off alarms at Sellafield. Many questioned whether the resultant radioactivity in the soil was not a relic of the Windscale fire in 1957, although the authorities stated the relationship between caesium 137 and 134 gave different fingerprints. Brenda Howard from ITE at Merlewood did valuable research at Woodend, Upha, on top of the fells, discovering that caesium followed the wet patches and in one two-acre field readings of 200 vegetation samples varied between 250 and 6,500 bqs. per kilo. Through peaty soils caesium moved freely, sheep droppings recycling through the grass, but when animals were moved to lower ground heavier soil particles bound it up, causing monitor readings to drop dramatically. The London NFU establishment were hell bent on keeping the Welsh and West Cumbrians apart which didn't prevent me attending two meetings at Llanrwst, and two years later a Commons Committee enquiry at Bangor. Joe Rayne, the National Livestock chairman, and the farmers beyond the fells thought we were kicking up a fuss about not very much.

That mid-summer the Pennington Research Association of America invited me to speak at their annual meeting in Charleston, South Carolina whither I went with Gretchen Stevens, still a US citizen, as my guide to ultimate America. My eye had a stye and the air hostess, Linda Cowderoy, produced a cold teabag to cure it, and champagne, and still sends Christmas cards. At passport control we were separated, Gretchen anxious in case my reply to 'What is the purpose of your visit' was 'To overthrow the US government!' The lack of humour in the eyes of hard faced officials luckily restrained me. In Charleston were every kind of Pennington 'relations' with antecedents stretching back to 1620 and the Mayflower, as well as unlikely legends. Pocahontas was reputed to be a Pennington, as was the last man back across the Alamo alive. John, aged 14, was there in a teeshirt announcing it had been presented by his President, Ronald Reagan, for being the Spelling B champion of the USA. That was too much for me and I had to find something he couldn't spell. 'Eschscholtzia' got him in one. The chairman, Vivien from Santa Fe, and her husband, R.C. Pennington, known as Preach were lovely people. When they returned to Muncaster they presented me with a sombrero and a letter announcing Tony Anaya, Governor of New Mexico, had made me his Honorary ADC. It gave me delusions of riding down Whitehall followed by a line of dark skinned men with large moustaches to tell the authorities where they could go! The Penningtons were kind and far more knowledgeable about Phyllida's ancestors than I. Charleston was hot, but moving to the humidity of Washington was worse. Grace da Palma who had visited Muncaster gave us lunch with her husband. They had a daughter whose Principal at Brynmawr University said none of her students were worth a degree until they had been on a demonstration. There were visits to the US Department of Agriculture, the Pentagon, and other sights before flying to Boston. Never feeling secure unless knowing where north is, it was upsetting when the driver said: 'In Boston it's East!' I felt even less secure when his card was pressed into my hand announcing E. Carlo Marotti, investment adviser and a smart name for taxi driver (– probably Mafioso!). Boston was wonderful, walking down the Freedom Trail with Connie Hill, a journalist, hearing about the War of Independence and places and people from history books. I ate Boston skrod and sat on a bench with the bronze figure of Mayor Curley, the Rascal King, who administered the city from jail. There was lunch in the Senior Common Room at Harvard and dinner with the Reeds. She worked for a famous firework family and was in love with her boss who blew himself up. There was a visit to the Glass Flower museum and a journey on the Metro to visit the Boston Globe, passing along the road with two delightful little coloured girls of ten and twelve who knew exactly what they wanted to do with their lives and couldn't believe I lived in a Castle. It reminded me of one early morning in the London Underground with three little white boys and one little black boy delighted with each other's company, going fishing.

Afterwards to New York, staying in the Algonquin, Dorothy Parker's old haunt, where Paco, the Bishop of Puerto Rico, came to visit. An old friend from Gretchen's Puerto Rican days, he later stayed with her when he preached in Eskdale, playing his guitar in the church. New York was amazing – we visited Bedford Paice, the BTA representative, and the Frick Museum; ascended the Empire State Building; and attended an outdoor concert at the Kennedy Centre with Robin Cohn. One night to dine with John Thomson, British Ambassador to the UN, who had a home near Castle Douglas. Ruth Prawa Jhabrala was there, the endlessly famous author of *Heat and Dust* of whom I had never heard. We were late and being unable to find a taxi, hitched a lift with a man called Daniel who, on the short journey, gave a rundown of his marital problems. As he needed a wife and we were visiting *Bride Magazine* the following day we suggested him as a suitable husband for the girl who interviewed us and was short of a husband. There being no subsequent wedding invitation it obviously didn't work. In 1985 *Bride* had sent Gustavo Martoramo and Janice Marsh to Muncaster on their honeymoon. She wasn't pleased, having thought their destination was Florida and dressed accordingly. They spent the whole time sitting arguing on the dining room floor, but perhaps it was all right as two years later they sent a photograph of a baby! Muncaster's American promotion was successful but I didn't like the food and couldn't get round the idea of deep fried ice cream. The Pennington Research Association came twice more to Muncaster under the guidance of Bob Laubach who also brought the American Watercolourists. Everybody was kind wherever we went, but it was a relief to return home to a more understated life.

That summer a minibus appeared at the Front Door with two men from the Ministry in Carlisle who I knew and liked, two men from the Ministry in London, two others, and a large policewoman to see if our loos were fit to sit on if the Senior Agricultural Committee from Brussels came to lunch when the Agricultural Ministers were meeting at Windermere. One man got out. 'How do you do? I'm Melville from EC2.' I'm sure he was a good husband, but I didn't know him and rapidly disliked him. 'You know, it's a great honour. The Minister is considering sending important guests from Brussels and wants you to tell me what you will tell them.' Phyllida's great great grandfather, John Charles Ramsden, who was sacked from school for fighting a duel over a girl in 1804 seemed a suitable introduction and in the family dining room I explained that the panelling over the fireplace came from the captain's cabin of the *Fighting Temeraire*, the French flagship captured at the Battle of Lagos in 1759, which later fought for the British at Trafalgar. 'Stop!' said the odious Melville. 'You will not mention Trafalgar – there will be French people there!' Anyone who knew me could have told him it was unwise. At the end of September, having dined with the Ministers, we reached home at 2 a.m., exhausted. The next morning was thick mist which cleared at 12 o'clock as the buses arrived. The first twenty to alight were French. I stood with a sweet smile on the doorstep, my mouth curved upwards at the sides, 'I'm told I'm not to cause an incident, but I cannot stick the French.' Everybody was appalled. 'We've had French students on our farm in Scotland and I have lots of lovely French friends, but as a nation you're awful!' They still looked doubtful until I explained that when, one Monday morning, my mother produced Mlle. Gras from Strasbourg, with large pebbly glasses, large bosoms and large legs, to teach us French, we weren't happy. By the following Sunday a pit was dug, filled with water, and covered with sticks and leaves. We got her on Sunday, she left on Monday. The visitors cheered, Melville from EC2 was nowhere to be seen, and the *Entente Cordiale* was sealed when I placed one *Eucryphia cordifolia* bloom on each wife's side plate for lunch. Much later Jack Cunningham brought Franz Fischler, the Austrian Agricultural Commissioner, and his wife Heidi, with whom we have exchanged Christmas cards ever since.

Harold Robinson took over as County Chairman in January 1987. As an outsider the support received from members and staff was astonishing and gave entry to many homes which would normally never have welcomed me. It was not Scotland – the lament of my life – but the needs of the farms were very close. On leaving, the comradeship of Roger Ward was most missed, but the

Young Farmers took me under their wing, making me their County President.
For their *Journal* in June 1986 I had written:

Young Farmers

She – or he – is very strange!
They're kind to all the old –
Including me –
And good to animals
But don't know what they want
And sometimes don't like doing
What they're told. They're shy
In company they do not know,
Not keen to join in agricultural politics
Which bore them stiff.
They do not always do
The things they say they'll do
But think that they know how to farm
Much better than their antique relatives.
Perhaps they're right, although
The young ones make the same mistakes
We made and go
To colleges less old than us.
They will not listen, which would save
A lot of time, and keep
Their banks and families
Happier than mine.
So when I watch the kindly eager faces
At the YFC they should
Better attend the words the old buffoon lets fly.
I tell them what to do – and think
There but for the grace of God go I,
Watching them go their own sweet way
To make the same mistakes I made
Those countless moons ago when I also
Was young and unafraid.

Meantime Muncaster preserved its state of malignant chaos. Students came
and went from Newton Rigg and Seale Hayne. David Turner from Sheffield
and Alastair Graham from Grange lived with us. David was shocked when
Alastair unpacked a dinner jacket, but they got on well, and never got on our
nerves, and when they left were greatly missed. David had a girlfriend, a fellow
student, also from Sheffield. His description of her taking off her earrings to
prepare for action when the going became rough in a home town bar was
hilarious. After their departure we were at the end of next year's Newton Rigg
queue with a man of forty with ringlets who looked like a New Guinea head
hunter and squatted in the back yard watching the swallows, and a girl who

didn't approve of the Queen and stuck stamps on upside down to signal her disapproval but came up trumps when the head hunter tried to cut his wrists. The third was a boy who ate three pounds of sausages every day for breakfast. The Bendells retired to Hollowstones, their place taken by Phil Heyward from the Parachute Regiment and his Rambo wife Anne-Marie. Mrs Simmonds retired from cooking and took up the no less demanding job of cleaning. The kitchen was manned briefly by Georgina Mackay-Fowler, an ample lady who sang arias with her four daughters as they swung from side to side over the Aga, putting a pinch of this and that into the pots in time to their singing. Georgie, who embroidered the truth with Irish charm, originally applied for a job as Curator. She had misfortunes in her life which she surmounted with verve and a fertile imagination. She had emigrated to a farm up Eskdale, which had to be sold when her partner died. Nothing daunted she drove a digger and worked as a bouncer in an Egremont night club. She had three boy friends. One, the dishy major from the gun-range at Eskmeals, was seen by a passer-by chasing her at night naked around a ploughed field. 'So earthy, dear boy!' she said as she related the story. She still lives in Ravenglass with her mother who is blind, has trouble with her hips, dyes her distinguished hair a ghastly mottled red, and has a heart of gold. She reminds me of our eldest daughter who would give her shirt away, even if she didn't have one. Americans came and went, one family preceded by a letter reporting an unspeakable twelve year old son who picked his nose, used his napkin as a handkerchief, and had various other undesirable habits. Unfortunately it was left on a hook in the kitchen. The mother, who had no business to be there, found it and threatened everybody with the law.

In 1987 Rowena married Robert Morris-Eyton from Beckside, who was working in Sussex as a land agent, and proposed to her up a tree. She agreed to marry him if he moved closer to Scotland, but thought a May wedding was unlucky, which proved unfortunate. Spring was immaculate, without rain for eight weeks, but the night before the wedding the heavens opened. As there were no marquees seven hundred steaming guests were crammed into the hall like sardines imposing a satisfactory social solution on many who had never met before. The following year, on a day of May sunshine, Iona married Peter Frost, a high class vet from Edinburgh, trained in Glasgow, who added Pennington to his name. It nearly didn't happen. One Bank Holiday the previous year, as I addressed the masses in the Library, he telephoned. 'Can I speak to Iona?' 'No, you can't, I'm busy!' 'Will you give her a message?' – I forgot. He continued with the practice at Broughton for a few years, but as demands of Muncaster multiplied, he joined his wife running the business. In 2001 he returned to his profession to help the Ministry in Carlisle with the foot and mouth outbreak. It was a terrible time causing him to write this very powerful poem, which he read out at the Prince of Wales's big concert in the Albert Hall.

Into the Valleys of Death

Damien Hurst has nothing on me.
I create ghastly pictures of death, officially sanctioned.

I have to believe this mass sacrifice of animals I love
Is worth it.
Or is it the farmers who are the real sacrifice?
Like the animals, they take it meekly and obediently
Often thanking me for doing it.
After I had killed all 356 cattle in one family's dairy herd
They sent flowers to my wife.
These are the people who are giving up all, in the hope it will save others.

But don't get me wrong
I have now seen plenty of this plague
And it is no common cold.
The animals suffer horribly, as the skin of their tongues peels off
And their feet fall apart.
We must try to kill them quick and clean,
As soon as it appears in a herd or flock.

The farmers' suffering does not end with the visit of the
Slaughtermen.

I must continue to do my duty
In these Cumbrian killing fields.
Quickly, efficiently and effectively.
Yes, the official papers must all be in place
Yes, the Health and Safety Man must be happy
Yes, the Environment Agency is only doing their job as best they can.

It is 6 a.m. Today I go out to kill again.
The worst is the young stock.
I thank God the lambs are not yet born with these ewes today.
I will have to kill a calf born yesterday,
The first beautiful calf from the farmer's pride and joy
His new Charolais bull.

This is not what I trained for.
I hope familiarity will never make me immune from the trauma of killing
But I do hope – for the animals' sake – to be good at it.

It is the virus we are trying to kill
With our disinfectants and culling policy,
Our imprisonment of farmers in their own homes.
All they have left is the telephone.

Perhaps today there is hope.
One soldier will meet me at the farmgate
I hope he, not I, will quickly arrange the funeral of the animals I love

Peter Frost-Pennington with Fraser, Phyllida GDP, Iona FP with Isla, PTGDP with Ewan FP. Dogs Mrs Hegel and mother Khyber.

Before their carcasses get so bloated they fall apart
Adding more to the farmers' anguish, trapped amongst them.
I should be free to move on quickly, find the virus
And kill again.

Into the Valleys of Death drove the 600
Or are we now 1100?
The countryside I love is bleeding to death
Mr Blair, please help.

Peter Frost-Pennington
Temporary Veterinary Inspector   23 March 2001

Chapter 14

Because of all the children we have met
We shall go back to our place
In search of the old beliefs.

Patrick Gordon-Duff-Pennington (1930-   ) *Patrick of the Hills*

IN SPRING 1988 for three weeks Aleksandr Shumsky from the Northern Caucasus, Ivan from Rostov, and Piotr from Siberia, bosses of Russian farm cooperatives, came with Frances Cooley, a sweet interpreter whose father made violins. Aleksandr and Ivan stayed at Muncaster, Piotr with Harold Robinson at Kendal. One morning our two guests appeared for breakfast after walking in the garden. Ivan said Aleksander wanted to write a poem for Iona's wedding, but wasn't doing very well 'so I took off my hat and poured my thoughts in, and here you are.' It wished all Iona's enemies to have hiccoughs and her to have more children than she intended. We travelled around Lake District farms and businesses, saw Michael Boothroyd, the Principal of Newton Rigg, visiting the College's hill farm at Mungrisdale with Andrew Humphries, and the creamery at Kendal. Once we went to Scotland to Anna and Colin Campbell, the current Scottish hill farming convener, at the Holm, Carsphairn, where they kissed the ground. The Russians didn't want to visit Sellafield and knew nothing of Chernobyl. When the Press pursued us, imagining they had come to study the damage it had caused the local economy, I always answered the questions to protect them. Wherever we went we caused chaos, singing in the Ministry offices in Carlisle, the boardroom of Preston Farmers, and for a hilarious interlude, accompanied by one, Bernie Gallagher, from Londonderry, at Asda in Preston. My mother told me never to sing in public, but our voices blended so well I began to consider myself a fine singer! There was a song about eagles flying high in the blue skies of the Caucasus and an old man meeting Lady Death. 'I want you.' 'Oh!' said the old man, 'I'm old and I suppose I could come, but I'll tell you what, let's have a drink on it on the way.' The upshot was he left Lady Death dead drunk in the ditch while he went marching on – and that is how the people of the Caucasus are so unending old.

One night, descending from Wasdale to visit Norman Ireland, Phyllida's tenant at Drigg, Aleksandr suddenly saw the sea. 'I've paddled in Lake Baikhal, the Arctic Sea and the Baltic; in the Black Sea, the sea of Azov, and the Caspian. Please, please can we paddle?' The three of us and Frances walked in line abreast down the beach at Seascale where Nikita Kruschev had kissed the babies in 1956. Aleksandr in black Homberg hat, black coat, black trousers, black marching boots, waded into the sea, picking up a stone for each of us, and offering a handful of seawater. It was such a basic gesture I wanted to cry.

In July Harold Robinson, his son Matthew, and I were invited on a return visit. On the plane, stretched out on two seats beside me, her smelly feet under my nose, was an American lady on her way to Yerevan. Going in to land at Moscow she awoke. 'Hi! I'm Lilian Rosengarten, a psychiatrist from New York.' The ultimate show off, I demonstrated my looking-glass writing as a suitable introduction to which she responded: 'Boy, you need me!' Moscow was horrid. In the hotel a wardress guarded each floor and as there was no loo paper I had to make do with a copy of the *Whitehaven News*. While we waited for the Agroprom office to sort out the mess they made with our visas we visited a pig farm in a forest so overstaffed it was no wonder our guests had been impressed by the Woodall's operation at Waberthwaite. After interminable delay at the airport we flew to Novosibirsk, as far the other side of Moscow as Moscow was from Muncaster. To the north we watched the drama of sunset and sunrise merging over the Arctic and in the darkness below, as we crossed the Urals violent jags of lightning illuminated the countryside. After a reception committee, which made us feel important, and breakfast we travelled forty bumpy miles to the east to the Kholkhoz of the Red Banner, Piotr's community. We rested in the cooperative's guest house through an afternoon with temperatures of 112°F. The countryside was flat and in the winter the thermometer sank to −85°F. Dairy cattle were hand milked under primitive conditions amid swarms of flies. There was a herd of horses bred for racing and a crop of barley. Although living was precarious, great care was taken of the young children, mothers dropping them at kindergarten on their way to work at early morning, collecting them on their way home at night. In the middle of the day they had bunks to rest under the eye of dedicated teachers ever mindful of the Russian saying: 'Our children are our future.' One evening we went on a boat on the great River Ob to catch sturgeon, afterwards cooking them over a fire on an island, bitten by midges. Another evening we spoke to eight hundred members of the cooperative about home. Before starting there were traditional gifts of bread and salt and an embroidered cloth. The children sang their own composition pointing at us and their parents. 'For goodness sake stop arguing and allow us to enjoy our animals and the peace of the Siberian countryside.' At the Agricultural College at Novosibirsk we drank *kumlis*, a mixture of mare's milk and fizzy water. My heart sank every time they said Cognac. 'Come on, Patrick, bottoms up!' but it probably kept our stomachs orderly. For the final meeting I wrote:

For the People of the Kholkhoz of the Red Banner

> You have taken us
> Who were strangers only yesterday
> Into your hearts.
> You have given us the feeling for your lands

And your love for your cattle
Which we can so easily understand.
In two short days
You have handed us so much
Of your kindness
That when we have gone away
To our own homes
We shall never forget
All the beauty we have seen,
Watching the sun and the moon
Rise and go down
Across the wide Siberian lands;
And if we should ever be given the great privilege
Of an invitation to return
We would ask that it should be
At a time of year
When we can plant a tree,
So that when we must leave again
We will have the thought,
Always in our minds,
Of the little birds in its branches
And the shade of its leaves
Over the children of the children
Who met us yesterday
In the kindergarten of your kholkhoz.

Too soon
Shall we go away to our own houses
And our own hills
But our hearts will always be full
Of your people;
And when we watch the moon rise
Over our fields again
We shall know
It is the same moon
Which shines on us
As upon you. We shall shed a tear
Because of the great distance
Which keeps us apart
When we are, in our minds,
So close;
For you, all the people of this kholkhoz
Of the Red Banner,
Have made yourselves a part
Of our own families.
We have so little to give
But you hold in your hands

Our hearts,
And a part of them will always belong
Only to you
And to the children who sang for us
Yesterday.

From Siberia we flew to Stavropol, before a Land Rover took us to Aleksandr's Kholkhoz of the October Revolution, stopping to eat a trout on the way in a place where Lermontov was killed. The community ran efficiently. Aleksandr, an engineer, member of the Supreme Soviet, friend of Gorbachev's with whom he had worked on the combines in their youth, heated the village from hot springs. Symmetrical 300-acre fields were surrounded by mulberry shelter belts to encourage silk worms whose thread was used for military uniforms. Machinery spare parts were difficult, but considering no fertilizer was used, production of wheat and maize was respectable. Because of stupid rules, worthy of central authority anywhere, no surplus grain could be exported out of the region despite production being double its needs. The result was that half the harvest lay in rotting piles. The large grey sheep were kept mainly for wool in the foothills, herded by hardy horsemen with dogs which looked like short legged Old English Sheepdogs. Our hosts took us to see the space capsule of Valentina Tereshkova, the first woman in space, which was strangely moving. We visited schools, danced in the streets with the children, and placed wreaths on war memorials. One day a local journalist took us to the Dombai National Park, usually only open to researchers, afterwards visiting the place where the Cossacks repulsed the German army. Agriculturally Aleksandr ran a well-ordered enterprise and one wondered how the grain producers of Eastern England would compete if the rest of Russia was as well organized.

Next we were taken on long dusty roads to Rostov, with tomato sellers by the side, coming at sunset to the marvellous statue of the Guns of Trachanka commemorating the turning back of the White Russians by the Red Guards in 1919. Along roadsides wrecked cars perched on high structures as a deterrent to careless drivers. We spent a day on a boat trip down the river for a picnic and visited the cooperative's modern medical facilities dedicated to monitoring workers' health in a community where time off was considered letting the side down. Ivan was experimenting with leasing land to private individuals with a guarantee that the kholkhoz would buy the produce, although the accounting systems would have defied a senior wrangler. At Muncaster they had had endless evening post-mortems about finance which were equally insoluble.

The last night at Rostov, Ivan wanted to introduce us to his best water-melon gang, a family who came each spring, camping in the 50-acre field in makeshift shelters until after harvest. A man approached, exact replica of the Cumbrian who had sold us the horse in the Cockermouth street, silk scarf around neck, cap over eyes those thirty years before. 'Good evening, I'm Rubin – not the pianist, you know, he's my son' (Rubinstein), which he wasn't. 'We would be honoured if you would eat with us.' He showed us a trestle table groaning with food under an awning, then from underneath produced a case of the finest Georgian champagne which we drank as the sun went down over the River Don. It was a special moment and we sang Scottish songs and Russian songs, and their folk melodies made me want the evening never to end. The following day we flew back to Moscow to meet the Agroprom sponsors whose crunch line was, 'When can we do business with you?' A correct answer was far beyond the diplomatic talents of three Cumbrian farmers.

In Moscow there had been a hash about hotel bookings and we weren't expected. The interpreter went home leaving us to doss down for the night in the lobby, pulling our hats over our faces hoping no one would notice us. At midnight an intruder appeared, shouting and hitting two bystanders over the head with a broken bottle. His wife was sent for and the police came but did nothing. We pulled our hats further down. When the interpreter, another Aleksandr, reappeared in the morning his only comment was: 'Must have been drunk. Not Russian. Probably Jugoslav.' We visited the Kremlin, but spared ourselves the queue for Lenin's tomb, and in the evening travelled through spotlessly clean metro stations with crystal chandeliers to see the Red Army dancers. Returning to Britain was like waking from a dream and the incredible memory was of the generosity of the country people who had so little, but were prepared to share it with strangers. I shall never forget the single voice starting to sing at the end of our Siberian evening, followed by the perfect natural harmony of eight hundred others, and the vanquished look of the one disagreeable visitor who had bicycled from Vladivostok.

Chapter 15

...dost thou not know, my son, with how little wisdom the world is governed.

Count Oxenstierna (1583-1654)

IN 1986 BOBBY DIED leaving a gap in the chair where he watched the racing in the Library, his back to the public as they milled around. They still remember him. He was always fit until slipping in the burn at Ardverikie eighteen years before as a result of which he had to give up hunting and most of the things he enjoyed. Veronica followed eighteen months later and their passing left an enormous hole at Muncaster even although their visits had become increasingly rare. Their virtues are still remembered not least by their rebellious son-in-law. My own mother having arrived at one grand-daughter's wedding by helicopter and landed on the lawn in a puddle of water, lingered until 1996, travelling to Sutherland each August out of habit, staying at the Navidale Hotel at Helmsdale to taste the salt sea air. One night, returning to the sleeper at Inverness, she collapsed in hysterical laughter at the Station Hotel when her skirt fell around her ankles in the reception. Her last years were fairly horrible, unable to do much with her bad back, unable to eat what she wanted – she had always been fond of her food – and unable to garden, detained in her downstairs rooms at the Stable Cottage whither she had moved after selling the Old House to the Benhams. Kate and Gordon Simmonds cared for her with great kindness and poor Elspeth, who lived an hour away at Nether Wallop, bore the brunt of family care. Suddenly she had had enough, ensured her affairs were in order, and took off, causing Milly, Elspeth's grand-daughter, to speculate upon which cloud she was sitting. She was most determined and without her there was a large gap in the lives of her wide acquaintance. Shish died shortly afterwards, and my half-brother Roderick in 1999, having smoked himself to death. He never believed in possessions – except books, which to Patricia's amazement he insisted on carting from posting to posting. We visited them in Hong Kong, Berlin, Ballykinler, Sandhurst, Kimpton, Netheravon and Rushall and there, sure enough, was his increasing supply of literature. Having left the army, after a brief and unhappy stint as Bursar of Hertford College, Oxford, he returned to an ERE job at Shrivenham where he was loved by his assistants and all the families he supported. In many ways he was like his mother, often intellectually arrogant which offended many less intelligent contemporaries, including his army superiors. Shish had moved to 10 Jameson Street, Notting Hill when Father died and was supported by friends, young and old, acquired through her membership of the Russian Orthodox Church. Our happiest memory of her later years was sitting cross-legged on the floor at Knott End Centre for Complementary Care in a circle of people while Arthur Paynter, the paediatrician at West Cumberland Hospital, taught us a deep toned Tibetan chant which went U, O, I, E, A. It remains suitable refuge in time of stress.

In 1987, having been interviewed by Derek Barber, I became one of ten Ministerial Appointees on the Lake District Special Planning Board (LDSPB), serving on the Development Control Committee and the Park Management Committee, of which I became chairman two years later. The Board Chairman, shortly replaced by Steele Addison, was Dick Shelton who ran a family joinery business in the Central Lakes. Vice-chairman was Jean Corlett, a kindly and knowledgeable fish researcher who retired to the Isle of Man. To describe Steele as kindly would be damning him with faint praise. Larger than life, he was a farmer, a robust chairman who ruled the Board with strength of character and common sense, and was quite capable of withstanding unreasonable demands from any direction. The Chief Planning Officer was John Pattison and the Development Control (DC) chairman, Richard Vane, later Lord Inglewood MSP, a young shaggy lawyer by training whose hair style varied between wild and a monstrously clipped back and sides. He was eminently qualified to unravel the complicated spates of planning applications and on joining the Board was asked by his brother what it was like being one of the thirty most unpopular people in the Lake District. Papers for monthly meetings became so voluminous that officers were eventually given delegated authority to deal with simpler cases. Planning Officers are universally hated and once or twice I found myself having to speak out for them in their very difficult job. One or two were less intelligent than they might have been in handling local opposition. Anne Brown, whose integrity I grew to respect, so incensed one Eskdale farmer driving his flock along the narrow road, that he kept her car behind him for more than a mile. In the case of Eskdale Estate, which was the conversion of a snipe bog into a small golf course for the owner's personal pleasure, my colleagues took a blatantly unfair decision to oppose it on the grounds that as it was going to cost so much he must be going to make money out of it! It was also considered too green when viewed from the Fells. The ensuing brouhaha more or less caused the death of Phil Jacobs, a very special human being and one of the last true gentlemen in the world. Although the course remains, so does the nasty taste in my mouth. John Pattison and the Board lawyer, John Chapman, were invariably considerate to me, but I was probably not their easiest member, often failing to appreciate the relevance to the problems of the natives of rules drawn up in London.

There were frequent site visits. I learnt to sense PVC windows and Welsh slates as out of harmony with the built environment of the Lake District whose integrity was a testament to the skill of past planners. Unfortunately insistence on local slates raised the price of all developments, most quarries being controlled by a single firm with a large export trade to America which doubled the cost not only of new buildings, but of re-roofing old ones. My position was considerably imperilled when Iona tried to re-roof the cook's flat at Muncaster with fibreglass slates! Another local farmer tried Vermont slates and compounded the felony by using red tiling roof ridges. The same problems subsist fifteen years later with housing too expensive for young local people who have to go away, unable to compete in the market with people retired with a bundle from London and the South East. The immigrants often purchased small cottages in the fells and sure as night follows day, six months later a planning application would arrive to double the size of the house, thus removing it yet further beyond the reach of local inhabitants. For all the pious talk of affordable housing the problem persists throughout the countryside. Agriculture's slump and the lack of small scale industrial development leaves few jobs in the National Park except tourism.

Meetings were not without humour. Ronnie Calvin, ex-miner from Whitehaven, attended DC meetings with field glasses to study plans on the blackboard as they were discussed. Wendy Kolbe, an animal artist, leaned over a steading gate at Bassenthwaite. 'What a lovely little bull!' Anne Hayton, a farmer's wife: 'Wendy, it's a cow!' Peter Phizackerley, ex-Board chairman, ex-shop steward, was the *gauleiter* of the Labour councillors who held pre-meetings. He talked a lot and was sometimes wrong, but so sincere in his commitment to the Park it was impossible to dislike him. He became a distant friend, even though he made constant digs disguised in heavy humour about people who lived in big houses (84 rooms counting the loos!). Development Control meetings were long, but leavened by a lunchtime break across the road for shepherd's pie and lemon sorbets at Brambles. We were conscientious scrutinising planning applications, but as their weight became heavier it was increasingly difficult to dispose of them as speedily as the applicants required. Timing of site visits irritated me. In other areas, which took me an hour and a half to reach, they were scheduled for 10 a.m., while those in West Cumbria were set an hour later to allow the large majority of members and officers time to get there!

The notorious case of my term was the redevelopment of Ambleside bus station. The bus company had sold it twice to itself under other names, adding £1 million at each exchange. They therefore needed a large increase in value to recompense themselves in any sale to developers. The planners said there were no valid grounds for objection. At the DC meeting nine of the seventeen present objected, because the locals disliked the development. I drew the short straw to put the Board's case at the enquiry. We were assured by Frances Paterson, a grey-eyed lawyer from Manchester in a long black coat, that we would lose. She had a gravelly voice, was deeply attractive, and terrified me. A large meeting was held in the church with two half cheers for our courage. Doreen Harrison led the protest, announcing they would show the Planning Board what was what and that a busload of angry inhabitants would demonstrate their displeasure if things didn't go their way. I hadn't the heart to tell them that from the floor of the Council chamber people in the public gallery were invisible. When the Enquiry eventually took place in the Methodist Hall at Ambleside, to everybody's amazement, we won. There was a young girl, attached temporarily to the Board, who fetched and carried all the papers and for her this was written.

The Gopher – for Lucy Bond
Ambleside Bus Station Enquiry, 8 February 1990

Sweet 21 – and a little bit more;
Beautifully dressed,
Undoubtedly bored,
She fetched and she carried,
For day after day,
The system's demands
To the Methodist Hall;
But when I am old
I shall always remember
The sweet wide smile
She gave to us all –
A flower bud in spring
As she dropped in her mouth
Her chocolate drops
In the Methodist Hall.

At the end I bought a box of chocolates for Frances Paterson's children who commented 'Mummy, when are you going back to Ambleside?!' The case was won on traffic grounds, although the traffic officials were most unhelpful. The applicants appealed and the Board won again, although at the third attempt, after my retiral, they won with modified plans. I never regretted our decision to object in the first place. Afterwards, for one brief night, Ambleside danced in the streets.

John Capstick, a robust countryman, was Director of Park Management, shortly replaced by Bob Cartwright from the North Yorks Moors National Park. Both were cheerful fellow fighters. The most irritating case work was dealing with applications to re-route footpaths, many running through farm steadings and a few through people's gardens, but guidelines were specific – any alternative route must be no less convenient and no less enjoyable to the users. On the whole we managed to negotiate the complications, even if not always to the satisfaction of applicants. Occasionally users neither liked nor understood landholders, and adopted an overt political stance which made the Agriculture and Forestry Advisory Committee an essential place to discuss differing views of the countryside. It was there that those representing outside organisations could promote ideas not always coinciding with views of the Board.

Six years as a Member taught me much of the meaning and working of

National Parks, the need for simple rules, and the ability to strain them occasionally in everybody's interest. I attended a two day get-together with the Northumberland and North Yorks Moors National Parks at Helmsley to discuss mutual problems, and also the National Parks Conference at Brecon when Barbara Castle gave a fiery address at the dinner. There were comical diversions. One meeting at Brockhole with Keep Britain Tidy was embarrassing. On arrival a girl was distributing papers around the table. Never having seen her before I thought she must be one of us. The KBT chairman spoke first, and went on and on. I passed a note to the same unknown girl sitting beside me. 'God! He is boring!' – which he was. She hissed in my ear, 'I'll blackmail you. I'm his secretary!'

When I left the Board in 1993 John Toothill and three of his officers came to Ardverikie for their annual weekend outing which was a useful change for them and a happy time for me, showing them the part of my life which made me tick. At the same time the LDSPB were setting up a joint venture with the Field Studies Council (FSC) at Blencathra where the old fever hospital was disintegrating. They asked me to help raise the £250k for its restoration. We were supplied with a pleasant but useless consultant from Craigmyle's who survived only two or three unproductive meetings. The money was finally raised without his assistance thanks to the generosity of many people, including various charitable trusts. My contribution was conditional on part of the syllabus concerning itself with the economies of the local agricultural community. Rob Lucas, the Centre manager, was an able young man, who, assisted by his wife Rachel, his eventual daughter Hannah, and Poppy their labrador, surrounded himself with a dedicated staff to supervise the construction of classrooms and accommodation. The FSC made me a Vice President and their executive meetings bring contact with distinguished academics and environmentalists which I enjoy. It was hoped Prince Charles would open the Centre, but because of his commitments a date was so uncertain that we persuaded David Bellamy to do the job instead only to be told the following week the Prince of Wales would be delighted to come. We arranged a second ceremony when he opened a rock garden constructed by the local school who sang for him in the pouring rain and thought he was wonderful. Fundraising committees were poorly attended but one stalwart was Mary Burkitt, ex-Curator of Abbott Hall in Kendal, who seems to have forgiven me for introducing her to Prince Charles as the maddest woman in Cumbria! Roger Chapman came regularly all the way from Epsom, and Mary Reckitt was a wonderful and knowledgeable support. Her first husband, Paul Holmes, died tragically, the warden of the first FSC Centre at Malham Tarn above Settle, whither I was beckoned next.

FSC is an organisation with Centres around the UK dedicated to Environmental Understanding for All, and keen that access to their practical courses should be within reach of even the most disadvantaged students. Staff, food and accommodation as well as laboratory facilities have become increasingly expensive and it is a neat equation between affordability and viability as education budgets come under increasing pressure. FSC next asked me to raise £350k for the renovation of Malham Tarn, their first Centre in 1947. The Yorkshire Dales Millennium Trust would inject a further £350k into the project. The property belonged to the National Trust who considered their vetting of planning applications was a sufficient contribution to the Appeal although they were benefiting to the tune of £700k. I sailed into Queen Anne Gate and requested a cheque for £50k from Martin Drury, the Director General, who said he would have to ask his people in York – which meant no! It left me in a fit of fevered resentment, but when the job was complete their woman in York, Tiffany Hunt, was so nice it was impossible to restrain a smile – which was perhaps as well as she is now Director of NW England, a huge and impossible job.

At the same time I started attending Scottish Landowners' Federation (SLF) meetings in Edinburgh and Inverness and it was with some astonishment when, walking along the street with Colin Dalrymple, he asked me to consider becoming Vice Convener of the Federation to take over when Peter MacDonald, Colzium retired in 1988. Having three names in increasingly republican times and being based mainly in Cumbria it seemed an odd request! In addition I was a member of an absent landowning family at Ardverikie, a situation of which I continue to violently disapprove. Many landowners in the Highlands are absent, needing to work in London, Geneva or Hong Kong to earn enough pence to mend holes in the roofs of ancestral piles, often listed buildings. They then take little part in day to day Scottish affairs and fail to understand the needs of Scotland or its inhabitants. I did at least have total and transparent commitment to the land and people of Laggan and from my work with the NFUS had gained considerable knowledge of problems faced by members of the Federation. The family had endured the trauma of having to sell Creag Meagaidh and the moor at Dalwhinnie to save jobs during the Thatcher revolution. The lands, which included Moy deer forest and half Aberarder Farm, were bought by Fountain Forestry, the obligation being on them to get planning approval. The world and his wife objected and the case went to George Younger as Secretary of State for Scotland who approved the planting of only half the area considered viable in the application. As a result the Nature Conservancy was forced to purchase the property at a higher price than we had been paid, not knowing what they wanted to do with the land. It is now a National Nature Reserve. Over the years there has been a lot of bullshit about how wonderfully it is run by slaughtering deer to preserve regenerating birchwoods, but the deer aren't stupid and disappear in daylight hours leading to requests for night shooting permits with all their animal welfare implications. Years later a letter appeared on my desk in the Deer Commission saying that sheep from the west were peeing on the regenerating birch seedlings to their great detriment. The farmer wanted to know how to prevent it and some wag had written in the margin 'Give them less water!'

Until the mid-1990s Ardverikie was regarded as an example of a well run family estate, integrated into a progressive view of land management and into Scottish rural society but now, with too many members of the family involved who know little about the daily life of Highland people, it is rapidly becoming divorced from Highland life. With the exception of our own branch, they have little clue about running a family business. To write this breaks my heart. It still remains the most beautiful place in the world. It may still survive for the next generation to ask their smart southern friends to kill deer, but for me it should be about more important things than status – it should be about local people and man's relationship with the land and the birds and beasts who share it. It was with that thought and the will to modernise attitudes and improve human relations that I entered on my three year tenure of office as Convener of the SLF.

It was an organisation with only 4,000 members, but with considerable collective wisdom. Its relevance was ignored by a population with largely republican sympathies, reinforced by Mrs Thatcher's well intentioned but ill considered gesture of imposing a poll tax on Scotland and not England. Two thirds of the members owned less than 300 acres contrary to Press insinuations that Scotland was owned by the Queen, a few dukes, overpaid London businessmen, and foreigners. It was vital to enter dialogue with not only the NFU, but crofters, ramblers, mountaineers, planners, and environmental campaigners which often went contrary to the prejudices of its members. It was vital, too, that the organisation's profile should be raised. In the *Scotsman* of Saturday 30 January 1993, Auslan Cramb inserted my foreword for 'Heading for the Scottish Hills' which emphasised the problem.

Image of a Highland landowner – by one

Lives in a large house, wears knickerbockers; controls – or thinks he does – everything that moves on the adjacent hundred thousand acres.

Is reported to be stinking rich, but mean. Drinks a lot – hereditary. Hates mountaineers and ramblers, and if he can't shoot deer would gladly shoot them instead if it wasn't for the precarious balance of the legal system. Destroys the habitat by driving hideous roads across the hills to allow his gin-slinging, gun-toting friends who have lost the use of their legs, access to the grouse moors in their Range Rovers.

Poisons birds. Plants trees for profit and doesn't care if his employees' houses leak like sieves, so long as there is plenty water for the fish to run – most certainly not for his whisky.

Makes a fortune from his crofting estate and bends Scottish National Heritage to his will by devious connections and subscriptions to the Conservative Party. Belongs to committees that control the population and, the ultimate awfulness, might even be foreign.

Many of us do live in large houses, built in an age of industrial wealth in another century. They cost a lot to maintain and are extremely uncomfortable. Most of us wore out the knees of grandfather's knickerbockers long ago.

Some of us even go to the hill tied together with a piece of binder twine, and most of us don't think we control anything – certainly not our children.

And those long hours away from home without food have ruined our digestions – so a sip of claret has to be taken with a packet of Rennies.

In that long ago the Press were very fair and always gave me good coverage. As at Muncaster there was an urgent need to reconnect with an outside world to which the Federation should make a major contribution.

The landlord tenant system was constipated by Agricultural Holdings Legislation. There were no opportunities for young entrants to the industry who should have greatly benefited from sharing of capital costs between landowning and farming. As a result landowners were reluctant to halve the capital value of their land by letting it to tenants whose family would have security of tenure into some distant unspecified future. If a farm became vacant they were advised to take it in hand which usually resulted in losing money. During my time as Convener negotiations started with NFUS on the basis that existing leases were sacrosanct, but they refused to budge on security of new tenancies. The result was partnership leases which gave some control over bad tenants but resulted in few new opportunities for young entrants to the industry, with owners mostly taking into partnership established farmers wishing to expand. Twelve years later the situation has not much improved. In the Scottish Parliament, George Lyon, Liberal Democrat MSP, ex-President of SNFU, politically ambitious, attempts to drive through a bill giving tenant farmers the right to buy whether the owner wishes to sell or not. This would be legalised theft. So far he has not prevailed, but as a tenant farmer in Bute, if he succeeds in taking over the land, it will increase his own capital value and borrowing potential astronomically. At a time of disastrous livestock prices tenants have been severely disadvantaged in dealings with banks who dislike the look of their security. Livestock farming in Britain as we have known it, has an uncertain future.

Peter MacDonald, my immediate predecessor, was married to Barbara of the Ballantyne family in Peebles-shire who came complete with two sons from her first marriage. A long-time bachelor, one guessed he might have been a difficult undertaking. He farmed Colzium at the western end of the Pentlands with a too small flock of Blackface ewes from which he bred tups. He knew everybody, had a reputation for remembering most keepers in Scotland – and their fathers – had a deep gruff voice, but was not a public speaker which was a liability. They often welcomed me in their home and waking to the call of the grouse and the peewits, lying in bed at the top of the house on a spring morning, made me happy. Neither was blessed with good health. They sold and live at Eddleston near Peebles whither Barbara had always been hell-bent on returning. Even before they left she had a shop, Butterflies, at Melrose to which she commuted daily. Peter remains a Vice President of SLF, a constant monitor, with more wisdom than anyone credits him. I became Convenor after the CLA Game Fair at Floors Castle where, after incessant rain, everybody was up to their oxters in mud, the Tweed in full flood

The office was in Abercrombie Place in Edinburgh, administered by the Director, David Hughes-Hallet of a nautical family who rode a bicycle for recreation. He was tall, slim, competent and kind to me, but shortly left for the Scottish Wildlife Trust. I suspected it was because I undertook many jobs such as dealing with journalists which had been previously his prerogative. The Federation legal man was Gerald Barrie, ex-colonial administrator in West Africa, charming, but too gentle to be a lawyer in modern Scotland. Anna Boreham ran the Land Use Committee and seemed to select suitable convenors from her clutch of protégés. Doreen Mackie edited the *Journal* about which she was fiercely proprietorial. I sometimes stayed with Doreen and her husband, Archie Graham, at Blyth Bridge but slept badly because the window wouldn't open. Once I stayed with the Hughes-Hallets at Balerno, where the Buchanan-Smiths also lived at the House of Cockburn. Alick, with Hector Monro, was the last of the old Scottish Conservatives who really understood the countryside and when he died too soon in 1991, knowing their love for Harris, I wrote a note for him and Jan:

Leaving on the Tide

Last night
My thoughts returned to Harris
And as I stood beside the tide
Watching the sun go down
And listening to the seabirds cry
I wiped a tear
Out of my eyes
Watching the speck of the boat
Raising its sails to the rising wind
Making for home
And in my mind
Standing beneath the white birds' wings,
I waved my handkerchief,
Learning to hope.

For all his boyish looks Alick had hard teeth in a political battle, and, having been a Minister at MAFF and in the Scottish Office, should have become Secretary of State for Scotland, but as he was not always – which means more often not! – in agreement with Margaret Thatcher she appointed Malcolm Rifkind instead. Malcolm had great intellectual ability and a political awareness which led him to becoming Foreign Secretary in John Major's Cabinet. Some of us hoped he might one day be Prime Minister and his loss in the electoral massacre of 1997 was tragic for the Scottish Conservatives. As his poor wife

Edith was often left to guard the family fireside and do other things, Simon Fraser, the new Director, and I thought it would be a nice gesture to ask both together to one of the quarterly dinners held before Council meetings at the New Club in Edinburgh to exchange views with the great and the good. Towards midnight they had to be asked to leave as his driver was waiting and the staff needed to go home which was a pity as they were enjoying themselves.

The appointment of Simon Fraser, a retired sailor, as Director, although second choice because of a bad interview, was the luckiest happening both for the Federation and for me. His advice was invariably considered and wise and he managed to work out a modus operandi with his wayward Convenor as the office moved to Palmerston Place and then, after a cramped spell, to Maritime Street in Leith. He never questioned my aim of making allies of the most unlikely people. Once I had even travelled to Glasgow to meet Campbell Christie, Secretary of the Scottish TUC, an outstandingly sensible man whom we also asked to dinner. Other times Simon and I met mountaineers, ramblers, academics, journalists and farmers, as well as Scottish Office civil servants, planners, and all political parties. People scoff at the need for personal contact in the computer age. It may be mathematically simpler ruling from offices, but it's far easier to forge agreements face to face, and to build trust from personal contact. I was 60, the job unpaid. It was 156 miles from office door to office door, but I usually did a lot of business between the Borders and Edinburgh. Three days a week were devoted to the work. It cost me a lot of money so it seemed important my successors should receive some honorarium to compensate for time away from home and business to enable younger, more able candidates to undertake the job. This was eventually agreed after initial apoplexy from some of the old brigade.

Requests to speak fluttered from the sky and usually commanded an after lunch slot as I established a reputation for not putting the audience to sleep. There followed in quick succession the Edinburgh College of Art, the Royal Town Planning Institute at Troon, Young Farmers' Clubs, the Scottish Ramblers' Association AGM at Kinfauns Castle where I thought to travel with a hearse in case my return was feet first, and the Scottish Mountaineering Club dinner, sat between two eminent professors, Donald MacIntyre, a geologist who I call Donald the Rock, and Geoff Dutton, a professor of something scientific at Dundee who had created a garden in the skirts of the Angus hills. There were NFU annual dinners; the AGM of the Scottish Women's Rural Institute (the Rural); prize-giving of ESCA, both in the McEwan Hall, a loathsome place to speak as one's words echoed round and round the ceiling; Burns Supper of the National Union of Journalists; and more nerve-wracking than all, proposing the Immortal Memory at the Burns Howff in Dumfries. Luckily my mother dropped me not short of a word and only once, in Cumbria, having agreed to write an article for the paper about the Ulverston Belly Dancing Troupe, did I take fright when faced with the prospect of having to attend a training session.

In Mrs Thatcher's time there was a reception for rural people at Downing Street. I meant to kiss her so that she would never forget the SLF, but couldn't bring myself to do it. There was another in John Major's time to which Phyllida was also invited. The variety of the guests was astonishing. Lord McColl asserted Stephen Dorrell would one day be Prime Minister. There was a Norwich Union footballer, the Bishop of Winchester, and Janet Holmes à Court, the owner of umpteen theatres who seemed unaccountably shy for someone destined to become Businesswoman of the Year shortly afterwards. To her I took a great shine. One day the IRA fired a mortar at No. 10 hitting the branch of a cherry tree in the garden. Cabinet and staff assembled outside and were told not to enter the building. The cook said she must. 'You can't! Why do you want to?' 'I've left the gas on!'

For all the entertainment of meeting famous men and women in famous places the pleasure of the work was with ordinary people throughout Scotland. Sir William Swan, past President of SNFU, notable for his integrity and common sense, had long realised the need for all country people to discover a unity of purpose. He set up Rural Forum, on whose Council I served for several years, as an alliance of country organisations to combat increasing forces conspiring to destroy their way of life. Jealous of its perceived prerogative of speaking for the countryside SNFU never really believed in it and SLF were lukewarm supporters because of a careless public relations gaffe. As a result the organisation gradually fell into the hands of local authorities and NGOs, moving further away from land based industries. Willie was succeeded by Barbara Kelly and afterwards Deirdre Hutton, both heads of the Scottish Consumer Council, with Deirdre moving to become national chairman in London. Both were powerful ladies used to getting their own way. Barbara eventually served as chairman of almost everything that opened and shut, was brilliant at taking a meeting, and very successful at achieving results.

The SLF office under the roof of 19 Palmerston Place was not ideal and like an oven in summer. Simon's secretary was Shelley who left to marry a young farmer from Peebles, when her seventeen year old assistant, Lorraine Alexander, took her place. Lorraine was a special girl who made everyone feel loved and wanted, and would have made an excellent PA to the managing director of a large national company or the chairman of a bank, but after thirteen years and two young children she has remained loyal to Maurice Hankey, Simon's successor as Director at the new offices in Musselburgh. She has been a distant but loving part of our own family life since Phyllida took her, dressed to kill, to a Holyrood Garden Party as an honorary daughter. There she encountered many of the people to whom she addressed letters. An excellent mimic, they might not have appreciated the subsequent tales of who she had seen! Over three years Lorraine was the only person who could translate my illegible handwriting swiftly and accurately to a typed script. Her father, Robbie, a slater, got piles from sitting on a wet roof and her mother, Marie worked in a chemist's shop near Musselburgh where they lived and where, at the reception after her marriage to Scott Caven, I watched Musselburgh Races from the hotel window while waiting for the bride.

After the move to 25 Maritime Street to offices under an imposing dome at Leith, which belied the fairly slum conditions of the first floor, Anna Boreham's husband died and she left to be replaced by Maurice Hankey as Land Use adviser. Maurice, an ESCA adviser before becoming a farmer, had had to give up because of ill health. Since becoming Director his job has been intolerable, responding to endless consultation papers and giving evidence to their own specialist Committees to which the Scottish Parliament does not always listen. Even though he is not a warm character his very precise brain has nursed the Federation through an impossibly difficult time.

The Mrs Fixit of the office was Sheila Sim, although she must have had an official title. She departed for South Africa, but later resurfaced when her father asked me to stand in at short notice for the Canadian High Commissioner at the Clan Maclaren Society dinner. Two Maclaren wives I know were telephoned for information. 'Oh!' both said, 'before we married we always understood they were cattle thieves!'

National AGMs were boring and predictable occasions, but I also tried to attend those of the five branches, which sometimes meant driving through the night after functions at Muncaster. Once I travelled by train for a Central branch AGM, and having given myself breakfast, while waiting to be collected by Ian Fraser, the Secretary, wrote:

Station Hotel – not Inverness!

Sitting, waiting,
A child of a lost generation in the lounge,
Watching the ghastliness of modern life pass by.
Women in spotless white jerseys
Bought in the knitwear shops,
Bottoms too big by far
For scarlet trousers tight
Which emphasise their ugliness.
Two old guests paying their accounts
And a loud-voiced man in shirt sleeves
Asking for a glass of water and an aspirin
For a migrained American wife
Upstairs.

Gone, gone
Are the men with grey moustaches
And Highland Brigade ties;
Gone are the mothers and the wives
In family tartan skirts
And sensible shoes
No one I know.

The breakfast was disgusting with
Synthetic sausages;
Marmalade with the taste of peppermint
In plastic trays;
And the eggs tasting
Of fried fish from the night before.

Lost among the modern decor and
The awfulness of modern life
I sit – and wait!
This, which was once a flavour of the Scotland
That we knew
Is now no more than a gross irrelevance
To the life of the people –
A tiny space from which
Those from another planet can return
Thinking the unthinkable,
Telling their neighbours
That they have 'done'
Scotland!

Alastair Strathnaver and his successor, Johnny Mackenzie of Gairloch, with Ken Hughes as Secretary, ran a vibrant Highland Committee on which I served for many years, its views being sometimes in advance of its members. Johnny MacDonald, Tote was disgusted by the Crofter Forestry Bill negotiated by Alastair and Angus MacRae of the Scottish Crofters' Union, so I went to stay with him and Imogen in Skye which was happy but failed to alter his views. It brought back an evening of almost forty years before when, as a young officer in the 4/5 Camerons, the weather was too bad to play soldiers and a key Jock had to leave early to attend his sister Obadiahina Mackinnon's wedding in Barra. We had sat after dinner with Johnny's sister Wychie, and Barbara Fell on sofas newly done up with Jaeger covers while old Mrs MacDonald told how it was as she watched the Lovat Scouts sailing away up the Minch in the war. The moonlight beyond the window gave the evening a special quality, which was repeated many years later staying with the la Terrières at Loch Garry in Rannoch, watching Schiehallion in the snow while Charlie Gore played his violin beside the fire. Michael Burton, whose grandmother's factor Ken Hughes had briefly been, disliked any liberalisation of access, a view endorsed by his neighbour across Loch Ness, Lady Serena Bridgeman at Dell who died tragically after much illness and was no less attached to her land, and no less difficult, being known as Lady Burton of the South Side. In bad fettle, she had shot a pigeon on a ledge opposite her London flat with a .22 before proceeding down the street to lift a brick from a skip which she lobbed through her ex-husband's window. They were all a vivid mirror of many of their colleagues throughout Scotland of the 1990s, and anathema to the land reformers, but if Scottish landowners were not to become a mere footnote to the past barriers had to be broken down between town and country, agriculture and consumer, landlord and tenant, academic and practitioner, environmental concerns and traditional land management – as well as the insane political divisions dedicated to underlining politicians' individual prejudices. However proud people were of owning land and however much money they poured into it, the fact was that much of the population felt excluded. The days when owners could say, 'This is our land,' were long past and it was essential to forge understanding with the many other majorities who considered it was their land. During those years Simon Fraser and I worked together I do believe we laid foundations for more constructive attitudes to face future inevitabilities. We certainly created a dialogue with many organisations of which our members had been reared to disapprove. It was understood there were certain limits beyond which we must not go, but people would come to the hills anyway, as witness the weekend cars parked along the A9 at Drumochter, and they should be made welcome however much the Director of the Ramblers believed his job depended on stirring up strife.

My vindication was in 2001. Driving up the track to lunch at Corrour one sunny summer Sunday I encountered five hikers. I wound down the window. 'It's a lovely day. Are you going far?' Having had our conversation it was astonishing to hear: 'We know exactly who you are and while you are there we want to say thank you for everything you have said over the past twenty five years which has made us feel so much more welcome in these hills.' The unexpected bouquet made me want to cry, particularly as they were planners from Aberdeenshire. I remain implacably opposed to the need for access legislation in the hills, particularly without some burden of insurance liability on those who come uninvited. Of course the Scottish Parliament thinks it knows better. In its short life it has wasted an enormous amount of goodwill as well as the energies of Robert Balfour, SLF's latest most energetic Convener. The Federation, having responded to umpteen consultations and given evidence to umpteen committees, has found its well reasoned advice usually ignored, probably on predestined doctrinal grounds. Recommendations of the Parliament's own committees are also overridden. I put my X for a Scottish Parliament and there are a few excellent MSPs, but too many are little better than low grade local councillors who have never run a business in their lives.

Isabel, married to Patrick, Earl of Glasgow, from Kelburn Castle was briefly Vice Convener after Michael Strang-Steel withdrew to become a Forestry Commissioner. To appoint a woman was unthought of, but it was very much in the spirit of the time. Reared in Surrey, having worked in the media, Isabel was able and politically aware, if to the left of most of the constituents. The Glasgows were having a difficult time keeping Kelburn going as well as rearing two young children and were particularly kind asking me to stay when working in the hinterlands around Glasgow. Isabel came on a northern tour to visit some of the players and we nearly fell out of the car when Andrew Dingwall-Fordyce, convenor of the NE branch, announced he had been trained as an actor – a useful CV for anyone engaging with national politics. He was courageous, worked hard, and when later Convenor of SLF went alone, despite having had a dog set on him, to speak to the Carbeth Hutters for whom he stood up against a preposterous landlord. He was, however, less courageous when asking me to approach Colin Farquharson to step down after a long spell as Regional Secretary. Colin married to Clodagh, a widow, was my friend, so he received a poem suggesting that as my convenorship was about to end he might also contemplate retiring – which he did, becoming Lord Lieutenant of Aberdeen-shire after long being factor at Haddo. Staying with him at the White House at Alford or Dallas was always special, and spelt an evening of peace, good food, and common sense. My roots went down easily and it was always sad leaving the following morning through ice and snow or along the summer roads of north-east Scotland with the wild roses in bloom in Upper Strathdon and the hedgerows full of birds. It was a revival of past youth and in some ways one yearned for an end to life before the future destroyed the images of people and place and before the clever after-thinkers who write books battered the reputations of those one had learnt to know and love in one's wanderings.

After SLF's move to 25 Maritime Street in Leith there were major commotions with the introduction of the Scottish Natural Heritage Bill which Magnus Magnusson, the newly appointed chairman of Scottish Natural Heritage (SNH), accused me unjustly of trying to sabotage. We had a grumpy meeting, much to the embarrassment of John Francis, the temporary Director, who attempted to mediate. Alexander Trotter, former Convenor of SLF and later its President, had chaired the NCC Scottish Committee and many of us were irritated that announcements about the Flow Country in Caithness came from London without any reference to Edinburgh. There were comments in the Press by Marion Shoard about the theft of the countryside by people like me who were accused of trying to corner it, and any grants to which it might be entitled, for our own selfish benefit. The insinuation was that we were environmental vandals who had wrecked it and should be restrained, yet at that time I would challenge anybody to drive from Wigtownshire to Wick and not think Scotland was – and still is – the loveliest place on earth. Deep down the argument was not about land, but about who controlled it. We held a Press briefing in London resulting in excited comment from Malcolm Rifkind as Secretary of State for Scotland. I have never been a Nationalist, although once described in Tynron as the Tartan Tory, but anyone who lives in Scotland has nationalistic sympathies, and to be lectured on the radio by a woman with an English voice like a cheese grater about the rights of Scottish people on a Scottish committee to announce their own thoughts without reference to London was intolerable. The scientific environmental lobby was incensed at the splitting of their agency, the NCC, and there was a meeting at the RSA where Scotland was described as the Dirty Man of Europe by a man in a kilt. The setting up of SNH seemed a move towards common sense devolution. Originally the designation of SSSIs in the Highlands was carried out from Aberdeen by young girls and men with beards and ethnic sandals with degrees from English universities, with no knowledge of Highland culture, and no time to identify with the natives who, as a result, felt antagonised by central authority. Most were nice people, but under such extreme pressure that they passed over the countryside like a heath fire, leaving the smouldering embers behind them. It was not that the system was wrong, but its administration and the personal ambitions of its administrators were seen as stretching back through Edinburgh, and London and ultimately to Brussels.

So the setting up of SNH with a devolved structure was welcomed by reasonable people, but the five regions did not have the independence our naïveté had assumed. Roger Crofts, Director in Edinburgh, schooled in the Civil Service, intent on the post long before his appointment, clever, devious, if a part time friend and a brilliant flower photographer, screwed the system so tightly to the middle that too many SNH employees, such as Mary Elliot in Fort William, were unable to use their local expertise to help parishioners who trusted them. Most landholders were deeply interested in discovering more about their environment and how to achieve the countryside both sides of the argument sought. The conversation was poisoned by overuse of the catchword 'Sustainable'. Nor was enough attention paid to the water situation which demanded more than the single marine biologist on SNH staff. The Chief Scientist, Michael Usher, was a charming man who once spent a day at Ardverikie highlighted by the vision of him rolling up his trousers and wading into Loch nan Earbh to investigate the water weed. Des Thomson, son of the ornithologist Desmond Nethersole Thomson, was the ubiquitous tentacle controlling heather from Edinburgh. A rascal whom I liked and who was always nice to me, I was never certain I trusted him. The Central Board in Edinburgh had Chris Smout, George Dunnet, and Roy Dennis, all sensible members, as well as the chairmen of the five regions. Magnus Magnusson, brilliant author, ex-journalist, renowned TV presenter, past President of RSPB, hardly seemed the person to be the creature of Government he was forced to become as Chairman. With hindsight it is easy to see some of the fault lines in the organisation with which, over the next ten years, I had a love-hate relationship. My own realisation that things were not as they should be with the land dated from standing on a hill at Ardverikie in a freezing east wind with Adam Watson, a renownedly cussed environmental scientist, doing a broadcast with the BBC. Farmers and landowners had never been trained how to achieve the alterations in habitats they wanted. They badly needed help, not a sermon, but the people in the middle continually referred to European Directives and Regulations which they asserted prevented them preaching the messages they knew in their hearts could bring harmony to the Scottish countryside. In my attempt to help I participated, dressed in my disintegrating overcoat, in making a video for the launch of SNH and whatever people said SLF tried to give the new organisation a fair wind.

In the office I insisted on a copy of the *West Highland Free Press* for people to read in the loo to digest the views of the radical left. An excellent paper, full of trenchant comments from the Highlands and Islands, it should have been compulsory reading for anyone who imagined life could continue as it had for a century or more. Its criticisms were often unfair, making it seem all the more appropriate when the SW Region, whose secretary was Richard Ellis, asked Brian Wilson, its initial editor but by then an Opposition spokesman, to speak at their AGM at Blairquhan. He raised applause for criticising Conservative agricultural policies, brought with him Joni, his wife and one small daughter, Annie, who left her anorak behind. It was forwarded to her with a note appreciating the gesture but suggesting she was perhaps too young to decide to join the SLF. Brian, then a fiery left winger, matured later into an able Government Minister. He left the meeting, no doubt encouraged by a Colonel's voice from the floor: 'You're absolutely right, we've always done better under Labour.'

We forged increasingly strong links with the CLA in London who, because of restricted finances, had represented our interests in Europe. James Douglas, DG, and Rodney Swarbrick, their President, a dairy farmer from Longridge, near Preston, became friends, as well as many of their staff. Pam Forrest, employed as PA, had a reputation as speed typing champion of Europe but was miffed when they found a single mistake at her interview. Susan Bell, later Director of the National Forest, married to Hans Helvig, a Danish artist, was land use adviser who, when we attended the Council of European Agriculture meeting in Cardiff, took me around that underestimated city in the dark. Later attending James' farewell dinner, the address was given by Geoffrey Howe who was far from being the boring lawyer one expected. Rodney and his colleagues dined me at Boodles on my retirement on what must have been the coldest June night on record.

We began to establish stronger links with the European Landowners' Organisation (ELO). Adrian Palmer represented SLF at meetings in Brussels. One night at Manderston Adrian and Cornelia entertained Guilio Pascucci, ex Italian ambassador in Israel and his wife Franca, with Luigi Fricchione, ex-Secretary General of the European Community, chairman and Secretary of ELO. We played a strange game on our hands and knees on the drawing room floor. Adrian, having inherited from an uncle, had a difficult life running the estate, trussed in financial tourniquets by trusts. They tried so hard to maintain their home with its silver staircase and its fantastic stables erected in the early 1900s with money from the Baltic herring trade. He became a conscientious peer in 1992 and remained as a hereditary after Margaret Jay's insensitive bloodbath.

Simon ran a happy office. He and Elspeth, a conscientious member of the

Dumfermline Children's panel, often had me to stay at 55 High Street, Aberdour where they gardened in a restricted space. Simon was fiercely competitive with his dahlias at the local show and walked in the hills at the weekends with their spaniel Tuppence. On a Cox and Box basis I shared a bed with Jane, their daughter, who lived in Surbiton, a formidable hockey player married to Andy Tyrell. We met only once – at the Highland Show – but each year she brought her team, known as Tyrell's Tarts, to play in Scotland. When, in 1991, it was time to leave it seemed the end of my public life. I had acquired an enormous acquaintance throughout Scotland, many of them knowledgeable and tenacious like Jean Balfour, whose son Robert later became Convenor, most of them well mannered, and a few disagreeable enough to make me want to wring their necks. It taught me if there was a complaint anywhere the fire should be tackled at source as quickly as possible. We watched the outside world as difficulties passed from pillar to post, in and between countless other organisations, leaving resentful customers littering the roadsides, furious when their persecutors hid behind regulations, unprepared to strain the law, using common sense – a quality conspicuously lacking throughout public life. There were a few exceptions such as the saga of the Cromarty Bridge. The proposed roundabout at the north end was on land claimed by two owners. Some sensible person in Inverness said: 'For goodness sake, pay both!' which saved state and landowners enormous legal bills, far beyond twice the cost of the land, and allowed the project to proceed immediately to everybody's satisfaction.

Chapter 16

The Barbarians who inhabit the Banks of the Thames.

David Hume (1711-66)
Letter to Sir Gilbert Elliot on the inhabitants of London

I WENT BACK TO Muncaster, and tried not to return to the SLF office. There's nothing worse than old has-beens revisiting the site of their former glory, wasting everybody's time, drinking the office coffee and giving unwanted advice. There were still speaking engagements to entertain NFU meetings, WRIs, academic gatherings, forestry outings and a host of other outrageous requests which appealed to my sense of the ridiculous. I maintained my contacts in Parliament knowing that, once relinquished, it would be impossible to regain the dialogue that had built up over the years, in a rapidly changing scene. Iona had come home and was running Muncaster with her husband, a practising vet, until that became too much of a strain on family life. I still kept the accounts and spoke to the public who by this time were equipped with Walkmans to go around the house. Otherwise I descended into serious eccentricity as old people are expected to do, pulling up brambles and pruning bushes. An article by Terry Cringle from the *Manx Examiner* gave an accurate assessment of where I was.

A good man got the better of me...

'Thank you, my good man. Yes, we have to admit it, this is a most delightful place. We've enjoyed our visit to the full.'

She fired a sudden sharpish look across my bows. It was the first time in my life I had ever addressed anybody as my good man. It's not a thing which rolls readily off the tongue in these egalitarian days.

But it didn't seem out of place as we took in the afternoon sunshine on the immaculate gravelled drive of Muncaster Castle, talking to one of the Gordon-Duff-Penningtons' gardeners.

We had encountered him in the grounds just after spending an hour looking round the historic splendours of Muncaster, at Ravenglass in Cumbria, where one of our great noble families has observed the passing of the centuries in unbroken continuity since the thirteenth century.

He had asked us politely if we had enjoyed our visit. We assured him that we had, and he had nodded quietly. Clearly he was proud of the ancient heritage of which he could claim to be an integral part.

Certainly he was in sharp contrast to the general run of visitors we had seen in Muncaster that day; persons in unbecomingly short shorts, and tee-shirts making primitive statements, observed with patrician disdain by ancestral oil paintings. He was sturdily-built and wearing a check shirt and corduroy trousers – which I'm fairly certain, looking back, were tied below the knee with binder twine.

He was carrying a rip-saw of the kind used for sawing logs for winter fireplaces. His honest features were ruddy and glistening with sweat and he mopped them with a large bandana. (No doubt, earlier in the day, the bandana had contained the bread and cheese he had enjoyed at lunchtime – what he would call his dinner.) I felt the obligation to chat to him awhile.

'Warm work today,' he said, waving a horny hand at the manicured lawns and trim flower beds, whose riotous colour was in dramatic visual counterpoint to the stern grey stone of Muncaster.

'But no doubt you'll be knocking off now,' I replied. It was getting on for late afternoon and he was by no means a young man. 'The faithful family retainer must have earned his rest by now,' I added. No doubt he had a little cottage, out on the estate.

He looked at me steadily for a moment, as if weighing something in his mind. Then he said with sudden roughness: 'No such luck, sir. They drive 'un from morn till night, so they do. Them in the big house.'

She stiffened at my side. She laid a hand on my sleeve. 'We have to go,' she said. 'It's a long drive back to Windermere.' She caught and held my eye and did one of those surreptitious little nods of the head.

'Just one minute.' I wanted to hear the fellow out. The old hack, off duty or not, had caught a whiff of ancient social injustice in the balmy air of the good English countryside. 'Do you mean to say,' I asked him, 'that this fine old family aren't good employers?'

He shook his grey head vigorously and waved his rip-saw with sudden violence. 'Oh, they'm an old family I grant ye,' he said morosely. 'But that don't teach 'em humility.'

He spat the word out. 'Yewmili'y,' he said, the glottal stop coming through strongly in his sudden access of emotion.

'If you don't come away this minute,' she ground out, 'I'll abandon you to your fate.'

It was an odd thing to say, but I just couldn't leave things as they were. 'This is terrible,' I said, 'my good man.' She drew her breath in sharply. 'This sort of thing should be exposed.' I added.

'Thank 'ee sir, thank 'ee,' he said fervently. 'Anybody can see *you're* a proper gennulmun. Not like *him*.' And he tugged his wispy forelock before hobbling away.

I watched him go. 'Good grief,' I said. 'He's going in the front door. They'll give him what for.'

But she was studying the guidebook to Muncaster Castle which we had bought on the way out. In it was a picture of Patrick Gordon-Duff-Pennington and his wife Phyllida. Mrs GDP was wearing a headscarf, her husband was in well-worn but exquisitely cut tweeds.

He was instantly recognisable.

'Now then, my good man,' she began. But I walked ahead briskly, closing my ears to her. She'll have to stop talking about it eventually.

That summer of 1991 seems a land of lost content, in the garden from early morning until dark, able to see the results of honest sweat, re-establishing links with favourite plants. Although Iona was starting to run everything, I still kept the accounts in longhand and paid the bills, sitting in hot afternoons in the cool of the nursery floor at the desk my mother gave me for my eighteenth birthday, working with gratitude in the methodical ways Uncle Edward and Judy Biggar had taught me. There was a calculator but mostly my mental arithmetic was quick and accurate, adding long columns of figures in my head, something incredible to grandchildren and their parents. Ten years later, on a train, watching a three year old tapping it out on her mother's laptop seemed equally amazing to me. The World Owl Trust had become an increasingly important part of Muncaster. Tony, the Director, with a mane of white hair, was a brilliant communicator, but a hopeless business man, with a strange consort who announced in the Ratty Arms one night that she could levitate, which should have made it possible for her to raise vast amounts of money for their captive breeding programme. This she conspicuously failed to do, telling me that she didn't need my assistance. She was a nervous person whose life had been unhappy. That the owls were an unquestioned asset was recognised by Third Millennium Muncaster (TMM) building new aviaries, a hospital, and a quarantine centre for them during the Millennium work. For years they had been unable to shake off a 'them' and 'us' attitude, but with the later appointment as administrator of Sheila Sloan, a lovely sunny character, the atmosphere completely changed.

Before the 1992 General Election Phyllida handed the bulk of the estate to Iona to ensure its survival if the seven years' gift rule for Inheritance Tax was revoked. Ardverikie remained the centre of my universe. I had become Chairman of the Scottish Committee of the Association of Electrical Producers (AEP) whose Director, David Porter, fast became a friend and with his wife Judith was always kind to me. He understood more about the industry than most people in it, and had once run a hotel in Cornwall. Scottish civil servants had taken minimal interest in the potential of renewables in Scotland.

In London I had become connected with the Industry and Parliament Trust (IPT), a non-party charity dedicated to educating Parliamentarians too often ignorant of businesses, large and small, for whom they legislated, which in their turn were equally ignorant of the Parliamentary process. Fellowships were set up and over the years I have taken nine MPs, Lords and Parliamentary Clerks for up to a week at a time, mostly in Scotland but sometimes in northern England, introducing them to problems of rural affairs, the environment, small business, agriculture, and tourism which has proved mutually beneficial. My one failure was with Ken Maginnis, who wasn't really interested, but the others, MPs Colin Pickthall, John McFall and David Drew, Baronesses Hazel Byford, Joyce Gould and Angela Harris, and Parliamentary Clerks Alastair Doherty and Andrew Mackersie proved model students, and have become friends. In 1997 my own European Fellowship was completed, and four years later a

Muncaster.

Parliamentary one, both giving immense insight into the process of government of which most citizens are completely ignorant. It entertained me at the latter to find that the others on the week's course were all bar two young enough to be my children, and two to be my grandchildren. The Trust's father figure was Jack Weatherill, the knowledgeable tailor, ex-Speaker of the House of Commons before becoming a cross-bench peer, whose wisdom and wit at the age of 82 is still in constant demand. The Director, Riki Hyde-Chambers, a Buddhist, has established relations with Parliaments around the world. The offices were at 1 Buckingham Gate at the top of three flights of very steep stairs. Riki's assistant, Peter Sharp, supported a luxurious mop of dark hair which was the envy of an old baldie like me. Sue Chaytor, éminence grise, presided over an office run by consistently friendly and helpful staff. The quarterly Fellows' dinner, officiated over first by David Arculus until he became chairman of the Better Regulation Task Force, and then by Mary Jo Jacobi, once special adviser to President Reagan, are expensive but always worth attending, with interesting speakers and good food. AGMs are boring formal affairs but usually an opportunity to exchange views with talented interested people which extends one's network, even if the cards pressed into one's hand are often mislaid. Why I was there in the first place I never knew, but now MVM is a member my presence has achieved a veneer of respectability. The Small Business Committee on which I sit will eventually need a stick of dynamite if it is to become a significant support to a sector which provides 50 per cent GDP, but it is still severely fragmented, despite sterling work by the Federation of Small Businesses.

Chapter 17

I would give him a night's quarters though he had a man's head under his arm.

Gaelic Proverbial phrase

MY RETIREMENT TO Muncaster was short-lived, leavened by Planning Board site visits and meetings in Kendal. In July 1992 a letter arrived from Ian Lang as Secretary of State inviting me to become Chairman of the Red Deer Commission (RDC). Three months before the Prince of Wales had held a meeting at Sandringham of people influential in the Scottish countryside, in an attempt to make them settle their differences and to support SNH. From then until now he has always tried to pour oil on the turbulent water of Scottish environmental politics. The trouble is many of the combatants are strong characters unwilling to yield one square inch of territory. The result has been prolonged tribal warfare which would have done justice to the fighting abilities of Afridi tribesmen in the Khyber Pass. RDC, set up by the Deer (Scotland) Act, 1959 had a low profile at a time of growing concern about escalating deer numbers, particularly in the Angus Glens, where they raided the arable lands to the south. Breeding success was spectacular throughout the northern hemisphere, and in Scotland, where forestry fencing erected during the grant led planting boom of the past thirty years was becoming increasingly porous, the sheltered habitats thus provided increased the fecundity of the herd. The ratio of stags to hinds was 1:3 and the desire of estate owners to maximise income and capital value which was geared to stag numbers led to many ignoring the hinds. In some places deer were more plentiful than others, and the campaign organised by the East Grampian Deer Management Group (DMG) whose secretary was Richard Cooke, the Dalhousie factor, was particularly successful. By 1999 a target ratio of stags to hinds of 1:1.3 had been achieved. RDC, whose remit was to advise Government on the regulation, management and control of Scottish deer, were also responsible for roedeer, fallow, and sika whose numbers were increasing rapidly, damaging forestry investment in southern Scotland and Argyll. The red deer herd, mainly concentrated in the Grampians and west of Inverness, was reported in 1992 in the Press to number 300,000, a doubling over thirty years. RDC counts had reduced to 7-10 year intervals because of a minimal budget of £300k – insufficient for necessary staff, vehicles, and equipment. By the end of my six years the budget had tripled. There were high winds and lashing rain through the winter of 1992-3 resulting in heavy spring mortality. That was succeeded by six mild ones with deer far out and rising public access driving them into huge herds highly visible to walkers who complained. Conducted at a time of decreasing daylight hours hind culls became difficult to handle and it was a tribute to stalkers' dedication that they achieved culls of increasing size which they never believed in their hearts to be necessary. Unfortunately, as culls rose, with the removal of more aged females and late calves, so did prolificacy, leading to further complaints from environmentalists who took little account of damage caused by sheep and rabbits. It seemed essential to raise the profile of the Commission, to establish close relations with estate stalkers and landowners, and to carry on a civilised dialogue with environmental and access lobbies.

Although politically impartial, having sent a bunch of red roses from SLF to John Smith, the Labour leader, when he was in hospital. I was lucky to have strong support from Ian Lang, the Secretary of State, and his Minister, none other than Hector Monro. The Permanent Under-Secretary at the Scottish Office was Russell Hillhouse, whose Secretaries at DAFs in my time were Muir Russell and Kenneth Mackenzie. My immediate and quietly able predecessors had each served nine years. The Scottish Office treated Ian Mackenzie disgracefully, only telling him his contract would end in January, one month before, although I had accepted the post in July. My appointment was for three years, renewed for a further three in 1996, covering the tenure of Hector Monro, Jamie Lindsay and John Sewell as Scottish Agricultural Ministers. Hector was an old friend, once Minister of Sport in Mrs Thatcher's government, unexpectedly returned to office under John Major, who eventually made him a privy councillor and then a life peer. Jamie Lindsay, a young hereditary of great energy, greeted his visitors at Dover House in his braces. His father-in-law, Nigel Chamberlayne-MacDonald, once owned Knoydart, a focus of considerable irritation at the time of the Land Reform uproar. Jamie's appointment was greeted by cries of 'Lord who?' but he rapidly developed into a highly effective Minister. John Sewell, an Aberdeen academic, newly translated to the House of Lords, although a hill walker, was reputedly lazy.

Andy Rinning, my minder, whose office I shared which was equally annoying to both of us, sat on the children's panel and would have preferred my job plus that of the Chief Deer Officer, Dick Youngson, better than being chained to a desk at 82 Fairfield Road, but he was a good friend. I was cross when, having waited for my retirement, the heavies from Edinburgh moved in, told him to empty his desk, and having suspended him, appointed a new Director, before subsequently clearing him of any wrongdoing. He and Jeanette, and their children Leanne and Scott, were invariably good to me, but he was perhaps a square peg in a round hole. Dick was nice to everybody, deeply knowledgeable, having served as assistant to the legendary figure of Louis Stewart, for many years, but very gentle which meant saying unpleasant truths was too often left to me. Dorothy Urquhart, Andy's deputy, administered the office and once ordered me down the street to buy new trousers. They didn't last long and at a barbecue in the street outside Blair Atholl station a small girl with a South

African accent approached the woman next to me, not my wife: 'Your husband's got a hole in his pents!' That evening I watched the swifts high above the village and longed for the freedom of flight, and often and often I watch the swallows and martins swinging around the Tower at Muncaster longing for release into the width of the sky. The Deer Officers, Colin Maclean and Ian Hope, and the Commission stalkers, Ian Mackay, Alan Corrigan, Harry MacNeal and Acky Dempster, knew more about the physical geography of Scotland and its inhabitants than anyone in the land. Ian was responsible for the plaque on the base of the stag the staff gave me on retirement. It made me proud: 'To Patrick – for annoying those who needed it.' In the office Carol Taylor and Ann Clarke did the donkey work, typing my awful writing, providing lunch on Commission meeting days, as well as the mammoth task of sending authorisations for out of season shooting and night shooting permits. The Commission were considered the enemy in many places, and the twelve other members who came from places as far apart as Wick and Wigtownshire were never given sufficient recognition, being paid only travelling expenses. I was paid £17k gross for two and a half days a week, but mostly did five, and have a Scottish Office pension of £1,600 p.a. to which I contributed.

My six years as Chairman were the happiest and most fulfilling of my life and brought me into contact, not only with the great and the good in London and Edinburgh, but with people from the Outer Hebrides to the Borders. Island people made me feel so close, one of my ancestors, unknown, illegitimate or otherwise, must have come from the West. Katie Mary Rankin, and Catherine and Roddy MacDonald in North Uist made me feel I belonged, and there were many others from whom the termination of my contract cut me off. I learnt to say 'a bagful overflowing with shit' in Gaelic and to regret having left it too late to write poetry in the language. One evening after rain at Fassfern, on Locheilside, where I used to go with Geordie Chalmer, who factored the estate for Lord Dulverton, to see Tommy John MacDonald the shepherd and his wife Jessie, a Gaelic singer, I walked down the road with her grandmother behind Catriona to whom this book is dedicated. Aged two, with tiny stick, she strode into the west behind Roddy the sheep and his dogs as he drove his flock before him. She seemed a light of hope.

Vice-chairman was John McDiarmid, old friend, and Aberfeldy farmer, an arbitrator, full of common sense and deep wisdom. Other Commissioners were Archie Macleod, ex Chairman of the Crofters' Commission; Johnny Mackenzie, endless purveyor of irreverent humour and contemptuous of self-important authorities, who sometimes had to go out to smoke; Alastair (Lord) Strathnaver, a Board Member of SNH, unjustly crucified for being paid for not cutting down mature trees at Dunrobin, both of them sometime Chairman of the SLF Highland Committee; Ricky Sidgwick, senior partner in West Highland Estates at Fort William; Angus MacRae, past chairman of the Scottish Crofters' Union, from Loch Carron; Sandy Calder, ex-Forestry Commission whose first job had

Catriona Bechtel, aged 11.

been collecting prisoners from Barlinnie to plant trees; Heather Gow, from Lochmore in Sutherland; Stephen Gibbs from Arran who, following Aylwen Farquharson, was a highly effective chairman of the Association of Deer Management Groups (ADMG), where he was assisted by Richard Cooke, the Dalhousie factor. ADMG was the most efficient method of liaison for the Commission and there were more than fifty groups in Scotland; Brian Staines, Director of ITE at Banchory, the only scientist whose language made sense to me; Ian Smith, a sheep breeder from the Angus Glens; Julie Crowe from Wick; and Ian Evans, Fraser's son, the NFU nominee from Wigtownshire, who blotted his copybook at my first meeting by using his mobile phone. Donald Smith from Stornoway was the lawyer, shared with the Crofters' Commission. He had a quiverful of children and was usually late or absent, one guessed as a result of sleepless nights! Alan Lowe from the Forestry Commission attended and Richard Grant, responsible for us at Pentland House, the DAFS HQ in Edinburgh. He, and Margaret Peterson, his secretary, always made me feel welcome when passing through Edinburgh, although they probably pulled out their hair because of their unruly lieutenant.

In the jungle, excluded from former conversations, people waited to ambush us, Simon Pepper from WWF being their leader but without his goodwill we would never have achieved the consensus needed to push the Deer (Scotland) Act 1996 through Parliament. John Lister-Kaye, Highland chairman of SNH, an amalgamation of the Countryside Commission for Scotland and the old NCC Scottish Committee, had an impeccable attitude to conservation but handled his victims with such uncompromising zeal, assisted by equally zealous supporters, that people's tempers were frayed long before problems were explained to them. There were the Scottish Wild Land Group, ramblers, mountaineers, crofters, foresters and landowners, and twice I had to take myself to London to speak to the lairds of Lochinver and South Eishken. Edmund Vestey was unexpectedly charming and receptive, Oppenheim misguided. He was at the end of his experiment of shooting no hinds, and even the considerable firepower of the poachers from Balallan had failed to curb their numbers, which were driving mad poor Tommy MacRae and his son Chris, whose family had been stalkers on the estate since the time of the Pairc Deer Raid.

John Lister-Kaye was deep down nice, but not a people person. I spoke at a dinner at Aigas to commemorate his twenty five years in the Highlands. Although an elegant writer, a natural speaker, a dedicated naturalist – everybody should read his book, *Song of the Rolling Earth* – his handling of the deer issue at Coignafearn was unwisely brutal which put up everybody's back before sensible solutions could be explored. In alliance with 'the boy with the buck teeth' he was legitimately worried about the destruction of salmon spawning grounds at the head of the Findhorn and the degradation of the hill habitat caused by enormous herds of stags congregating on the flood plain in winter to be fed large amounts of purchased feed by the stalker, Frank Stewart, who ran a prosperous venison business for the owner, Thierry d'Huarth.

The 316 miles from office door to office door were used to call on customers with problems throughout Scotland, which took me into corners known only to few. Red stags were seen up to their necks in fields of oilseed rape beside the A9 at Blackford. Fallow bucks which the keeper was reluctant to control ravished Matt Bailey's early grass at Murthly. Escalating and unseen, sika barked the Border forests, notably the Altarstone plantation near Peebles where there were elders with red berries planted by some forest officer who didn't know what to do with them. Hitherto RDC had insufficient funds to address perceived escalating financial problems in the woodlands. From Kielder, where Bob Mackintosh, later head of Forest Enterprise (FE) had done an outstanding job with roe deer, we travelled by helicopter to Ronnie Rose who had set up at Eskdalemuir successful control measures based on proper understanding of the relationship between deer and forest design. Reared on Deeside, where his father was stalker at Balmoral, he talked a lot, was rubbished by many conventional foresters who didn't want to listen, but preached eloquently a strong environmental message people ignored at their peril. Travelling to

Newton Stewart we listened to concerns about deer and goats at Clattering-shaws. The scattering of a great herd of grey goats as the helicopter cleared Cairnsmore of Fleet was a wonderful sight.

Eventually sufficient funds materialised to set up operations in southern Scotland with an office at Stirling University manned by Mary Crawford. There were three Deer Liaison Officers. Dave Goffin whose Englishness – he came from Lincolnshire – upset some – was energetic and highly successful in activating deer control in the Borders forests. John Wykes, an experienced stalker based at Dalry, Kirkcudbright, whose daughter did research on midges, was a pillar of practical common sense. Peter Kirk, near Lochgilphead, who kept hawks and a Border terrier, had the task of motivating some rather somnolent deer managers who considered their sporting had been wrecked by too many of their stags being shot out of season in the FE forests under authorisation from RDC. Dick Youngson oversaw the whole business with Gareth Lewis, the Buccleuch factor at Langholm, a Commissioner who had replaced Ian Evans of the Mobile Phone, keeping his conscientious eye on the problems.

Stalking in the Borders was let for a song to contractors who sublet for twice as much to people as far away as Kent and Southampton, unable to spend sufficient time in the forest to know the land and the deer, and with little commitment except to their own pleasure. The Swiss owner of Hearthstanes in the Upper Tweed Valley allowed Joseph Laughtenschlager, a nice Bavarian, followed by George Cattanach, the Rosebery grouse keeper, to sell the deer they shot on their own behalf with no money changing hands. As a result many more were culled than the total population assessment and as many again remained. In Argyll red deer were hybridising with increasing numbers of sika. SNH were keen to establish refugia in the Outer Isles to preserve the integrity of Scottish red deer, while it was hoped to stop sika crossing the A9 eastwards in Inverness-shire and the M74 westwards in Dumfriesshire. It was a case of barring the stable door after the horse had bolted, and there were still no figures to assess economic loss caused by deer damage in forestry. In the wider world, besides reluctant landowners were reluctant stalkers, some still believing 1950 hind culls from herds, drastically reduced in World War II, were appropriate for the 1990s, although their open range had been reduced by forestry expansion. Tourists enjoyed seeing dense herds of red deer, 'Britain's largest mammal', unseen anywhere else in the world on an open hill. The problem remained that they were destroying their food supply and much of the flora for which everybody had found such sudden enthusiasm. Press guesstimates of Scottish red deer populations varied between 300,000 and 360,000, but it wasn't numbers that mattered so much as the habitat in which they ran.

In my new role it seemed imperative that deer managers should be shielded from public abuse; hind numbers should be reduced; and that public pro-nouncements be prefaced by 'too many deer only in *some* places'. This demanded dialogue with politicians and guardians of the public morals such as

SNH, RSPB, WWF, ramblers, and mountaineers even though I was warned it was a dangerous waste of time. It called for research and a public awakening to difficulties faced by land managers. Above all it needed a higher profile for the Commission. An interview with Nancy Nicholson provided a good introduction to my problems.

Omens were awful. A Scottish Office consultation document concerning new deer legislation was circulated to all the environmental world who regarded RDC as pathetic guardians of the status quo. We were condemned before opening our mouths for never having used compulsory control powers under the 1959 Act with the sole exception of Glenspean where 250 stags were killed in one bloodbath after a verbal battle with the owner, a Durham lawyer of considerable charm and little tact. There was a dreadful meeting at Perth in 1993 where environmental bodies were rude about deer forest owners, saying they could never be trusted with the voluntary principle. The cry was for compulsory control which the Commission was equally adamant would end in failure and in the Courts because, with existing resources, it could never be enforced. The prospect of agreement was remote and without it the Government were unprepared to draft new legislation. At evening I departed dispirited to speak at the annual dinner in Glasgow of the Scottish Furniture Trades Benevolent Association, coaxed there by Keith Frost, authority on Persian rugs and uncle to our son-in-law. It was an unhappy ending to a dreadful day and prelude to a sleepless night but out of it arose the formation of a Deer Round Table to which any organisation with deer interests could contribute. RDC sent out the notices and took minutes. No other organisation submitted agenda items and some said they felt cowed by me sitting in the middle, after which we agreed to rotate the chair. As nobody else seemed to want to organise the meetings we continued quite amiably as before with Simon Pepper providing a sensitive lead from the Scottish Wildlife and Countryside Link which had been regarded as such a tiresome waste of departmental time.

The matter concluded with the drafting of the Deer (Scotland) Act 1996, but before it could be passed Andy Rinning and I had to embark on an extensive education exercise with politicians, many with no idea of deer or deer management. On endless visits to London Andy never used the Underground, insisting on walking from Euston to Dover House where he appeared well known to the inhabitants from some previous incarnation. He understood the law making process and its financial implications, worked long hours, and generally kept me out of trouble. The Bill started unusually in the House of Lords where the Committee was chaired by Lord Wilson of Tillyorn, recently retired as Governor of Hong Kong, both of which tasks he fulfilled with skill and sanity. Neil Carmichael, ex-Gas Board man, was a particularly apt pupil, and George Mackie's knowledge, humour and common sense helped. Once the Committee, breaking its tradition of meeting in London, met in Edinburgh, and in the later stages the Commons Committee convened in Dundee.

Through that summer and early autumn of 1996 Andy and I worked almost weekly with the Bill team at the top of Dover House up eighty five steep steps where no tea came to our roasting eyrie below the roof unless we collected it ourselves. Colin Imrie was in charge, assisted at times by Richard Grant, Andy McKeand, and a young girl, Sam Kibble, who worked endlessly on streams of amendments in a space unfit to swing a cat. Having worked so hard to broker a seemingly impossible consensus it was dispiriting when Malcolm Pearson lodged an amendment stating the Commission should be composed of not less than one third members with a knowledge of deer and deer management instead of the proposed quarter. Malcolm was right and the environmental interests enraged, but the Bill passed. Control measures were strengthened and all night shooting made subject to authorisation by the renamed Deer Commission for Scotland (DCS). The Voluntary Principle remained largely intact. The single dissident note in the final stage was struck by Roseanna Cunningham who used the debate for a vitriolic attack on landowners and deer managers. She can't be as unpleasant as she sounded then, but Ray Michie, the wholly loveable MP for Argyll, pointed out that the Hon Member for Perth and Kinross was wasting everybody's time as the matters raised had been discussed and settled at Committee meetings she had neglected to attend. John Swinney and Alasdair Morgan, other SNP MPs, had been extremely positive in our conversations.

In January 1996 the Secretary of State, by then Michael Forsyth, had extended my appointment for three years during which much progress was made in strengthening communications between deer managers and the scientific world and in raising the Commission's profile. John Milne and Iain Gordon worked hard to develop Hilldeer, a computer programme based on the Sheep Decision Support System at MLURI. It was designed to help deer managers, but was treated in its early stages with deep suspicion by DMGs who worried Government might use it as a tool for future interference. Meanwhile estate stalkers deserved highest praise for continually raising hind culls against their inner convictions. Stephen Gibbs, still a Commissioner, and Richard Cooke at ADMG were leading influences in acting as a conduit between deer management and the wider world. Gareth Lewis, a new Commissioner, provided a valuable lead in the Borders where, as factor for the Duke of Buccleuch at Langholm, he had considerable knowledge of woodlands throughout south Scotland. Ravages of uncontrolled deer suddenly became a major irritant to Forest Officers who worried about balancing costs of employing sufficient rangers with unquantified financial loss to their crop, hitherto considered insignificant. Relations between Commission and staff were on the whole harmonious and the fact that Commissioners were unpaid was testimony to their dedication to public service. In a rash moment, having spoken to a meeting of Crofting Assessors at Brora, I undertook the task of visiting all grazing committee clerks, little realising, until the Crofters Commission sent

Buckingham Palace with Iona and Anthea.

the address list, that they numbered seven hundred. It was a mammoth job. By the end of three years I had ticked off less than two hundred, but journeys to distant places most people never visited, through snow and ice, and wind and lashing rain, taught perspectives far beyond the comprehension of family and friends who thought me mad. Contact with enlightened environmentalists on remote edges made one ever more conscious of essential connections between man and nature, and of the ignorance of most land managers of how to achieve environments they knew in their hearts they needed, but from which they were frustrated by the necessity of making sufficient income to keep their families.

There were speaking engagements at NFU and DMG meetings throughout the country and unforgettable moments crossing the spine of Scotland through winter nights with moonlight blue on the snows of Cruachan or flickering on passing lochs as the car moved through trees; sunshine fractured by passing showers making rainbows on the Ross-shire hills and lighting the wake of the boat crossing the Minch; the lights of Stornaway; the seabirds' cry and the sound of young pipers travelling to Mainland competitions on the way from Lochmaddy to Uig in Skye; deep snow in Helmsdale for a night at Borrobol with the Wigans or staggering past Auchentoul to Forsinard to see David Cotton troubled by poachers at the top of the Halladale. Through snow at early morning on Drumochter with the Proud Ones above the road scraping for grass; after a night with the Blacketts, their four daughters, and a lovely hairy dog called Mabel at Invercauld, crossing from Braemar to Perth with a boot full of severely shaken contents of two dozen stags' stomachs for analysis in Edinburgh via a Scottish Gamekeeper's Association meeting at Scone, and an unfortunate discussion when the car skidded into the bank at the steep hairpin bend where the Kirriemuir road joins Glenshee.

Perhaps most vivid of all was a day with David Laird who sometimes gave me hospitality and patronised Tom Brown (tailor) aforementioned. We sat, David, Andy Rinning, Dick Youngson and I, eating our piece one early spring, high above Glenogil, a perennial source of complaint to the Commission, where two thousand stags had wintered since the start of time, eating out the heather of an exasperated Simon Woolton and the Campbell Adamsons who wanted their grouse moors. The squatters were never at home at the start of the stag season on 1 July, but provided a huge economic resource for other members of the East Grampian DMG. The eviction of the deer was likely to cause major problems of winter shelter, require drastic reductions in the stag herd, and the finding of long term solutions. As we sat, the North Sea sounding through the wind in our left ear and the imagining of the Atlantic in our right, we watched hinds brown in the snow below, and lower still the white mountain hares dotting what remained of the heather. Suddenly, from nowhere, a golden plover pitched on the rock beside us. In that one second plucked from time all doubt of magic vanished.

Another May Jim and Margaret Payne from Ardvar took me around Handa in their boat to see the sea black with wings of guillemots and razorbills before I visited Jean Urquhart at the Ceilidh House in Ullapool, where she gave me spinach soup. Heading for the Pattinsons at Couldoran, the car was filled up at Dundonell by Evander Morrison who left Harris to join the Army in 1955 never to return. Asked whether he was a Cameron or a Seaforth he said he became a gunner, fearing having to wear a kilt he would be bitten by midges.

One night, in the middle of all this wonder, Lisbet and Joseph Koerner from Corrour brought Michael Aris to dinner at Ardverikie. The husband of Aung Sung Suu Kyi, the Burmese democratic leader, Michael was distressed. She was besieged in a car on a bridge in Burma, their sole means of contact through a nurse in Rangoon by e-mail which didn't work at Corrour. It was special being able to take him up to the bedroom to dispatch his message. His description of eyes meeting across a room at a party at Oxford and knowing they were meant for each other was very poignant and when he died, even though hardly knowing him, there was a terrible sense of personal loss and a questioning if any cause was worth such sacrifice.

There came requests to speak once more at the College of Art in Edinburgh, at Charles Gimingham's 70th birthday celebrations at Aberdeen University when we visited Dinnet, at Forestry meetings and the Crofting Assessors seminar in Brora; at the dinner of the Crown Commissioners in Glenlivet; at the RICS at Hopetoun and again at Aberdeen to address the young surveyors on Public Policy and Private Landownership where Archbishop Desmond Tutu's comment was recalled – 'When the missionaries came they had the Bible and we had the land. They said go down on your knees and say your prayers, and when we opened our eyes they had the land and we had the Bible!'

There were countless forays into the media usually giving my minders the heebie jeebies and when Richard Grant was replaced by Isabelle Low she invited me to address her Land Use Division B, at Edinburgh Zoo, about my life on the land. On being asked how many didn't eat red meat one hand shot up – Isabelle's. I had already blotted my copybook by sending a postcard with a stag congratulating her on her appointment and reminding her of my mission, but addressing it to Isobel Lowe. By then my days were numbered. Many landowners regarded me as a pinko – which I am not. Those on the left saw me as an arch-Tory stooge, prop to a redundant land policy. My faith in the land and those who work it is undiminished, but also a disbelief in the will or ability of politicians to improve the lives of those for whom I have fought. Along with legislation to abolish hunting with dogs the Land Reform debate has been a shocking waste of time in Westminster and Edinburgh, giving satisfaction only to majorities disconnected from the economic realities of the countryside and the needs of its people.

The annihilation of the Conservatives at the 1997 General Election concluded eighteen years of Government which had achieved much but was past its sell-by-date. In Whitehall there was a tangible frisson of excitement at change. Gordon Brown, as Chancellor of the Exchequer had inherited the benefits of his predecessor's policies. The nation appeared in safe hands. His portrait was painted by Charlie Whelan, his spin doctor, as a man of prudence, a Scot, son of the Manse, and thus all right. Six years later his financial inheritance is squandered, the economy faltering, and his initial raid on pension funds causing misery to people who had relied on their savings to give a reasonable standard of living on retirement. The armed services, superbly trained though they may be, have been cut to pathetic numbers insufficient to protect us in emergency as well as fulfilling their peace keeping role around the world to accord with aspirations of a Prime Minister wanting to be seen as a world statesman. In Scotland one civil servant services every two and a half members of the population. The Press, intent on selling newspapers rather than providing reliable information, see themselves as necessary counterbalance to a huge Parliamentary majority, a position making it contemptuous of the real Opposition, and more powerful than it should be.

The mixture of working with people on the ground, and with politicians and civil servants suited my limited abilities and allowed my inherited nature to be developed to its full potential. Leaving Muncaster on Sundays after lunch with a feeling of guilt and freedom I usually took the road to the north where all the people in the countryside cared for me. There were days and nights of terrible tempest, hill burns foaming white. Once I said goodbye to someone with a tear in my eye taking to the road at 3 a.m., arriving at Couldoran by seven to find Gillian Pattinson looking awful. The pony boy, a family friend, had drowned in the swollen burn the evening before. I was glad to be there at that time, and at the end of the day Jennifer Murray, Gillian's sister, flew us to Applecross by helicopter, her hands on the controls like a Dürer drawing while the geese flew beside us. The following day the road took me past Loch Carron and Attadale, and over the hill beyond the head of Loch Duich to the Campbells at Glenshiel to meet Andy and Dick and three or four members of the Commission, before travelling to Uig in Skye, crossing by ferry to Lochmaddy where the place was in uproar. Four enormous stags were reported to be holding up the children on their way to school, ripping up the incomers' wallflowers, destroying the trees Dr John had planted outside the Community Centre, and threatening a woman from far away, hanging up her washing at Grimsay. Calum MacDonald, MP for the Western Isles, was unhappy, as, too, a journalist, Alasdair Morrison, tiresome son of the Wee Free Minister who had persecuted Pat Ford, hell-bent on stirring trouble against the lairds. He later became MSP and Tourism Minister until being replaced by the equally tiresome Lord Watson, architect of the anti-hunting bill in Edinburgh. Nobody had mentioned the problem to DCS.

First call was the Estate Office to George MacDonald, the eminently sensible factor who drove us around the problem areas. An Agricultural Development Programme had enabled reseeding by crofters of their apportionments from the common grazings. Unfortunately fences were erected for stock, not deer, and the long headed stags of Uist soon learnt the first bite of grass needed for lambing ewes was a good way to improve their diet. At evening eighty people attended the meeting in the hall, including the antagonistic ex-factor returned from his new job in Angus for the night. The Granville boys, schooled in Lochmaddy, had played a considerable part in Island life, but were not pleased when I explained agricultural occupiers' rights, under existing legislation, to shoot marauding deer. Reluctantly, however, they agreed to shoot the four offending 20-stone stags Angus Alec was keeping for high paying foreign guests instead of pursuing their shoo-ing policy. The meeting was slightly mollified, but I retired unhappily to bed with agonising swelled and itchy legs as a result of a tickbite months before. Three months later, landing on the pier at Lochmaddy to check, by strange coincidence three of the stags had been shot the week before and the death warrant was still out for the fourth. In inferior verse the episode was recorded

Angus Alec – the Master Stag of North Uist

This is a tale of impossible beasts
Who colonise lands from Balleshare east
To the streets of Lochmaddy where gardeners fear
The nightly excursions of free thinking deer.

For quite a few years the land was reseeded
With species of grass that the deer thought they needed;
Nor lochan, nor stock fence defied their sweet teeth
From stealing the titbits when they crossed from North Lee.

Alec Angus would try to give them a fright,
But his namesake who watched from his post every night
Could mastermind strategies made to defeat
The wily old stalker's attempts at deceit.

Each evening he counselled each one of his troops
To look for their pick of nutritional need –
The incomers' wallflowers would suit his best friends,
And the ones who liked fighting would serve their best ends.

If they tasted the trees Dr John had devised
To beautify patches before he surmised
He'd never outsmart the impossible beast
That commanded the deer on the slopes of North Lee.

So he swore at us men from the far RDC
Who had taken the trouble to come him to see.
John thought they were useless, unfit for the beast
Who sent every night his troops for their feast.

And the hardiest hinds were the worst of the lot;
He sent them to picket to the west of the loch

Where the slaughterhouse stands in its mantle of green,
The sparkiest spectacle deer could have seen.

It was there that we met them awaiting command
From Angus the Mastermind up in the mist,
And all we concluded the doctor could do
Was curse at the deer, and us he could sue.

Our statutory duty will never defy
All the deer of North Uist who'll never comply
With state regulations forbidding the hinds
From thumbing their noses, expressing their minds.

As they picket the slaughterhouse night after night
And eat the reseeds and spoil for their fight
For the burgeoning wallflowers, the doctor's good trees,
While the Mastermind Angus sits safe on North Lee.

Katie Mary was waiting when we men had returned
With food beyond wanting, while Will he did stand
With a bottle of whisky to toast the old stag
Who commanded his army from the top of some crag
While considering his troops and their culinary needs –
He'll be there when we're dead, the old King of North Lee.

The moral of this is it never will pay
To plant wallflowers in Uist, and trees in Lochmaddy
Unless you're prepared to put up a fence
And protect your investment from deer that belong
To no one by law – and that is my song!

The Commission helped Lewis MacRae, the NTS stalker in Kintail, with his cull which was regarded as useful training for the stalkers who also conducted the whole operation in Rum, where the deer had been extensively researched since the 1950s, and SNH claimed to be recreating an old Island economy. They had calving Highlanders with no stockman and it was with amazement I discovered that Harry MacNeal, an RDC stalker, was having to travel the long journey along the bumpy track to Harris Beach to check the calving cows by the Bullough Mausoleum, where for one owner's interment lawyers and mourners travelled from London in top hat and tails to be greeted by an Atlantic gale and lashing rain. One spring morning we counted deer on the section going down to Kilmorie Bay where the birches beside the track were lined with primroses and violets. Kinloch Castle remained a sump for the cash of an over-ambitious public agency. Once my stay coincided with the annual visit of an endless man come to service the unique orchestron and I felt uneasy having to eat with the paying guests in the dining room while the Commission staff were billeted in less salubrious quarters behind. One night I slept in Lady Monica's bed, her hunting boots in one corner, her silver hairbrushes on the dressing table. The bathroom across the passage was like the engine room of a ship and took much understanding. I hope SNH's rumoured intention of annihilating the deer to renovate native woodland is untrue, because it would be a shameful waste of half a century's research on a self-contained population. On my first visit, having been ferried to an ailing steamer, we had to return to Mallaig via Canna whose beauty was spoilt by graffiti on the rocks sailing into the harbour. I miss the Islands now. After each homecoming several days were needed to pacify the blessed memory of the tangle, the salt wind, and the cry of the seabirds behind the boat.

Highland Venison (HV), an intelligent attempt at cooperative marketing by seventy landowners, not usually renowned for cooperation, failed. Some estate stalkers succumbed, with the aid of a rumoured backhander, to the offer of an extra penny or two a pound and persuaded their employers, often extremely rich men to whom the price was of little consequence, to jump ship for another dealer who sometimes went phut or reduced the price as the season progressed. The chaotic situation of different dealers lifting single carcases from adjacent road ends meant unnecessarily high collection costs, with low prices acting as further disincentive to increase hind culls. Prompted by Hugh Oliver-Bellasis, chairman of the British Deer Society (BDS), Highland Venison launched a promotion in London where I sat next to the cooking guru, Prue Leith, but there was little sustained enthusiasm by Safeway for such a low volume, variable, and seasonal product. Although HV failed at the time it did much to upgrade presentation of carcases. Hitherto stalkers who handled with care were paid no more than those whose deer were dropped over rocks or piled on top of each other in airless vans. After some years the efforts of ADMG and the dealers have introduced a little stability to the market, even if not at a price reflecting the cost on a restaurant menu. Christian Nissen, whose family had an aerospace and cement business in Denmark, took over much of the HV business and Mitchell's in Dundee. Forest Enterprise (FE), on a twin fork of descending timber prices and low venison returns, were led to abandon good silvicultural practices and thinning regimes which must prejudice the value of final crops. Raymond Johnstone and Peter Hutchison as successive chairmen of FC and Robin Cutler and David Bills as Director Generals in my time all well understood deer problems and much DCS time was spent vetting planting applications and deer control recommendations but they had to be all things to all men to satisfy their political masters. FE contributed a high proportion of the annual cull in Scotland and the approachability of their Forest Officers, particularly Howard Embleton at Lochgilphead and Charlie Miller in Oban, as well as those in the Borders, increased the pleasure of my travels. As for SNH, Lesley Cranna, the Portree Dragon, became Establishment and, although likeable, her perpetual war with Michael Burton in Glensheil was a major irritant incapable of solution by sweet temper.

I took to calling on SNH offices, meeting excellent ecologists deeply frustrated by increasing bureaucracy of an organisation straining to conform with EEC Regulations and Directives. The Crofters' Union (SCU) with their office at Broadford in Skye were helpful and mostly much less antagonistic to private landownership than the Press suggests. Three times I attended their annual conference, the most noteworthy being in Stornoway where Donald (Footsie) Macleod, Professor of Systematic Theology in Edinburgh, addressed us for forty-five minutes instead of the advertised twenty. Calling before dinner, a friend from Lewis said they hoped he wouldn't say grace or there'd be scum on the soup. The gentle George Campbell, from Ullapool, Director of SCU, moved to Dingwall to work on the Leader project and married Fiona, a lawyer in Inverness. John Mackintosh from Banavie became chairman of SCU, and both eventually sat on the new DCS after my departure. Catherine Robins, working at the Eden Court Theatre, gave me a bed once or twice and there were comfortable nights at the Station Hotel where food and the terms were good. Heather at Reception, Pat from Wales in the restaurant, and Robbie, a permanent fixture behind the bar, always made one feel the most important person in the world. There were acquaintances old and new, and it seemed more like a club than a hotel. Most often though my head rested at the heart of Scotland whence routes to all parts of the country radiated.

There were many personal challenges, not least the verbal diarrhoea which cascaded through the Civil Service and it gave perverse pleasure amending the wasted words and abominable prose.

One summer we visited the Irish government's deer problems in Killarney and the Wicklow Mountains, staying for a night between with Rory Harrington and Helena, his Scandinavian wife who had a herd of sika. Sandy Calder fancied them and imagined four in his garden at Inverness until having to spend the whole morning blocking holes in the fence where they had rolled underneath. At Bray we met Mick O'Brien from Coillte, the Irish FC, and the Irish Deer Society, discovering the disastrous division of responsibility for growing trees and setting culls split between two different Ministers. Many hundreds of hectares were planted each year, 75 per cent grant aided by Brussels. Mostly unfenced sitka spruce they were ravished by escalating sika populations, leaving a large proportion ring barked and foresters in tears. One evening we counted a herd of sixty, a huge number, grazing outside the forest, and left with the unhappy conclusion that the EC and the Irish government were wasting a great deal of our money.

Andy Rinning was very internationally minded and some months before I left office we went to Hungary to see problems in the Bükk National Park, which wasn't as daft as it sounded as over the years the Commission had become worried about damage deer were doing to British woodlands.

Met at Budapest by Joe Simon who had left Hungary after the 1956 Rising, we passed through streets with the old bullet holes still riddling the buildings on our way to the Castle where he described how he and his colleagues had faded into the surrounding woods after their last stand. We travelled north-east along straight roads with miles and miles of dead flat land deer fenced with acacia stobs, marvelling at the undeveloped agriculture and fearful of its potential production if Hungary joined the European Community (EC). We stayed in a large guest house in the middle of a beech forest where the authorities were more concerned about moufflon than deer of which we saw few. We inspected ex-closures where ungrazed vegetation smothered the seedlings and the natural flora was unable to compete without grazing animals. On the border with Slovakia was a large house to let at £800 p.a. where the owner disliked the treaty settlement in 1918 and arranged for the line to be redrawn to include his house in Hungary. Discussions were held with the very competent National Park Officer and his assistants at Eger. They explained how local culture was geared to a long tradition of a forest economy with which they were entirely in tune.

We spent another day in the Aggtelek N.P. and visited caves before crossing the border for a day and a night in Slovakia, entertained in a hunting lodge among magnificent forests of silver fir and spruce by Anton Barbierek, a monstrous man, previously encountered in Inverness with an international delegation, and Deputy in those parts to the Prime Minister. He gave me a bear hug on meeting and throughout the lengthy dinner party insisted on murdering his guitar and the songs he sang. Bob Dunsmore, FC Conservator, who accompanied us, asked if he wanted the instrument tuned. It was surrendered with ill grace, but snatched back when Bob began to sing in his beautiful voice. The following day we drove through neat farmland and well kept houses to visit an old Esterhazy house with pleasant gardens and stiff central European ancestral portraits, interesting but ugly, before returning to Hungary to be shown a roedeer hanging in an insanitary larder. Somewhere there must have been the heavy red deer for the shooting of which foreigners were charged astronomical sums, but for us they were conspicuous by their absence.

We went then to Miskolc, the provincial capital, via the Tokay cellars and were given a bottle with our names printed on the labels. We visited Admiral Horthy's house, and the ruins of a historical castle. In Miskolc there were discussions with Officials, before being shown their Council Chamber and the lovely churches of a town where the empires of Austria-Hungary and the Ottomans had collided, the Turkish influence still surviving in many buildings. At evening, exhausted, we entertained our hosts to a good dinner at a ridiculously low price. Afterwards, returning to our billet, Gareth Lewis, who had never been parted from his wife for more than a night since their marriage, was horrified when a lady of the night slipped from a doorway and grabbed him. Luckily Stephen Gibbs was at his side and the woman was told, 'Not tonight, thank you!' Our guides, quizzed about their rulers, said they were the same old Communist officials regenerated under a modern name. We said farewell to Joe Simon, his cousin Erzsebet, and her family, who had arranged such a generous visit, before Andy Rinning drove us back to the airport between the 100km of deer fences with their acacia stobs. We left with a warm feeling for the people and places that had made our visit possible and I am sure it built bridges for the future – even if I had a slightly guilty conscience about how few deer we had actually seen.

Returned to Scotland, Bob and Ann Dunsmore visited Ardverikie, where we succeeded in stranding one of HMG's vehicles on top of a branch of a tree, fallen in a gale, until Ali Moir rescued us with his monstrous tractor.

Chapter 18

See our street?
You were middle class if you wore
Your dentures in mid-week.

Gordon Williams 'See Scotland' in I. Archer and T. Royle,
We'll Support You Evermore (1976)

DOING JUSTICE to all the friends made by the roadside, to their songs and stories, and the smiling of their children's faces is beyond the compass of a single book, but I never met a single unkindness in all my travels through those six years with the Commission. Alasdair Macleod in Lewis asked how it had been possible to be friends with so many opposing people. Not everyone was likeable, nor trustworthy, but the innate good manners of Highland people made dealing with them not a job, but a privilege. Many treated me as family and all seemed to sense our talks were a pledge to try to find solutions to their sometimes insoluble problems. There were simple unforgettable memories – Frances Ann, helper to Johnny and Philippa Grant at Rothiemurchus, baking me a cake with lemon icing for my birthday. Rory and Marion MacDonald at Blarour plucking me out of a tempestuous night when the surface of Loch Oich was in turmoil and the wind blowing the spray across the road. Crossing Loch Maree by boat to Letterewe where Paul van Vlissingen and Caroline entertained me for a night before the DMG meeting at Garve. Arriving late for dinner at Dunlossit after a hectic journey from Galloway via Arran, Kintyre, and the Islay ferry, to find Leonie Schroder having taken the trouble to leave the dining room to brief me about who was who in case I put my foot in it. Joe Goodburn, John Sewell's private secretary, who everybody loved asked if she could use one of my poems at her wedding to Brendan Hawden, and kissed me goodbye under the marble pillars of Dover House when her boss emerged from his room. 'I really can't have all this sexual activity in my office!' He didn't seem to know life would have been far livelier when Lady Caroline Lamb chased her lovers round the same marble pillars more than a century and a half before. Occasional visits to Kenneth Mackenzie, lonely in London having moved to the Cabinet Office. Then there were the Chalmers who had been such a central part of my life for more than thirty years, guarding the gateway to my Land of Heart's Desire. There were the people of Laggan and the McCalls in Sutherland, who had given me my first chance of life among the hills in Glenlyon. In my mind I see Brian Staines, the first scientist to teach me to appreciate scientists, explaining at ITE how the guillemots on the Isle of Mey had thirty nests per square metre and the blue guillemots in South Georgia had eyes adapted to withstand the pressures of diving 400 ft. deep for food. There was Peter Fraser, head stalker at Invercauld, telling a DMG meeting in Braemar how the stags no longer grazed the tops of Ben Avon in summer, driven elsewhere by constant pressure of walkers. Angus John MacDonald, arch poacher of Balallan, related tales of his outrageous exploits while I did a healing on his leg.

Andrew Gordon flew me from Atholl across Ardverikie to land on a field at Invergarry on our way to a meeting at the Cluanie Inn where many moons before Dick Youngson had released two surplus pigeons as a peace offering to Michael Burton's eagles. Archie Gibson, the new factor at Ardverikie, took me to speak to the Community at Knoydart but visiting first Sandy Morrison, retired head stalker, who disapproved of their attitude. He had been marched by the Germans from St. Valery to Poland in 1940 and forced to work three years down a salt mine without seeing the light of day. Mrs Strutt of Kingairloch gave me lunch, shot her last stag aged 89, and practised crawling on her bedroom floor. Calvert McKibben, arch controller of deer and rabbits, highly experienced with terrorists in Ireland and game in Africa, gave me prawns for lunch in Aberdeenshire. Andy Rinning, whenever we went west gazed longingly towards St. Kilda, but perhaps the most important memory of all was the kindness and thoughtfulness of all the Commission staff.

Of course it had to end; and the dream concluded one terrible summer day at Coylum Bridge when Donald Dewar, Secretary of State for Scotland, outlined his plans for Land Reform. He was a decent man and likeable, but that day I didn't like him at all. Our conversation went:

'You're going to Nolanise me. I've travelled a thousand miles a week around Scotland for the last six years on your behalf. I've kept the crofters happy, the landowners happy, the farmers happy, the foresters happy, the stalkers happy, and even the bloody politicians happy. Find' – I think I said please – 'me another job.'

'Our trouble with you, old chap, is you're about 100.' (Only 69 and new Labour say they're not ageist!)

Afterwards I sent him a nasty little sticker declaring 'Age and Treachery will overcome youth and skill' and the poor man died – too young! Scotland badly misses his ability.

In August 1998 at the Moy Game Fair, the British Deer Society asked if I might be prepared to be proposed as their chairman the following May in succession to Mike Squire, a retired Brigadier with a small farm in Cornwall. My agreement was an error of judgement. Although the following 2^1/$_2$ years brought new friends, it was accompanied by exasperation with an organisation composed of too many people with personal agendas. In England there was no statutory body like DCS, and little cooperative effort.

Remaining months in office at 82 Fairfield Road were filled, travelling the hedges and ditches on farewell journeys. There were stays with Robert Balfour and his wife Janet Morgan at Brucefield, admiring their clear minds and the

Phyllida and Patrick Gordon-Duff-Pennington.

lovely flowers all through the house. I had met them sitting on his Heritage Committee at Robert Gordon University. He had been Chancellor of Stirling University, and she was bright – very, but nice with it, which doesn't always follow. Saying goodbye to the Western Isles was the worst farewell, and felt like an end of living. The Scottish Office, apostles of so-called open government, set about above-board ways of finding my successor. John Graham was by then head of SEERAD. There were many unsuitable applicants, almost as unsuitable as the Secretary of the Albany Club who applied for the job as shepherd at Sandringham in 1958. The list was whittled down to five or six for interview by John, Isabelle Low, who probably devoutly hoped for a more predictable successor, Hugh Maclean, ex-Crofters' Commission chairman, and me.

In the end we chose Andrew Raven from Ardtomish, thirty years younger and far more able than I, and in tune with their new policies. He had been Lands Director of the John Muir Trust, was a landowner with deer interests, past Vice Chairman of Rural Forum, and was equipped with a modest smile. He did not communicate easily with people on the ground and would obviously run the Commission differently. I had regarded myself as a servant of the people and not of the state. He understood the importance of IT even if it meant discarding my own intensive personal contact built up over thirty years to a lower place on the agenda. He was good to me and made leaving easy, my only regret being that DCS, probably inevitably, has become a bureaucracy which appears to have lost some touch with the realities of land and people, placing its whole thrust on science and organisation.

We worried Andrew Raven had too much work. Member of the Scottish Consumer Council, Forestry Commissioner, and shortly to become Chairman of the Macaulay he had a clear mind and the support of both the Establishment and the environmental bodies though some feared, at the ripe old age of only forty, he might be too modest to stamp on toes which crossed lines in the sand the Commission had so clearly drawn over the past six years. We worried, too, about SNH's territorial ambitions, but halfway through his second three-year term, despite our fears, he has successfully acquired a budget of £1.5 million. There were new Commissioners and it was noted with regret that little priority was placed on promoting the concerned attitude towards people with deer problems in faraway places which had been the hallmark of the old regime. Times had moved on and in retrospect Donald Dewar was no doubt right to find a younger head to guide the Commission into the uncharted waters of the twenty-first century, but the countryside was fearful and four years later the new order has removed all photographs of past Commissioners from the walls of 82 Fairfield Road – a minor act of vandalism.

Transferring energies to BDS was a traumatic change. It was an organisation not short of ambition but perpetually short of cash, administered by Sarah Stride who, with husband and daughter Charlotte, rapidly became a friend. She had an office the size of a shoebox into which were crammed Sue Varvill plus Alice her dog, Felicity Anastasiadou named by me Peleponnese, and Graham Judd, together with mountains of paper. The list of members was kept by Margaret Bellingham, an employee of the Game Conservancy. The President was Jamie Ramsay, shortly to become Lord Dalhousie on his father's death, courteous, robust, with a sense of humour and a devastating smile capable of disarming most opposition. Mike Squire, retiring chairman who remained as English Secretary, was a most uneasy man married to Nancy, student of Classical Theology at Lampeter University, nice but rarely seen. He was extremely resentful of life – and me. Having been a brigadier with a budget of umpteen millions he had left the Army, commuting most of his pension to buy a small farm in Cornwall, the farmhouse being a listed building in poor repair, at a time of acute agricultural depression. It was intended to produce sufficient income for him to take part in public life and pursue his interests in deer and firearms of which he was extremely knowledgeable. I felt sorry for him, but whenever I suggested visiting his home he always said no, and whenever a visit to the South-West branch was proposed he always promised to ask me, but never did. Treasurer was John Thomas, very kind to me, but so engaged in audits for the Army he had insufficient time to conduct business promptly for BDS, of which he was also Vice-chairman. The 1999 AGM at Exeter elected me as Chairman. Arriving early I took Torquil Gordon Duff who was studying Sports Science at the University out to tea before meeting Phyllida off a train. Luckily we encountered a retired Professor from Reading who pointed us to a tearoom, because Torquil hadn't a clue. Two years later, repeating the operation at Durham with his sister, Jemima, she was far more streetwise.

The AGM outings had been beautifully organised by the SW Branch Committee. Returning to Exmoor revived happy memories of visiting the Yandles with Hugh Oliver-Bellasis at Riphay where none of the walls of the rooms were at right angles. John Willett, a VP, showed us his herd of sika and a natural hospitality that made one sorry not to know him better. The same applied to Cecil Kilpatrick and Dudley Forwood, the former met on a visit to Northern Ireland to set up a new branch, and Sir Dudley, equerry to Edward VIII at the time of the Abdication, at his home in the New Forest, just before his death. The Exeter meeting witnessed the first instalment of perpetual commotion from Desmond Lionel Hughes in what is engraved in my mind as the Wytham Wood Incident which wasted the whole of my two years with BDS, as well as a great deal of the Society's funds. A preposterous man who did his best to wreck both the British Association of Shooting and Conservation (BASC) and BDS, he was married to a wife whose father was, so he said, a colonel in the KGB and friend of President Putin. Des espoused causes. This one concerned a Dr Dowie who had managed the deer in Wytham Wood for Oxford University, lost his job, bought from Mike Squire a rifle for which his certificate was removed, and lived in Botley where he kept a feral cat that gave me asthma. Mike Squire should never have allowed the Society to be drawn